THE SINNERS
ALL BOW

THE SINNERS ALL BOW

TWO AUTHORS, ONE MURDER, and the REAL HESTER PRYNNE

KATE WINKLER DAWSON

RANDOM HOUSE
LARGE PRINT

Spelling, capitalization, and punctuation in some historical quotations have been slightly modernized where necessary.

Original cover design: Evan Gaffney
Design adapted for Large Print
Cover images: (woman) © Rekha Garton / Trevillion Images; (barn and tree)
Elements partially generated by
Adobe Firefly generative AI

The Library of Congress has established a Cataloging-in-Publication record for this title.

ISBN: 978-0-593-94911-5

https://www.penguinrandomhouse.com/

FIRST LARGE PRINT EDITION

Printed in the United States of America

1st Printing

To my mother, Frances Lynn Lefevre,
who taught me how to advocate for
other women, as well as myself

CONTENTS

THE SINNERS
ALL BOW

PROLOGUE

~⁓~

THE ADVOCATES

CATHARINE READ ARNOLD WILLIAMS was a fearless woman. Her multilayered skirt firmly in hand, she gingerly stepped over ground littered with broken maple limbs before coming to a stop and gazing down at the green, well-trodden grass. Hoofprints marked various spots where cattle had grazed. I hovered nearby, settling beneath a towering maple tree. It seemed surreal as we both stood where a young woman, gifted with ability and loyalty, had lost her life. We stayed hushed for a bit, out of respect for Sarah Maria Cornell.

The tiny lines on Catharine's alabaster skin around her eyes deepened when she expressed concern. We were the same age, but my freckles revealed years of sun damage from working on my father's farm in Texas as a teen. Catharine, on the other hand, had never done a bit of manual labor in her life—though her wrinkles seemed perhaps more pronounced than mine, her worries etched deeply on her face. Our lives were an illustration of extreme contrast, but our divergent experiences had led each of us to similar writing careers propelled by diligence and necessity.

Catharine's life up to that point had not been easy. The forty-six-year-old had contended with an abusive marriage and a humiliating divorce, before settling into life in New England as a single mother. Through it all, Catharine had nurtured a writing career that she cherished, penning a short list of novels, poems, and biographies that braided religion with history. Despite almost immediate professional success, Catharine tended to be an impatient wordsmith who fretted over financial stability and never seemed content with her creative output or the resulting earnings.

I understood that concern. As the main breadwinner in my own home and the mother of two young children, I was also continuously on the lookout for the next opportunity, the next assignment, the next book. Authoring is a tricky craft, one that feels risky even at the best of times and positively precarious during uncertain economic moments—when recessions loom, pandemics rage, and politics threaten to upend our social structure.

Aside from all that, writing is horribly tedious. I've often compared the art of narrative writing to the act of conscripted self-reflection. Yet Catharine claimed it was meditative for her—as I said, we had varied experiences despite our similarities.

Writing a book with another person can be tormenting, melding two voices, two sets of observations, two life experiences into a single narrative. That was certainly my experience working on this book, **The Sinners All Bow**, with Catharine. Each of us saw things the other did not, and while our observations lined up perfectly much of the time, we each had to contend with the occasional blind spot or different interpretation of the same event. Still, I think the sum of our work together is greater than its individual parts. The collaboration process can be strenuous, but the fruit borne can also be satisfying.

As Catharine and I wandered beneath the graceful branches of the magnificent maple tree that summer, we surveyed the precise spot where the victim had exhaled her final breath. In most documents, our protagonist, Sarah Maria Cornell, is referred to as Sarah, even though she signed her personal letters with a variety of names over the years, including Maria and Sally. Catharine and I call her Sarah in our pages. Another quick note: Sarah was discovered on a farm in what was Tiverton, Rhode Island, about fifty miles south of Boston. In 1856, the town of Tiverton would vote to rename its northern section, where the Durfee farm was, Fall River, Rhode Island. Five years after that, the U.S. Supreme Court moved the state of Massachusetts's boundary to include that area, which is how 1833's Tiverton, Rhode Island, became Fall River, Massachusetts, by the twenty-first century.

Sarah's story held many mysteries for two avid true crime writers like us. Standing on that same field where Sarah had walked years ago, Catharine and I could almost see her before us. When Sarah herself had slowly navigated through the dark December night, it had been deep into a cold New England winter, just below freezing. She had wandered across Fall River without the assistance of streetlights—only starlight and moonlight. Catharine and I braced ourselves against the imagined western wind that rushed across Mount Hope Bay, which was just a few yards away down a gentle slope. Sarah must have felt chilled as she made what would become her final walk—the dead grass crunching under her boots, the wind swooping beneath her cloak and seeping into her bones with every step.

My coauthor and I were standing at the location of a tragedy that had perplexed and shocked the residents of nearby Fall River for nearly two centuries. As nonfiction authors, Catharine and I thought it was critical that we make the trip. We needed to see the site of this tragedy firsthand. We both noted our impressions of the area, initial thoughts that would—we hoped—eventually translate into spirited, visceral descriptions on the page. We knew how to tell a story, yes. But we also were reporters who believed in telling the truth and retrieving all the facts. These were facts, we would soon learn, that could be interpreted many ways, by those with many different agendas.

In the years ahead, Catharine and I would carefully evaluate the clues to a maddening mystery—why was Sarah Maria Cornell, a thirty-year-old woman with seemingly so much to live for, found dead on this spot on a crisp December morning? Catharine and I would scour the scores of unpublished original documents, mining for clues in the extensive testimonies of people who sought to protect Sarah. We also had to consider the damning narratives from those determined to condemn her. Catharine and I would interview Sarah's family and her close friends—though, admittedly, Catharine was granted greater access than I (luckily for us). We would soon visit Sarah's humble gravesite, the spot where she was finally able to rest in peace after being buried three times in two different locations.

Ultimately, we hoped that our writing would serve as a lesson in criminal investigation. There was discussion about victimology, motives, witnesses, criminal profiling, physical clues, and legal arguments. We both had our own forensic experts, though my list was more extensive. Catharine's side of the investigation had its weaknesses; she refused to interview the suspected killer's family, much to my dismay. But I did.

And Catharine didn't realize it, but once I detected her biases, I began investigating **her**. What were

Catharine Williams's true intentions for writing a book about a murder that might not have been a murder at all? Unbeknownst to her, I spoke to Catharine's own family to evaluate her motives and delve into her personal history.

But the focus of our narrative was the distraught young woman found dead on a remote farm one winter morning. Regardless of the cause of Sarah's death, Catharine and I both wanted to answer **why** it happened. Together, we would investigate a sad, pitiful end to a troubled life; we would dissect the dynamics of Sarah's family that led her to that bleak spot; we would study her past paramours, as well as scrutinize several sexual predators who crossed paths with her. We would examine the overt, odious assertions about Sarah's so-called promiscuity as a cause, even a justification, for her death. Catharine and I noted the misogyny that has always pervaded America, the enduring impulse to excuse a man's behavior at the cost of his victim. Our aim was to offer a true crime narrative that might reshape how Americans regarded the demise of a flawed, victimized woman . . . and how our society exploited her, even after death.

While Sarah Cornell's story has largely been forgotten, its legacy remains. Echoes of her narrative—which was as omnipresent and infamous in its time as the stories of women like Nicole Brown Simpson and Gabby Petito are in ours—made their way into all aspects of society upon her death. In fact, the details of Sarah's story inspired an author to write one of the most important novels in American history, a reimagining of the exploitation of women. But more on that later.

True crime, I believe, is overdue for a broad reckoning. For every authentic, empathetic professional in the genre, there is an endless supply of seemingly callous true crime creators whose work exploits a victim's past, re-traumatizing and re-victimizing their families (and the victim's reputation) in the process. The genre seems to be at an inflection point, a moment that demands self-evaluation for all of us who venture into true crime storytelling.

Catharine Williams and I want to do things differently. We aim to offer readers a victim-centered reclamation of the "wanton woman" in the true crime narrative. As a crime historian, I found that working with a gifted, galvanized writer like Catharine was a blessing. Alongside her, I wasn't alone in my determination that true crime could help restore the public character of victims who suffered harm not only at the hands of perpetrators but at the pens of writers who recounted their stories. That impulse is at the heart of **The Sinners All Bow**.

I consider Catharine Williams my coauthor, and she and I were determined to get to the heart of the mystery of Sarah Cornell's death. The only catch: we were working on the same case almost two centuries apart. Sarah Cornell was found dangling by her neck from a haystack pole in what is now Fall

River, Massachusetts, in the year 1832. Catharine Williams began her investigation the following spring.

What's singular about **The Sinners All Bow** is that my coauthor has been dead for more than 150 years.

———

These are the basic facts of the case:

On a frigid day in December 1832, the body of a young woman was found hanging at a farm in Tiverton, Rhode Island. She was identified as Sarah Maria Cornell, a worker in a nearby textile factory. Evidence implicated Methodist minister Ephraim Avery, a married man and father of four. The community was outraged that a man of God had apparently seduced and murdered an innocent mill girl.

But as more evidence emerged, this picture grew murkier, more complex. If she **had** been murdered, was someone other than the minister responsible? Could Sarah Cornell have planted evidence against Avery before taking her own life? Who was Sarah Cornell, really? Was she truly a victim, as many would paint her—or did she have secrets and an agenda of her own?

Sarah's story resonated with Catharine Read Arnold Williams, who went on to write America's first widely read true crime book, **Fall River: An Authentic Narrative**, in 1833. Most true crime aficionados (me included) have long believed that Edmund Pearson's 1924 **Studies in Murder** was the first true crime narrative in the United States, but that's not the case. True crime narrative had its origins within the pages of Catharine Williams's book.

Fall River was "written to convict a murderer in the court of public opinion and published as an 'Authentic Narrative' in 1833 as perhaps the first extensive 'true crime' narrative in the United States," wrote Shirley Samuels in **Reading the American Novel, 1780–1865**. Catharine Williams, a poet who never intended to be a reporter, had made true crime history.

With her pious character and adherence to the strict social norms of Puritan New England, Catharine seemed an unlikely colleague for me. But her book was an outstanding, deeply investigated narrative of a death that outraged a country.

Catharine penned about two hundred pages in **Fall River** with the aim of dismantling Reverend Ephraim Avery's defense. Catharine was, I believe, also the first author-advocate for the crime victim, which is an unusual perspective for a true crime author, even today. Her point of view was unflappable: she labeled Avery as the sinner and Cornell, while certainly not a saint, as the imperfect woman who had been victimized by her spiritual guide. He had exploited her recent indoctrination to the church to gain control of her. In contrast to the crass, big-city newspaper articles in which female victims often were said to get what they deserved, Catharine offered Sarah Cornell some crucial sympathy—and in doing so shifted public opinion.

But did Catharine get the facts of the case right all those years ago? **Fall River** is remarkable in its ability to synthesize a compelling story with accurate details of the crime, social context, and impeccable reporting, like any true crime story should. But in **The Sinners All Bow**, I'll reexamine Sarah Cornell's death using the tools of a twenty-first-century journalist; I'll evaluate Catharine's evidence and weigh whether her clear biases against Reverend Avery and the Methodists affected her judgment in this case.

The story of Sarah Cornell's death inspired another author in his quest to craft a scathing social commentary. Several scholars believe that Sarah was Nathaniel Hawthorne's inspiration for Hester Prynne in **The Scarlet Letter**, among literature's most tragic fallen women. Six years after Sarah's death, Hawthorne referred to the case in his journals after he visited a touring wax display with a scene that depicted the murder in Salem, which was a popular tourist destination in the 1800s. "July 13th—A show of wax-figures, consisting almost wholly of murderers and their victims," Hawthorne wrote in 1838. "E. K. Avery and Cornell—the former a figure in black, leaning on the back of a chair, in the attitude of a clergyman about to pray; an ugly devil, said to be a good likeness." Being featured in a wax exhibit indicated that the person had achieved a certain level of fame or notoriety or infamy. And indeed, the story of the minister and the mill girl gripped the nation. Hawthorne would have certainly known the details of the case—he was an avid reader of popular newspapers. His son, Julian, even called it a "pathetic craving," how he was so consumed by news. Hawthorne even used newspaper copy in some of his own writing.

The Scarlet Letter was published eighteen years after Sarah Cornell's death. Within its pages, Hawthorne unravels the tragedy of a needleworker, Hester Prynne, in Puritan New England. When her adulterous affair is revealed, Hester is forced to wear a scarlet letter "A" as public punishment while raising her daughter, Pearl, and being pursued by her wrathful husband. Hawthorne's work has endured for almost two centuries as an illustration of both penance and perseverance with shades of disdain for the Puritan beliefs of intolerance and public punishment. Once you learn the contours of Sarah's story, the parallels are hard to ignore.

Both Hester and Sarah were seamstresses embracing sexual independence, and these autonomous women frightened provincial New England society, where the patriarchy leveled punitive shame on those who unmoored themselves from a husband. And yet, both Sarah and Hester selflessly shared their gifts, despite the public ridicule that sometimes followed.

"Hester's needlework also enables her to practice

charity, for which she, like Cornell, eventually becomes known," wrote Kristin Boudreau, professor of English and the head of the Department of Humanities and Arts at Worcester Polytechnic Institute in England. She wrote a paper called "The 'Scarlet Letter' and the 1833 Murder Trial of the Reverend Ephraim Avery," detailing how Hawthorne drew inspiration for his fabled character by examining the life of Sarah Maria Cornell. "Indeed, whatever their sexual transgressions, both women significantly rehabilitate their characters by performing benevolent acts with apparent humility." We'll see the parallels between Hester Prynne and Sarah Cornell drawn throughout this book.

"Nathaniel Hawthorne's greatest novel owes its inspiration in part to this public discussion of seduction and murder," wrote Boudreau. "Hawthorne's novel is less concerned with Hester's actual crime . . . than with the people's response to that crime."

The people's response to Cornell's death is the issue in our case: Was the minister guilty of murder? Or the recipient of unwarranted public judgment?

———

The Sinners All Bow also draws on hundreds of pages of unpublished material. There are more than a dozen accounts during that time period of the case, including letters from family and friends, reports by investigators, and notes from the prosecutor. There are also letters between Sarah Cornell and Ephraim Avery, offering an inside look at their tortured relationship. Sidney S. Rider's biographical essay about Catharine Williams included her own memoir, in which she detailed her struggle as a single mother and an emerging writer in a male-dominated field.

Catharine Williams and Sarah Cornell were confined by the still-powerful vestiges of Puritanism in their society: propriety, devotion to the church, the commitment to marriage. . . . But Catharine was able to disentangle a few of those knots. She dared to divorce a man from a respectable family in New England, an affront to the traditional norms of the times. She persevered and eventually gained a level of respect offered to few women in New England in the early nineteenth century. Both Catharine and Sarah made a choice for independence, despite the consequences. Sarah Cornell dared to gain autonomy through mill work, and she refused to settle with a husband and raise a family; she had been devoted to a church that seemed to contradict the restrained roles of women that much of America subscribed to.

Together, Catharine Williams and I will rewrite the tale of Sarah Cornell and Reverend Ephraim Avery—and this version, drawing on the conventions and fact-checking of twenty-first-century crime reporting, will present the reader with all the facts, no matter the conclusion. It will serve as a reckoning for all true crime writers: how to avoid the mistakes of the past and how to move forward by respecting the victim, no matter their background.

Catharine Williams crafted a new genre: a victim-centric, story-driven, fact-checked narrative meant to bewitch an audience and shift their belief system about women and their burgeoning independence. She believed that women could protect one another—and she demonstrated that in her own life, because, after her marriage, she shunned all dependence on men. A narrative focused primarily on the victim was unique—and her commitment to thorough reporting was exceptional.

But Catharine's own troubling history with men, along with her rigid religious ideology, posed a problem for our project because those factors **might** have influenced her judgment; this was a narrative she had framed as "authentic," starting with the title. But Catharine Williams despised one of the central characters—the vitriol she had reserved for Reverend Ephraim Avery litters the pages of **Fall River**. She viewed him as little more than a despicable predator; a greedy, venal man stalking the young women of New England; a brute who was halted only because of his connection to Sarah's death. **He murdered Sarah**, she declared in her pages.

Catharine refused to investigate alternate theories, but a journalist who offers readers a nonfiction narrative **must** examine all sides of the investigation, and a controversial story demands a responsible, unbiased pen. I offer that pledge to my readers and my listeners: if you trust me, I will do my best to provide you with the full story in this case, no matter the outcome. Did Sarah Cornell die by her own hand, or was she the victim of a killer? And if she was murdered, **who** was the killer? Catharine Williams was stubbornly, foolishly steadfast in her conclusion, well before all the available evidence was submitted. But I'll offer a more complete picture of one of the most important cases in American history . . . that you've likely never heard of. **Will Catharine and I arrive at the same conclusion?**

CHAPTER ONE

~⌇~

THE DURFEE FARM

IT WAS JULY 1, 1833, and the moon was just beginning to rise over the small town of Tiverton, Rhode Island. Catharine Read Arnold Williams stepped onto the wooden front porch and rapped on the door of the old home. It swung open, and a tall, thin man in a top hat greeted the writer, steeling himself for what he was certain would be a solemn visit.

The man who answered the door, John Durfee, nodded respectfully to Catharine as she stood in the darkness. The farmer was known for his hospitality, and Catharine was familiar with his reputation. She was grateful that he had agreed to this meeting, morbid as it seemed. Both hoped to gain some understanding of what had happened on his farm the previous December. Durfee closed the door and stepped outside.

The thirty-five-year-old Durfee was an important, anxious witness—he had been the first person to find Sarah Maria Cornell's body that cold day half a year earlier. Catharine was determined to record Durfee's story accurately, so she reported to his farm that night for a tour.

This property was owned by Richard Durfee II, John's seventy-five-year-old father, who was a well-liked deacon and a retired captain with the Rhode Island militia. But it was John who ran the day-to-day operations. John Durfee was a profitable farmer, a justice of the peace, a widely respected town councilman, and a member of one of the most influential families in the area. Because of Durfee's seemingly sincere benevolence, the town leaders had appointed him "Overseer of the Poor." The overseer, a position originally created in England and later adopted by governments in the fledgling American colonies, was tasked with protecting the destitute in their parishes. Traditionally, the overseer would control a small budget for this purpose funded by collecting a tax from residents, but his duties also included distributing food and money and managing the local poorhouse.

As the pair stood together, Catharine inquired about John's family. His father, as well as his mother, Patience, would remain inside the house this evening, along with John's wife, Nancy, and their six children. The Durfee family had been in this area since the mid-1600s, beginning with Richard

Durfee Sr., a descendent of several passengers on the **Mayflower**. Eventually, John's father married Patience Borden—a member of the later infamous Borden clan. (That family plays a prominent role in this story too, as you'll read later.) The Durfees and the Bordens, Catharine wrote, were two of the three families who had established Tiverton.

"The land in this vicinity belonged principally to the families of Borden, Bowen, and Durfee," she wrote in her 1833 book, **Fall River**, about this tragedy, "three families from whom the principal part of the stationary inhabitants sprung." It was a prosperous, fertile area; "so flourishing has business been there, that there is scarce a mechanic, trader, or even labourer, who has been there for any length of time, who has not acquired an estate of his own," Catharine wrote.

The Durfees and the Bordens would remain pillars of the community for generations. But all families are flawed, and some are plagued with characters with a penchant for brutality. The Bordens, who would come to infamy a few generations later when Lizzie Borden was tried and acquitted of the infamous axe murders that killed her father and stepmother, were clearly not immune to violence.

John Durfee, by all accounts, was prosperous, compassionate, and altruistic, a rare intersection of traits in the 1800s. It was important to Catharine and me to establish both Durfee's reputation and his apparent character because he had been a crucial witness—he had sounded the alarm about Sarah Cornell's death.

Catharine Williams was determined to record everything involving this case, including an extensive interview with John Durfee. The farmer described what he had discovered that frigid December morning. Durfee needed coaxing to recall such a traumatizing sight. He might have felt reticent because such horrid details surely would offend his guest's feminine sensibilities, yet he responded to her questions candidly, starting with a trip he'd taken with his horses early that day.

"On the morning of the 21 of December," began Durfee, "I took my team to go from home to the river, and passing through a lot about 60 rods from my house."

He descended the hill, careful to avoid burrow entrances dug by gophers and groundhogs the summer before. As Durfee approached a haystack, less than a quarter mile from his home, he gasped. "When I arrived within ten yards of the haystack, I discovered the body of a female hanging on a stake." Suspended by a cord, swaying slowly in the wind that blew from Mount Hope Bay, was the body of a young woman. Sarah Cornell was dressed in a long black cloak; her shoes were laid neatly on the ground. In the dim light of the sunrise, he could see that her short, dark hair was frozen to her face and covered in frost. John Durfee cried out and three men responded, including his father, Richard.

The woman was young, attractive, and dead—but that's all Durfee knew at the time. The farmer told Catharine that he had never seen the woman before. As the sun began to illuminate the yard, Durfee braced himself.

"After taking more notice how she hung, I attempted to take her from the stake by lifting her up and slipping the line," said Durfee. "I found I could not well do it, at arm's length, and my father said, 'cut her down.' One handed me a knife, and I cut her down, and let her down."

Her body slumped; the cord was still wrapped tightly around her neck.

"I then went after the coroner," Durfee said, "and brought him to my house."

As the first person on the scene, Durfee wasn't just a witness—he was also a de facto investigator. He had initiated his own inquiry by collecting valuable evidence, and the picture that he and the investigators painted was a disturbing story, one Catharine was at the farm to hear about firsthand and examine further.

———

But first: safer subjects. That evening in 1833, Catharine began peppering John Durfee with queries about the property and its history. He replied as she jotted down notes. He resided on his 57-acre family farm on the main road of Tiverton, about a half mile from the Massachusetts border, across the water and less than two miles from the factory village of Fall River. As I noted earlier, that part of Tiverton was renamed Fall River, Massachusetts, about thirty years later.

The town was located on the Quequechan River, the last tributary at the mouth of the Taunton River, which made it a perfect spot to take advantage of the burgeoning industrial revolution that was sweeping across New England and reshaping the economy and landscape. The river was slow moving, even stagnant, except near downtown Fall River, where it flowed quickly down into Mount Hope Bay—the perfect fuel for textile mills and ironworks.

"Starting as early as 1811, cotton and woolen mills were built and put into operation," reported the Advisory Council on Historic Preservation. The Durfees were at least partially responsible for Tiverton's growth as a mill town.

Water is featured in both Sarah Cornell's story and that of Hester Prynne. "Fall River can be understood in relation to . . . **The Scarlet Letter**," wrote Shirley Samuels in **Reading the American Novel, 1780–1865**, "as a narrative about an itinerant female laborer whose restlessness and employment depends on the vagaries of water. As the river waters that turn the mill wheels rise and fall, so does the employment of factory girls at the mill's ebb and wane."

Working women in the mid-1800s often needed

to be near water. Joseph Durfee had built a simple spinning mill in the area at the turn of the century, and through the first few decades of the 1800s that holding had grown to contain even more mills. As the family's wealth increased, so did their influence. By 1833, Richard Durfee II's farm was a vast estate boasting a fantastic view of Mount Hope Bay—a clear symbol of their wealth and influence. The Durfees remained so important to the area for generations after that eventually a high school was named after them, as was a street in the town. There is still a mill complex in Fall River that bears the Durfee name, as well as a house designated as a historical home. The Durfees were Fall River and Tiverton royalty. Catharine Williams described their land at the time:

"Fall River, which in 1812 contained less than one hundred inhabitants, owes its growth and importance principally, indeed almost wholly, to its manufacturing establishments: which, though not splendid in appearance, are very numerous and employ several thousand persons collected from different parts of the country."

All these mills required workers, and towns like nearby Fall River began attracting men and increasingly women from the surrounding rural landscape. Women, in particular, were deemed well suited for mill work, because they tended to work hard without complaint; they also drank infrequently, mostly because they were tightly supervised in their boardinghouses. And many came from strict religious households, which meant reverence to men was mandatory. Most "female operatives," as women mill workers were called, were compliant, and if they weren't, they were forced to move on.

Sarah Cornell had been in many ways the ideal prototype for the female mill worker: husbandless, without a child, and untethered to her parents. She could toil for long hours without the need to tend to a family. Sarah was also a proficient weaver, seamstress, and tailor. The thirty-year-old had been professionally trained by other women in her youth, and by the time she reached the Fall River mills, she had logged many years of mill-work experience. Throughout her twenties, Sarah had traveled from village to village across New England, plying her trade year-round with few holidays and little respite. Anthropology professor David Richard Kasserman, author of the 1986 academic book **Fall River Outrage**, discovered that Sarah had moved more than sixteen times in twelve years to various jobs around Rhode Island, Massachusetts, and Connecticut. Yet this sort of movement was not necessarily unusual for a woman like Sarah. Factory work was often seasonal, and workers might be shifted to and from mills if owners decided to downsize.

As America rapidly expanded in the first few decades of the 1800s, factories emerged in cities and towns all along the eastern coast, transforming their owners into millionaires. Smoke spilled from the factory chimneys as soot floated toward the roofs of the town churches. There were many new job opportunities for young women yearning for independence—"at least forty thousand spindles in operation" throughout the region, Catharine wrote—each filled with women praying for respite from servitude in the cities, or hoping to escape the trying life as a farmer's wife.

Catharine seemed quite fond of Fall River and its history, both recent and more ancient. She wrote: "It requires no great effort of imagination to go back a few years and imagine the Indian with his light canoe sailing about in these waters, or dodging about among the rocks and trees. The neighborhood of Fall River has been the scene of frequent skirmishes among the Picknets, the tribe of King Philip, and the Pequods and Narragansetts. Uncas too, with the last of the Mohicans and the best, has set his princely foot upon its strand."

But while Sarah Cornell's death was the focus of the first narrative book of macabre murder in America, it would not be the last in Fall River. In the years after Catharine first told Sarah's story, other dark events occurred in the surrounding streets. That's where I'll contribute to Catharine's observations of Fall River's history by adding more context with darker details.

After the village was renamed in 1856, its population grew, as did its crime rate. It has been referred to in the modern press as a "cursed city," though I'm not certain that reputation was earned. Less than a twenty-minute walk from John Durfee's farm (now Kennedy Park) is a section of the city measuring about two blocks, where a series of freak, media-grabbing tragedies occurred spanning a century. These were not simple domestic disputes or botched bank robberies. They were deaths that seemed so out of the norm that they were triggered by a cloister of demons hiding in the shadows (or so some local tours claim).

The most notorious tragedy in Fall River happened in 1892, when Lizzie Borden was tried for murdering her father and stepmother with a hatchet in their multilevel Fall River home. The case grabbed headlines across the nation for its brutality, and also its aftermath—Borden was eventually acquitted by a jury, an all-male panel unconvinced that a respectable middle-class woman could butcher her parents. Later investigators weren't so sure about that. The Borden murders still draw countless tourists to the house every year, particularly around Halloween.

But tragedy had long stalked the Borden family. Four decades earlier, Lizzie Borden's great-uncle Lawdwick Borden and his wife, Eliza Darling Borden, lived next door to the Borden house on

Second Street in Fall River. Eliza had three children with Lawdwick in quick succession, and afterward she grew increasingly depressed, apparently suffering from postpartum depression that went untreated. In 1848, after months of despair, the thirty-six-year-old Eliza drowned two of her three children, Holder and Eliza Ann, in the home's basement cistern, before slitting her own throat with one of her husband's straight razors.

There were five horrific, violent deaths at two locations just feet from each other, all involving the Borden family. But preceding those fatalities, the block was touched by another doomed event, a seemingly innocent accident directly across the street from both homes. On July 2, 1843, a deadly fire ripped through that section of Fall River, nearly destroying a large portion of the city; historians believe it began with two boys who were exploring the back of a three-story warehouse near the corner of Main and Borden Streets. The boys discovered a small cannon that was going to be used for Independence Day festivities in two days, and, being curious, they fired it. The blast ignited a scattering of wood shavings on the ground, left behind by workers in the warehouse. The shavings flamed and the fire spread quickly, thanks to the dry summer winds caused by months of 90-degree temperatures. Within five minutes, the fire raged. Fall River's fire bell clanged as terrified residents evacuated onto the streets, including those at the Borden home across the street. A sheet of fire pushed onlookers backward.

"Showers of sparks and cinders, carried by the heavy wind, kindled many buildings before they were reached by the body of the fire," detailed the author of **The History of Fall River**. "The whole space between Main, Franklin, Rock and Borden streets was one vast sheet of fire, entirely beyond the control of man."

Mother Nature intervened. Despite every effort from responders, only a change in wind stopped its spread. But in the end, the fire had destroyed almost three hundred buildings. Although no one died in the fire itself, the blaze was blamed for four deaths, including someone who died of "fright."

"They looked upon their village in ruins, and felt that it must long bear the marks of this fearful calamity," concluded **The History of Fall River**.

And here's another coincidence involving that fire. Eliza and Lawdwick Borden were living in the house across the street during the fire. Eliza had two sons from a previous marriage who would have been about the same age as the boys who were suspected of starting the fire. Did the Borden boys ignite the inferno that nearly destroyed Fall River? Maybe, but we can't confirm it because newspapers at the time never revealed the identity of the boys. But it was quite a coincidence.

Fall River, Massachusetts, **did** seem to be cursed in the 1800s, the nexus for an evil entity bent on

committing murder and provoking fear for generations. Gory stories permeate the pages of Fall River
history books. But in 1833, as Catharine Williams
stood on John Durfee's porch that summer evening,
all these tragedies were years in the future. Fifty
years before "Lizzie Borden took an axe," Sarah
Cornell had died on a bitterly cold December night,
on the Durfee farm, swaying in the wind from a
tight cord. She was a wayward planet with nothing
to orbit, Catharine wrote, a tragic spirit that now
haunted the lonely property. Sarah had been abandoned in death for hours, far away from her family,
with only the hooting great horned owls in the trees
as witnesses before John Durfee discovered her. The
death of Sarah Maria Cornell was, at the time, Fall
River's most significant murder.

But was it even a murder at all?

———

Catharine stood outside the farmhouse in the warm
night air on the Durfee farm and breathed in. She
could hear the waves on the rocky shore of Mount
Hope Bay down the hill as she and John Durfee
left the farmhouse and started walking. Her visit,
she felt, was shaping up to be a success. There was
nothing like seeing the scene of a crime for yourself to paint an accurate picture of the events. And
Catharine was, above all else, a stickler for accuracy.

The air felt a bit humid, she noted, and it smelled

of sea salt mixed with livestock. On this warm summer evening, with the moon barely rising, Durfee's cattle shuffled in the paddock in the distance, confined by a maze of short stone walls. The farm's horses whinnied. Durfee's farmhands had housed for the evening several large carts for hauling goods and ranch supplies. The wind blew across the fully leafed limbs of the massive maple trees that peppered the land. Catharine took notes for the opening of her book, glancing at the outside of the home and then turning to look at the hill to its side. She would later write about her surroundings:

"There is a large old-fashioned farmhouse belonging to a family by the name of Durfee. The land descends from here towards the bay with a gentle slope and is probably about 150 or 200 rods to the water. The house stands in the state of Rhode Island, and near the line that marks the boundaries of the two states."

Catharine and I both lean on deeply rich scene-setting in our books, a writing technique meant to draw readers into a world we are reconstructing to offer them a visceral experience. But she also understood how important evaluating the accessibility of a crime scene is for investigators. It's often the first step in modern policing: examining the area and marking it for clues. And this is where Catharine and I will start with our own investigation.

Today, investigators can, of course, detect a wealth of useful information from the scene of a crime;

these clues are the basis for prosecution, and the police and other investigators serve a vital role in evidence collection after a suspicious death. "Crime scene investigators document the crime scene," according to the National Institute of Justice. "They take photographs and physical measurements of the scene, identify and collect forensic evidence, and maintain the proper chain of custody of that evidence. Crime scene investigators collect evidence such as fingerprints, footprints, tire tracks, blood and other body fluids, hairs, fibers, and fire debris."

Investigators also determine what forensic tools might be useful before turning over clues to forensic experts. Killers often unknowingly leave behind physical evidence that can be forensically tested later and leveraged in trial. Forensic investigator Paul Holes told me that assessing a crime scene can yield invaluable tools if detectives know what to look for. "Oftentimes there's physical interaction, there's physical violence," he said. What crime scene investigators are looking for is, "Is there evidence of somebody else present?" Holes is also a cold-case investigator, known for helping solve the famous Golden State Killer case in 2018. He's also my cohost on our podcast, **Buried Bones**, where we dissect cases from history that need to be viewed through a twenty-first-century lens. We'll hear from him throughout our story.

Some techniques, like fingerprinting, shoe-print examination, and handwriting analysis, have been available for more than one hundred years. "Plan and plan, as he may," wrote true crime author George Barton in 1926, "the criminal invariably leaves some gap in the machination of his scheme, some rift, minute though it may be, some crevice through which the detective may insert the little probe of his specialized knowledge, and thus discover the truth."

The skilled evidence collector can secure clues and catalog them to be used later by forensic investigators. But detectives go a step further and evaluate accessibility; they're trained to note who might enter the area easily: Are there locked doors and latched windows? Are there secured gates? Is there a night watchman to avoid? Is there some kind of security system? Detectives interview people nearby: neighbors, domestic staff, and workers. Did the victim share a key or a security code with someone? Was there maintenance work recently done where laborers might have observed the victim's habits? Is there transportation nearby that would aid in a getaway? Establishing access is crucial. A locked door, bolted shut, that shows no signs of tampering might indicate that the offender was either known to the victim or found another way in, including force. Investigators can narrow their list of suspects by establishing the level of access.

Catharine, of course, had none of these modern tools. But peering into the darkness that July night, she realized one detail immediately: the Durfee farm was easily accessible. There was no night watchman wandering around the property. No farmhands lived near the barn. If the offender had been a member of the Durfee family, then access was assured. But an anonymous offender could also observe the Durfees' nightly, predictable routine. Drawing a victim to a quiet farm, in the darkness, might seem private. That section of the property was tucked away, cloaked by large trees, down the hill from the main house. With the family secluded inside the home, they were unlikely to hear a struggle, even in the quiet of a winter night. Certainly, Sarah Maria Cornell, if she had arrived there alone to die by her own hand, would have had access. The crime scene's relative accessibility wouldn't help us narrow our list of suspects.

Catharine scanned her notepad to check. She noted what the weather conditions had been on the night that Sarah had died—below freezing. An elderly man from Newport, Rhode Island, named James Taylor was a retired druggist who referred to himself as a "scientific apothecary," a kind of nineteenth-century meteorologist. Taylor would later be interviewed by investigators because he kept the habit of noting the area's weather three times a day in his journal. He observed the conditions at sunrise, then 2:00 p.m., and then 9:00 p.m. year-round. Taylor reported that it had been 29 degrees around 9:00 p.m. on the night of Sarah's death. And there had been clear skies, no snow or rain, though the ground had been muddy.

Modern forensic investigators understand how crucial weather can be to a case. Cold weather can slow the decomposition of a body and help investigators preserve evidence. Warm, wet weather can accelerate decomposition, making it difficult to establish the time or cause of death. Bugs might arrive sooner or later in certain weather conditions, telling forensic entomologists how long the body has been at the scene. Rain might wash away crucial clues, like blood pooling, semen, shoe prints, or other physical evidence.

"Rain is horrible to work in—it's horrible for the crime scene. You have blood patterns that are being washed away," Holes told me. "So much is affected by water at a crime scene. And so, when you have the spray of the water, everything is damp, that prevents some evidence from being left behind. Or it also will destroy evidence."

Poor weather conditions can also prevent investigators from even reaching a crime scene. "I've been in situations in my jurisdiction in which our crime scene vehicle could not get close to the crime scene," Holes continued. "So now there's having to get equipment out to the location, and you forget something. And now you're constantly going back and forth."

Analysts generally follow a standard set of steps

when they're dispatched to a crime scene: They create a sort of perimeter around the "main action," and concentrate on collecting evidence in that area first. They secure the crime scene, often with yellow crime scene tape. They determine the type of crime they're investigating—is this likely a robbery, or a sexual assault, or an execution-style murder? They process the scene, which includes photography, and then go back and examine it once again. Finally, they collect and preserve the evidence. All this happens before the bulk of the investigation begins. Crime scene collectors have a trying job.

Of course, we have access to none of this sort of information on Sarah Cornell's death. And neither did Catharine—she was visiting the Durfee farm six months after the discovery of Sarah's body. But Catharine does provide us with something valuable: the notes and impressions that she recorded from the first eyewitnesses. It wasn't ideal, but Catharine did the best she could to gather intelligence from John Durfee's firsthand observations.

Durfee smiled at Catharine as he gripped a gas lamp in one hand that warm summer night and led her back down the main dirt road, toward an isolated spot not far from the bay. Tufts of black hair escaped the tight top hat on his head. As the dirt path crunched under their feet, Catharine and Durfee slowly and quietly walked down a sloping hill toward a massive round haystack—at least a building story tall. The mound of hay was flanked by four sturdy metal stakes, over which a burlap cover was suspended—offering the haystack protection from the wet wind that plagued Massachusetts, even in the mild summer months.

As she stood near the farmer in the moonlight, Catharine realized that it would be improper for her to remain at the Durfee farm too late—besides, she and John Durfee, both devout Christians, were committed to reporting to their respective churches for Sunday services early the next morning. The church bells would toll, beckoning for their reverence. She noted in her book that there were seven houses of worship in the small village, all hosting devotees of Christ.

The breeze from the water felt cool. Catharine glanced down at the ground to the green grass, which, the previous December, had been brown and wet. The writer gazed at the section of land where the haystack pole stood. This was the location they'd been heading toward. The very spot where John Durfee had found Sarah Cornell's body.

She looked down at the area where Sarah's shoes had once been placed, close to her body—**did Sarah lay them there neatly before taking her own life? Or did her killer leave behind that curious clue?** It seemed strange for a woman in the throes of depression, determined to take her own life, to take the time to arrange her shoes in an orderly fashion, yet Sarah Cornell was a young lady trained to be orderly. Catharine was amassing information about the crime scene as the moon glowed, illuminating the tree limbs above. An artist sketched the scene in the late 1830s, and the drawing matches Catharine's description of the area as secluded—a fitting place for a suicide . . . or a murder.

Catharine thought often about dying, which wasn't an unusual practice in the 1800s, considering how frequently fatal tragedies visited families. Death was a part of everyday life for people in America in the early 1800s. Men and women were not expected to reach their fiftieth birthdays, and deaths—whether from childbirth, illness, or accidents—were terrifyingly common. If one was lucky (or unlucky) enough to make it to a doctor, anesthesia during operations was rudimentary—many times it involved opium or alcohol and a rag to grip between your teeth. Doctors were not even trained to regularly sanitize their hands before surgery. Often, patients never recovered.

New England's mill towns, in particular, were known for their high mortality rates. The growing multitudes of dangerous textile operations created immense financial opportunities for some . . . but that growth largely came on the backs of young women like Sarah Maria Cornell. Women sometimes died from accidents in those mills. Even if they were lucky enough not to be injured, the work was hard and punishing. But, Catharine knew, it hadn't been the mills that had killed Sarah—at least, not directly.

Catharine stood in silence with John Durfee, hovering near where Sarah Cornell had spent her final moments alive. There was a macabre romance swirling around Catharine that night. A poet by nature, she found the location oddly mesmerizing. Her eyes welled.

"Few have visited that spot without tears," she wrote. "There seems to be a spell breathing around that none can withstand. The effect is absolutely irresistible."

Little else beyond religion and her daughter had ever moved Catharine Williams. With the stalwart stoicism characteristic of a proud, noble New Englander, she had long internalized her pain—the pain of a failed marriage, the isolation she felt afterward by judgmental contemporaries in her social circle who had once proclaimed to be her friends. It was perhaps Catharine's knowledge of what it felt like to be judged that gave her real compassion and insight into Sarah Cornell's situation.

Often, poets allow their emotions to spill upon the pages of their work, refusing to be refined and ashamed. But until she had discovered the sad, pitiable life and death of Sarah Cornell, Catharine had been a stoic, even reserved writer who restricted her passions to her adoration of the Bible. But Sarah's pained life and premature death—and the unconscionable reaction from society that followed—had evoked a fury in Catharine that had been long repressed. **After all**, many at the time whispered, that Cornell girl was no better than she ought to be. It's a shame she's dead, but she got what was coming to her.

Catharine was appalled by New England's pretentious snobs who shamed Sarah Cornell and disparaged her life. Catharine wrote in her book, "One person went so far as to say that 'he did not think such a drab worth having a trial about.'" That abhorrent admission sickened Catharine, though many in her upper-class circles would admittedly feel the same. She reserved little judgment for Sarah Cornell . . . only for her suspected killer. This made Catharine Williams unique within the blue-blood society of New England: she could look beyond class discrimination and see Sarah as a victim worthy of justice.

––––––––

As Catharine Williams and John Durfee talked under the light of the moon, the silhouettes of the massive oak trees faded while the cobalt summer sky darkened; their thick branches veiled the sleeping finches and robins. Durfee whispered as she nodded and scribbled notes on her pad in pencil. It was an unorthodox time to survey the property, but it was important to Catharine to visit the scene around the time of night that it was estimated Sarah Cornell had died.

This was an impulse that I, as a fellow true crime writer, could understand. After all, here I was, almost two hundred years later, at the exact same spot. As I surveyed the slope of the old Durfee farm, just as Catharine Williams had done nearly two centuries earlier, I sighed. The breeze was still cool off the water and gently tugged at the massive maple trees. The space between that night in July 1833 and my visit in 2021 seemed to melt away.

Catharine felt haunted as she imagined Sarah's final moments. She prayed that Sarah had died quickly. Death by hanging could be agonizingly slow—the sufferer might be strangled rather than have their neck broken quickly if the rope were not placed correctly. They could also die in less than five minutes, according to Paul Holes. Is that what had happened to Sarah? Had the young woman walked to this isolated spot, in the dead of night, in December 1832 and hanged herself? Or had she been drawn here . . . by another person who had a hand in her death?

That was what Catharine and I were both trying to understand by coming here. The trip to Durfee's farm had convinced Catharine that this story was worthy of her pen; she had written nonfiction historical accounts before, but never about so unseemly a subject. The world of crime reporting, in which God's commandments were regularly violated, felt seedy to Catharine. But she was seduced by the story of Sarah Maria Cornell—a young woman with promise, who had been rejected and dejected at every turn, including by her own family, because of a handful of poor decisions early on in her life.

Catharine Williams, too, was leery of Sarah's connection to the Methodist Church—a trendy new religion in the 1830s, with its rambunctious, ill-educated ministers and their flock of naive, sexually charged female congregants. A staple of the Methodist denomination in America was the infamous "tent revivals," which were loud, days-long parties where young men and women came together to sing, pray, and get swept up and away by the Holy Spirit. This probably doesn't sound like the Methodist Church that you're familiar with now, the sedate mainline Protestant denomination with its tiny cups of nonalcoholic red grape juice referred to as "Methodist wine." But as we'll see, the early Methodists had a scandalous reputation in starchy, tradition-bound New England, and not everyone was a fan of this seductive new religion.

Catharine was one of the skeptics. Her devotion to the old-guard Protestantism moved her to denounce what today we might call "charismatic evangelicalism"—ministers standing onstage and preaching as if they were on fire. Catharine's ire was particularly focused on the Methodist Church and its so-called blasphemous ministers. Methodism, Catharine feared, was spreading across America like an unrestrained contagion. In her writing, she highlighted the stark differences between respectable, old-school Congregationalism, which was referred to as a Protestant movement, and Methodism, a new Protestant denomination.

Congregationalists had carried their conservative faith with them on the **Mayflower** and were seen as a staple of provincial, conservative society. The shift toward these new denominations like Methodism, she feared, heralded the rise of fanaticism in America. "There are daily and hourly opportunities for the real Christian to shew forth the beauties of holiness, without disgusting people," Catharine wrote.

Sarah Cornell had attended some of these infamous Methodist tent revivals. Was it Sarah's infatuation with the Methodist Church—and her reverence to one magnetic preacher in particular—that had led her down a dangerous path?

As I read Catharine's words, I could tell right away she was biased. Could my cowriter be trusted to supplement my research if she harbored hatred for one of the largest characters in this case: the Methodist Church?

As I familiarized myself further with Catharine's work, I noticed other biases as well. We'll explore more of them as the story progresses. But some of these might be explained by the fact that, before her reporting on the story of Sarah Cornell, essays on crime were not Catharine's specialty—rather, her reputation had been established through her poetry, prose, and biographical narratives. But the story of Sarah Maria Cornell resonated deeply with Catharine. She felt compelled to seek out details and uncover exclusive information. Despite (or perhaps because of) her biases, Catharine transformed herself from a poet and a historian into an investigative reporter, even though she lacked what we would today call formal journalistic training. In the 1830s, Catharine had no guide to writing a true crime story—there were no contemporary authors in this genre to admire. Her book would be groundbreaking. She was pioneering true crime journalism, and she didn't even realize it.

As she stood at John Durfee's farm, she knew what her opening pages of **Fall River: An Authentic Narrative** would be.

"A fair and candid statement of facts, connected with the late unhappy affair is desirable," she insisted. "A narrative, therefore, that would embrace the facts, without any of the odious details in the trial, is highly necessary."

But Catharine Williams, armed with scathing words on a page, seemed incapable of keeping that promise to write a "fair and candid" statement of facts. She would instead write a story where her biases and preconceptions were on the page and evident for all to read. Whether those notions were in fact accurate—well, that's what I'll investigate alongside her.

———

In July 1833, standing where Sarah Cornell had died six months before, Catharine Williams felt saddened as she considered the short life of the wayward wanderer without proper influences.

"The deceased, it appeared, had been a moving planet, which she accounted for in one of her letters to her friends, by saying, 'she belonged to a people who did not believe in staying long in a place,'" concluded Catharine. "She seemed to have adopted for her motto, the text, that 'here have we no continuing city' and she adhered to it in the spirit and the letter."

That quote came from Hebrews 13:14, the King James Version. Catharine Williams quoted the Bible with ease and enthusiasm; the text served as her moral compass—a bright lighthouse in a storm of uncertainty born from a challenging life. Catharine wished that Sarah had listened to the Bible's teachings; in her writing about Sarah, there's an undercurrent of judgment of anyone who didn't heed her book's lessons; her unsolicited advice bordered on preaching, frankly.

"She probably had never read that admirable fable of the Fox who was advised to remove on account of the swarm of flies who beset him," she wrote, "and who wisely chose to remain where they might after a time get gorged with his blood."

Catharine admired **Aesop's Fables**, particularly one titled "The Fox, the Flies and the Hedgehog."

The fable goes that a hedgehog encounters a fox who is the victim of a swarm of flies, devouring him as he lies on the ground. The hedgehog offers to help, but the fox decides to stay with the current swarm of offenders that have almost finished feasting on him, rather than take a chance that he will encounter another fresh and hungry set of flies that might finish him off. The tale is meant to illustrate how greedy politicians are so prevalent that replacing one with another only weakens their constituents. But Catharine believed that young people should heed its lesson: straying too far from home could put them in tremendous danger.

Blaming the victim is never appropriate, and yet that method is often used in true crime writing because reflection is meant to offer the reader a lesson in how to avoid a similar fate. In Catharine's era, the mid-1800s, absolving Sarah of all responsibility would have met with outrage from her own readers, so the author straddled a fine line in her writing—an ounce of criticism mixed with plenty of pity; I'll aim to avoid that in my own book. Catharine's greatest skill as a writer was a devotion to her subject, whether it be a biography, a history, or a supposed murder case. And Sarah Cornell had been her focus now for six months. Sarah's death both inspired and dismayed the poet.

"For some time I stood wondering, without dreaming of the cause, but upon looking up, discovered the moon was in an eclipse," she wrote. "There was a singular coincidence in it certainly, and it forcibly reminded me of the dark and mysterious fate of her who reposed beneath."

Catharine stared toward the heavens above and imagined justice.

"I watched it as the shadow slid from the moon's disk, and I felt that confidence which I have ever felt since, that the mystery of darkness which envelopes the story and hides the sad fate of that unfortunate victim will one day be dispersed."

———

Catharine had already interviewed another crucial witness: Sarah Cornell's most trusted confidant, her physician Dr. Thomas Wilbur. He was not only Sarah's doctor in life; he was also one of the first men to examine her body upon her death. Dr. Wilbur's statement to Catharine became invaluable firsthand knowledge. It was also, as we'll learn, not without controversy.

The doctor told Catharine that he had been preparing to have breakfast with his family just a few blocks away from the Durfee farm the morning of December 21, 1832. "The doctor observed some people running up the street, apparently in great haste," Catharine wrote. "He stood at the window watching when they should return, to know what the matter was, but nobody came back, while another and another party followed close upon the heels of the former."

Dr. Wilbur watched from the safety of his home on South Main Street as more people rushed toward the farm. He felt uneasy—he couldn't smell the smoke of a fire, which seemed the most likely explanation for the panic. But then he became especially surprised and then alarmed when he spotted another group gathering nearby.

"The women appeared to be horror struck as they collected in groups at the doors or in the streets," Catharine reported Dr. Wilbur saying in their interview, "and many leaving their families just as they were, (it was about breakfast time) and hastily throwing something over them pushed on in the direction of Durfee's farm."

Observing women in a panic was troubling to Dr. Wilbur. Still, he stayed inside his home and watched the chaotic scene, determined to not become involved, until he was forced to by a concerned neighbor.

"Presently someone came running into the doctor's saying a young woman had just hung herself up at Durfee's," Catharine wrote. He hastily got dressed and ran out the door toward the farm, having no idea who he might discover. When he reached the crowd, he stood startled, and gazed at the body.

"He perceived a female lying on the ground, for they had taken her down," wrote Catharine. "She lay with her cloak, gloves and calash on, and her arms drawn under her cloak.

"'Does anyone know her?' asked one.

"'She is well dressed,' said another, 'I think she must be somebody respectable.'

"'Yes I know her,' said the Methodist minister

who had arrived on the ground a little previous to the doctor."

The words had been spoken by a local reverend named Ira Bidwell; Sarah Cornell was one of his devout congregants. Bidwell turned to Dr. Wilbur and John Durfee and declared solemnly:

"She is a respectable young woman, and a member of my church."

Reverend Bidwell seemed saddened by her death; she had been lately at his church services in Fall River. The identification was also verified by John Smith, the man who was called "the overseer" of Sarah's weaving room; Smith was essentially her supervisor. Dr. Wilbur, of course, had recognized her too. His patient's outcome had distressed him.

"Hastily lifting the profusion of dark locks that had fallen entirely over her face, he discovered with grief and astonishment the countenance of his late interesting patient," wrote Catharine. "Horror struck, he endeavored to loosen the cord from her neck."

Dr. Wilbur was shocked to find that the cord was embedded nearly half an inch into her flesh. He struggled to free it. It was a grim, gruesome scene.

Sarah had not died in peace or with relief, Catharine insisted to her readers—she had suffered greatly. There was no use in Dr. Wilbur's trying to save her, wrote Catharine. It was clear that she was dead and had been so for a while.

"But alas! There was nothing in the usual remedies

to produce resuscitation that would have availed anything here," she concluded, "for the young woman appeared to have been there all night and was frozen stiff. And is this the end of thy sorrows, poor unfortunate! thought the kind physician, as bending over the hapless victim."

"Hapless victim"—Catharine Williams would repeat that phrase in her book often as she leveraged her gift for sympathy toward Sarah in idioms filled with compassion.

———

That night in July, six months after Sarah's discovery, Catharine Williams visualized the woman hanging by her neck, hovering just above the twigs and muddy grass, as Durfee had described it. At the end of her introductory chapter of **Fall River**, Catharine would frame her story as an indictment not only of many men but also of the judgmental women who doomed Sarah to a legacy of shame.

"Here at this lonely grave, whose plain and unobtrusive stone just tells the name and age of a female cut off in the prime of her days—and tells no more—shall the young and the beautiful read the warning against the wiles of man," wrote Catharine. "Here the prudent mother shall bring her lovely daughters to read those lessons of prudence and caution."

Standing near Sarah's grave on the Durfee farm,

Catharine felt bitter over the young woman's fate . . . and she focused her vitriol squarely on the man she blamed, our main suspect. He had been the worst kind of offender: a demon in disguise.

"Pointing to this place, the drunkard, the swearer, the Sabbath breaker, the gambler, and even the highway robber, shall exclaim, 'that grave attests that monsters have lived worse than me!'"

Catharine's journalist writing, rooted in deep research and rigorous reporting, veered into the poetic as she unfurled the beginning of the narrative. Catharine mused about how well Sarah's body had been preserved, thanks to the cold weather. She also described in clear detail the Durfee farm's location in Tiverton—"about half a mile from the centre of the village of Fall River, in a southerly direction, on the direct road to Howland's Ferry and rather remote from any other dwelling." But while the country nights were dark and the farm was quiet, its proximity to town meant that it was easily accessible to anyone nearby. Catharine's detail about the farm being off the road to a ferry is also notable, because virtually anyone could have arrived on (or escaped by) the nearby ferry boat, a vessel that was likely to be deserted late at night.

And yet, while her narrative was factual and true, she also admitted to making a few adjustments to the story—mostly involving Dr. Wilbur's encounters with his patient Sarah Cornell. Catharine doesn't explain exactly what she changed, and insisted it was nothing of consequence. Here's how she explained her notes: she made changes "where it is said the phraseology is improved without altering the facts. If the error is on the side of delicacy we hope to be pardoned." Catharine continued, almost defiant:

"With respect to embellishment in this book, no person acquainted with the facts, who has seen it, pretends to say there is any, except in the first interview between the physician and the unfortunate heroine of the tale," Catharine disclosed. What "delicate" changes she made are left to the imagination, but one wonders if she left out graphic or salacious details that she considered both offensive and superfluous.

This "embellishment" by the author is another sign of innovation in true crime writing, a genre, according to modern scholars, that Catharine began to shape: creative nonfiction.

"Williams is really acting as lawyer in **Fall River**, offering her own narrative, timeline, and evidence meant to exonerate the victim of a crime for which she somehow became responsible," wrote Leslie Rowen in her essay "True Crime as a Literature of Advocacy." "This is another technique anticipating a new convention in the true crime genre—the synthesis of many different documents, styles, and pieces of evidence into one digestible narrative."

The synthesis of different documents and evidence, like interviews, is a hallmark of good narrative nonfiction writing, but are "flourishes" problematic? Perhaps, if we're using them to weigh a man's guilt or innocence.

As I left the park where Durfee's farm once stood, I knew I needed to keep my factual-reporter hat on as I continued my investigation. The next task: understanding our victim, Sarah Cornell, a bit better. This next section is about victimology, one of the most powerful tools of the investigator.

CHAPTER TWO

∿

SARAH MARIA

THE AGED WOODEN PLANKS CREAKED as I walked across the floor, trailing behind the curators of a unique museum known as the Leffingwell House, built in 1675 on Washington Street in Norwich, Connecticut. Heavy rain pelted the black wooden-shingled roof as sheets of water slammed against the row of four windows facing my rental car. The married couple guiding me on today's tour, Greg and Cam Farlow, swiftly drew me from room to room, explaining the significance of the two-and-a-half-story home as we ducked under low doorways. The cramped parlor of the Leffingwell House, featuring a large fireplace, seemed too modest to have hosted the Founding Fathers of colonial America. Its startling deep red exterior, contrasted against the muddy, cloudy sky, was a beacon from the monsoon of storms I had just driven through. The home is crucial to our story . . . and it was critical in history. It doesn't seem like Catharine Williams ever visited, however—she never mentioned it.

Centuries ago, the Leffingwell family hosted George Washington for breakfast. Notable, yes, but then half the old New England houses have a "Washington slept here" plaque out front, so this designation is hardly unique. But the Leffingwell family appears to have distinguished themselves in other ways, as well: they cloistered and fed Patriots during the Revolutionary War and established themselves as part of an emerging New England aristocracy.

They were also the family from which Sarah Cornell, our victim, came. Her mother, Lucretia Cornell (née Leffingwell), had been born and raised in this esteemed home. How did poor Sarah wind up alone, abandoned, and helpless if she hailed from such a prominent lineage? I was here at Leffingwell House to find out.

While Catharine Williams may not have visited the exact spot where I was standing, she had examined the Leffingwell family for clues about Sarah Cornell's lineage. In 1833, Catharine researched the family's rise to power in the 1600s. It was part of her investigation as she constructed a profile of the victim, a deep dive into her personal history that was a practice in victimology before that term was coined in 1946. This was a rarely used technique in early 1800s true crime newspaper stories.

"Christopher Leffingwell [Sarah Cornell's grandfather] was the direct descendant of that Thomas Leffingwell of Saybrook, Connecticut," wrote Catharine. Several generations earlier, Thomas Leffingwell was born in Essex, England, and he arrived in the colonies in 1637 with no fortune but full of drive and, it seems, some important skills. A hunter in his youth, Thomas befriended the legendary warrior Uncas, the sachem (or chief) of the Mohegan Tribe during most of the seventeenth century. This might seem like an unlikely connection, an Englishman and a Native American. But Thomas Leffingwell learned the tribe's language, survived in the forests of New England with the Mohegan, and forged a real connection with Uncas and his men, sharing resources and displaying bravery to help protect them.

In 1645, as the story goes, Uncas and the Mohegan were surrounded during a siege from a rival tribe, the Narragansett. Fearing his friends would starve to death, Leffingwell loaded a canoe with food and came to Uncas's rescue, helping him stave off his enemy. For his help, Uncas and the Mohegan rewarded Leffingwell with nine miles' worth of land in Connecticut, which eventually became part of Norwich. Within a decade, he had thrived there and started a family.

"It has been said that Thomas Leffingwell may

have been the living inspiration for the fictional character Hawkeye in the story **The Last of the Mohicans** by James Fenimore Cooper," wrote his biographer, Russell Mahan. "He was an English immigrant, an early settler of Saybrook and a co-founder of Norwich, a Puritan, a family man, a farmer, a soldier in the Pequot and King Philip's wars, and a surveyor of the wilderness."

Thomas Leffingwell was a prominent frontiersman in the Northeast in the 1600s, but his descendent, Christopher, might have had an even greater impact on New England in the 1700s. "Christopher Leffingwell was a well-known businessman in Connecticut, and not only that, he was an outspoken Patriot," as Amirah Neely wrote on the blog **Digital Farmington**. "He was connected throughout the war and commanded the 20th Regiment of the State Militia, where he was a colonel. He was highly skilled at war strategy and became an advisor to Governor Trumbull."

During the Revolutionary War, Colonel Leffingwell became a confidant and advisor to General George Washington. "Washington, who made several stops in Connecticut during the war, would stay in Norwich and Leffingwell would provide him with provisions," according to Neely. "Connecticut provided the best prices and supplies on goods such that even John Hancock would often write to Leffingwell about goods."

Before the war, in 1766, Leffingwell had built the first paper mill in Connecticut, a decision that seeded the rise of mills across New England; the industry ushered in an era of massive economic growth and prosperity for the mill owners. Over the next decade, Christopher Leffingwell built numerous factories that made everything from felt to combs to clocks. He also established a chocolate factory—and he fed Patriot soldiers sweets during the war. But then, he also became critical to the war effort in other ways.

"When news of Lexington and Concord came around, Leffingwell signed the Lexington Alarm, which was carried by Israel Bissell from town-to-town warning that the war had begun," according to Jason Mandresh of **Founder of the Day**. "He then became one of six men (others included Silas Deane and Samuel Parsons) to pay for Benedict Arnold and Ethan Allen's notable capture of Fort Ticonderoga." (That last bit is quite a coincidence, because Catharine Read Arnold Williams was rumored to be Benedict Arnold's descendent, though it wasn't a connection she publicly acknowledged. These old New England family trees are tangled, indeed.)

Catharine, it is fair to say, was awed by Sarah Maria Cornell's family legacy. "New England is under lasting obligations to the name of Leffingwell," Catharine effusively wrote in **Fall River**. What wasn't immediately clear, though, was how the family had gone from New England aristocracy to poor, itinerant mill workers in just a generation or two.

The roots of that story go back to Norwich, Connecticut, and Leffingwell House, where Sarah's mother was raised. Inside the Norwich home, just after the Revolutionary War, Christopher Leffingwell's children scurried from room to room, never quite appreciating the affluence and influence of their father. But one of Christopher's daughters, Lucretia, would learn at age twenty-six about his high expectations.

Christopher Leffingwell yearned to cement and grow his already substantial power, and he understood that the key to this was that his children marry well. Like most other colonists, Leffingwell was in debt. It would serve him to marry his children into a moneyed family.

I had spent months locating a Leffingwell descendent who might offer me more context to the family's history, and then I found Roy Leffingwell. The sixty-eight-year-old's family has lived in New England for hundreds of years—and he didn't venture far from his roots, because he now lives in Rhode Island. I called him at his auto repair garage in Bristol in 2022, and when we talked about the Leffingwell family, he spoke frankly about their history and elite attitudes.

"The Leffingwells only married the who's who in New England," Leffingwell told me. "And if you didn't, you were an outcast."

Catharine Williams concurred. As she penned her book in 1833, she lamented Lucretia Leffingwell's unfortunate marriage "mistake," one misguided enough to seemingly doom her daughter, Sarah Maria, before she was born. In the pages of her book, Catharine framed Sarah's decisions as an adult as a study in victimology—how did her early life shape those decisions?

———

"With the greatest care and impartiality, the author of the following pages has collected together all the facts susceptible of proof relating to the life of Sarah Maria Cornell," Catharine wrote about her reporting. "Some of these were gained from her own family—others from strangers."

Catharine and I began structuring Sarah's profile to help understand **why** she died, not how she died. Victimology might help us.

Victimology is the study of crime victims, a subset of criminology, and, according to forensic psychologists, an important tool for both criminal investigations and academic research. Forensic investigators often use victimology to examine a victim's inner circle, to help decipher the killer's identity. The suspect list might include jilted lovers, violent spouses, disgruntled business associates, or something even more complicated. Determining who had a motive to murder the victim is crucial to preventing the case from going cold. Victimology as well as criminal profiling also save lives by identifying killers before they murder again.

" 'Victimology' is a very broad term," forensic investigator Paul Holes told me. "It refers to, of course, who the person is—you know, their name, their background, where do they work, their education. The victimology also encompasses their social circles and their personality."

Holes said that victimology helps investigators determine how a victim might have responded if they were confronted by an offender: "Are they a fighter? Are they somebody who would go passive and basically allow the offender to command them?" mused Holes. "That plays into not only the investigative side [who's in the victim's social circles]; it also plays into the **behavioral** assessment of what happened between the offender and the victim."

As Catharine and I explored the case, it was particularly salient for us both to determine if Sarah had been vulnerable during those final days of her life . . . to either suicide or murder. Who would Sarah Cornell have trusted if she **had** been murdered? Was she emotionally stable during her final days if she had died by suicide?

As she sat nightly at her desk at home in Providence, Catharine noted in her manuscript that Sarah Cornell's mother, Lucretia Leffingwell, was "a well-educated and good principled woman, a daughter to one of the first families in the State." Lucretia had enjoyed her family's affluence and had been a part of Connecticut high society until she met a paper-maker who was charming and handsome—James Cornell.

"Mr. Cornell was a person employed in one of the manufactories belonging to her father," wrote Catharine. "Good looking and of pleasing address, he succeeded in captivating the affections of a daughter of his employer."

James Cornell charmed Lucretia, and in 1796, the two planned to marry. But Christopher Leffingwell forbade it. James's low station made him an unsuitable suitor; her father refused to agree to the union and argued with his daughter about James's dismal prospects for supporting a family. As a woman reared in an upscale family in the 1700s, Lucretia had an edict to marry **up**—not down. Christopher catastrophized about Lucretia's future and refused to offer the couple any future financial support. He warned Lucretia that marriage to a lowly laborer would be grueling; James couldn't offer his daughter the future his family deserved. But Lucretia ignored her father's warnings, and she and James married. Lucretia Leffingwell became Lucretia Cornell, and her father was left dejected and heartbroken. But he couldn't quite cut ties with her.

"Upon being assured by his daughter that she was firmly and irremovably attached to Cornell and could never be happy with any other man, the old gentleman gave up the contest, and suffered the union to take place without further opposition," wrote Catharine. "His daughter removed after marriage to Vermont, where her children were born." Lucretia and James had three children, and in the fashion of the times, the first two were named after their parents: James and Lucretia. Sarah was the youngest.

Lucretia's marriage to James Sr. was ill fated; as predicted by her weary father, James seemed duplicitous nearly from the beginning. With his trio of children as pawns, James demanded that his father-in-law fund his life of leisure. James no longer wanted to toil in mills, as he once promised Christopher Leffingwell he would. "In pursuit of this determination he worked upon the feelings of his wife to get her to draw money from her father," wrote Catharine.

Catharine Williams pitied Sarah's mother. Sarah's sister described their mother to Catharine as kind, but easily influenced by her scheming husband; Catharine called Lucretia a "gentle, unresisting character." Sarah was an infant when her father relentlessly pressed her mother to plead with Christopher Leffingwell for financial support.

"[She] repeatedly drew large sums of money

from her indulgent father, to supply her husband's demands," wrote Catharine.

Lucretia Cornell wept as her elderly father reluctantly issued her funds at her request. Christopher was disgusted with his greedy son-in-law, but he yearned for time with his grandchildren and his distraught daughter, so he softened his stubborn stance against providing money. He could not cast his beloved Lucretia out . . . until he felt he had to. After years of pleading, Christopher Leffingwell finally had enough. The patriot and innovator who had survived and then thrived after the Revolutionary War surrendered to a more stalwart, cruel enemy.

"The old gentleman resolutely refused to advance anymore," wrote Catharine.

Christopher had, finally, released his daughter and his grandchildren for good. Lucretia delivered the unhappy news to her husband. James reacted angrily before retreating alone to Providence, Rhode Island, with the promise to search for work. When he failed, James returned to Vermont, packed up his wife and children, and traveled to Connecticut. The family arrived in Norwich, where James Cornell, the self-professed colonial gentleman, promptly abandoned Lucretia and their three children on the doorstep of her father and left for the West, never to be heard from again.

"[He] relieved himself forever from the task of supporting a woman whom he had probably carried without the least sentiment of affection whatever, and abandoning the children in their helpless infancy," Catharine wrote with disgust.

James Cornell was a cad, Catharine declared, a swindler who had used Lucretia until she was no longer useful. Any father who could abandon his responsibilities, his children, was a disgrace and a pathetic excuse for a man.

Christopher Leffingwell looked mournfully at his daughter, his grandson, and two granddaughters. It was too late: Lucretia, his beloved daughter, had depleted her part of her inheritance. She had betrayed her respectable family to marry a grifter. Lucretia, Leffingwell believed, lacked common sense and would inevitably make more costly mistakes. Her blunders could risk the future of the Leffingwells and imperil their enduring legacy. Lucretia was an embarrassment. After their years of separation, there was now a gulf between father and daughter. Lucretia and her three children, abandoned by James, were now shunned by the Leffingwells too. She would remain a Cornell for the duration of her life, living in the shadow of her distancing family.

When Christopher Leffingwell died in 1810 at the age of seventy-six, he left Lucretia nothing. Lucretia and her children are only briefly mentioned in the robust book **The Leffingwell Record**, published in 1897. Sarah's entry reads: "Sally Maria, b. Jan. 31, 1803; d. suddenly, Dec. 20, 1832." There was no mention of the media blitz surrounding Sarah's death, of his granddaughter's tragic life. Sarah and her siblings were simply a footnote in their family's storied history. They didn't even get her birthday correct. Lucretia and her three children had been deserted, left with few resources. But fortunately, they did have extended family.

"She and her children found a home with some of their relatives, and appear to have looked chiefly to their own exertions for support," wrote Catharine. The boy, James, was sent to live with relatives—he eventually became a merchant in New Orleans. Sarah's sister, Lucretia, was also sent to live with family members and later married an ambitious minister named Grindall Rawson.

"They were separated, being all brought up at different places, and not even knowing one another for several years," wrote Catharine. The pain of that separation would have a lasting effect on Lucretia's youngest daughter, Sarah Cornell.

———

Years later, in 1833, when Catharine requested Sarah's personal papers from her family in the months directly after the young woman's death, the family was only too willing to oblige. Catharine thought Sarah's correspondence might hold some key to her fate. The family offered the author a stack of letters, and as Catharine thumbed through them, she realized that they offered clues—not just because of what they contained but because of what they **omitted**. The letters began in 1819, when Sarah was sixteen and living in Norwich, Connecticut. But some of her missives were missing.

"Other letters, written at different times may have been lost or mislaid, but not by design," wrote Catharine. "Her sister's family informed me that they were all of a like character, and, resembling her conversation, full of Methodism, and relating mostly to her religious feelings."

As I looked through Catharine's notes and reportage, I wondered if Sarah's family had withheld those missing letters for a specific reason, perhaps out of propriety. As we'll learn, Sarah had been accused of scandalous things involving theft and men, taboo in the early 1800s. Or maybe the missing letters hinted at Sarah's deepest insecurities—including thoughts of suicide. Sarah's family believed that she was murdered. But if Catharine discovered any sense of despair, would she think differently? Or perhaps Catharine omitted some letters herself, trying to sway public opinion toward Sarah's innocence and away from her suspected murderer?

We'll never know where those missing pages went. But as she pored over Sarah's letters, Catharine realized they offered access to Sarah's most intimate thoughts. She was impressed with the Cornells and their love for Sarah. They also painted a picture of a family who was anxious for Sarah, who had spent years worrying over her transitory life as she traversed New England in search of weaving and tailoring work. Her family begged her to stay in one place and make a home—**please find a husband and remain still.**

"They gave her excellent advice about her disposition to rove from place to place," wrote Catharine, "and cautioned her of the danger."

According to Sarah's own words, she was also a bit of a seeker—a devout Christian in search of a flock. A home church seemed elusive until she was introduced to the Methodists. In one letter, Sarah assured her mother and sister that she was following God's plan, much to their relief. Sarah's growing devotion to religion was evident through the letters—they were filled with accolades for the Methodists; her correspondence mentioned her charity toward the church.

"I received yours dated March 18th and was glad to hear you was all well, my health is pretty good at present," Sarah wrote to her mother four years before her death. "You mention you expect to visit Norwich this summer, I wish it was so that I could come and go with you, but I do not think it will be possible, as I have lately given five dollars for the purpose of erecting a new Methodist meetinghouse in this town."

This would be almost $200 today, quite a donation for a young working woman. It was emblematic of Sarah's devotion to the church, something that would be repeated often by her defenders. Sarah Cornell, like Hester Prynne, was devoutly altruistic—kind, and giving, and humble to a fault. Sarah, it seemed, was "a pious and quite intelligent young lady," observed Catharine. The writer was pleased—Sarah Cornell would surely be a sympathetic victim, particularly to female readers. This would serve her narrative well.

"[Her] letters should speak for her," wrote Catharine, "and the author has been at the trouble to collect all of her correspondence that can be found, consisting of sixteen letters written to her mother and sister . . . between the year[s] 1819 and 1832."

Catharine assured her readers that she had accurately recorded Sarah's notes herself. Their transcription was rigorous—it had to be for authenticity: "Her letters here follow, copied verbatim. The originals are now in the hands of the author of this book, and can be seen by anyone who has the curiosity to see them in her own handwriting," wrote Catharine.

Catharine Williams was a reliable companion-researcher for our project—she was the only person who had access to the family's letters; the full collection hasn't been found in any archive. I would rely on her accurate reporting throughout my own research. She presented as a nineteenth-century journalist should: constantly assuring her readers that her book was grounded in facts. But that wasn't entirely true. And soon, her prejudice would shift our investigation.

———

"My dear Mother," began Sarah Cornell's letter. "Once more I take up my pen to write a few lines to my parents, as nearly six months have again elapsed since I have heard from you."

As she sat at her small wooden desk, Sarah looked down at her letter, pen in hand. A cold spring wind blew outside the home on Sunday, March 2, 1828. It shook the fragile window frames of her boardinghouse as she sat bundled in loads of clothing. Sarah was just twenty-five years old as she wrote these words, but her body often ached like that of a woman twice her age after years of toiling in mills and factories across New England. A friend once described her physically as having "dark hair, dark eyes, light complexion, and red cheeks." She was petite and said to be attractive. There are only rough sketches of her, in cartoons depicting her death.

In her darkest hours, Sarah felt abandoned by her family, her friends—everyone. "I cannot hear from any of them oftener than once in six or seven months," she lamented. "Sometimes I think they have lately forgotten me."

She was living in Dorchester, Massachusetts, in early 1828, one of many stops she made in her seven years of factory work.

"My work has been very hard the winter past," she said. "And I have got almost beat out; I have been weaving on four looms at the rate of 120 or 30 yards per day, at 1 half cent per yard."

Women like Sarah worked for up to fourteen hours a day (along with a half day on Saturdays), often in grueling conditions. Yet many female textile workers saved money and gained a measure of economic independence. The mill owners, predominantly Congregationalist men, regulated the moral compass and social behavior of their female workers. In the boardinghouses reserved for female factory workers, matrons enforced curfews and strict codes of conduct. A typical house consisted of eight units, with twenty to forty women living in each section. Women were expected to observe the Sabbath, and temperance was strongly encouraged. The clanging factory bell summoned workers to and from the mill, constantly reminding them that their days were structured around work. The stringent discipline enforced at the factories often brought criticism among civil rights activists.

"We know no sadder sight on earth than one of our factory village presents, when the bell at break of day, or at the hour of breakfast, or dinner, calls out its hundreds or thousands of operatives," wrote Orestes Brownson in 1840's **The Laboring Classes: An Article from the "Boston Quarterly Review."** "We stand and look at the hard-working men and women hurrying in all directions, and ask ourselves, where go the proceeds of their labors? The man who employs them, and for whom they are toiling as so many slaves."

Despite her skills at tailoring and sewing, Sarah Cornell found that she could make more money by working in the textile mills that were rapidly expanding throughout New England. But toiling in the mills was tedious, stressful, and even dangerous. "Lowell, Massachusetts, named in honor of Francis Cabot Lowell, was founded in the early 1820s as a planned town for the manufacture of textiles. It introduced a new system of integrated manufacturing to the United States and established new patterns of employment and urban development that were soon replicated around New England and elsewhere.

"By 1840, the factories in Lowell employed at some estimates more than 8,000 textile workers, commonly known as mill girls or factory girls. These 'operatives'—so-called because they operated the looms and other machinery—were primarily women and children from farming backgrounds," according to the article "Lowell Mill Girls and the Factory System, 1840."

The Lowell mills were the first hint that the industrial revolution had arrived in the United States, and with their success came starkly different views of the factories. For many of the mill girls, employment brought a sense of freedom.

"Unlike most young women of that era, they were free from parental authority, were able to earn their own money, and had broader educational opportunities," Catharine Williams wrote.

But many observers saw this challenge to the traditional roles of women as a threat to the American way of life. Others criticized the entire wage-labor factory system as a form of slavery; they actively condemned and campaigned against the harsh working conditions and long hours as well as the increasing divisions between workers and factory owners.

"Female operatives were some of the hardest working employees in mills and factories, but also some of the most exploited," according to the American Antiquarian Society. "Drawn by the prospect of freedom and money, they often logged twelve-hour days and there were few codes and regulations to ensure their safety."

There were hazards seemingly around each corner: poorly designed buildings, deadly machinery, and sheer exhaustion resulted in frequent accidents. From fires to floods to machinery malfunctions, accidents occurred regularly in factories around the

United States. And the local newspapers covered all of them.

"Saturday morning, between 9 and 10 o'clock, the paper-mill of Beckett & Laurie was the scene of a terrible accident, in which a young and interesting girl was hurried into eternity without a moment's warning," reported **The New York Times** on February 9, 1871, in a piece titled "Shocking Accident at a Paper-Mill." "Margaret Kriegenshafer, an employee in the mill, was engaged in carrying rags on the third floor, when she fell through a trap-door on the whirling machinery below, and was instantly severed in twain. The spectacle of the mangled body, it is said, was the most horrid one. The ribs were torn on the right side from the backbone, the body was almost cut in two in the back just below the shoulders and there were numerous other bruises and lacerations. The face, however, was not touched, and it presented an appearance of peaceful repose, as though she had fallen asleep."

The managers of these mills, the overseers, were often cruel and shameless, like the man in charge during a fire at a cotton mill in Allegheny, Pennsylvania: "All the operatives were at work when the fire broke out and great excitement was caused among them by the act of an overseer, who locked all the doors of the mill, thus preventing their easy escape," according to an 1873 story titled "Fire in a Mill" in **The New York Times**. "The same man also refused to admit the firemen till a stream from a hose was turned upon him. Many of the girls jumped from the second-story windows to the ground, but fortunately none were seriously injured."

The everyday experience of the female mill workers in these factory towns—even if they escaped the most grievous harm of injury or accidents—was nonetheless quite punishing and demoralizing. It was also, despite the hard work and the wages these women earned, not altogether respectable labor.

"The great mass wear out their health, spirits, and morals, without becoming one whit better off than when they commenced labor," wrote Brownson. "Few of them ever marry; fewer still ever return to their native places with reputations unimpaired. 'She has worked in a factory,' is almost enough to damn to infamy the most worthy and virtuous girl."

Catharine Williams was conflicted over the factories she had toured in the 1830s as part of her research for **Fall River**. She was concerned for the safety of workers, especially the children who were also frequently employed in the mills. But she also found value in the opportunities these same mills offered young women.

"There is no person who deprecates the practice of sending little children into a cotton manufactory more than the author," insisted Catharine, "but when she [Catharine] has again seen healthy, sprightly and well educated girls, labouring to assist some widowed mother, or to give education to some half dozen little brothers and sisters, her feelings have received a different impulse."

Catharine acknowledged that opportunities for women during this time were limited, and that factories—for all their ills—offered an option. "There is no way that grown up girls in the present state of society can get better wages—nor where their payment is so sure," she concluded. "And the privilege of working in manufactories to such is a great one."

Sarah Maria Cornell's journey into mill work was not unique. When Sarah was a teenager, she had apprenticed as a tailor altering men's jackets and suits. This would have been grueling and tedious but satisfactory work for a young woman reared with little financial support from either parent. In 1819, she wrote to her sister, Lucretia, about her burgeoning career.

"My dear sister," began the sixteen-year-old. "I am learning the tailors trade, I have been here seven months, and expect to stay 17 more. I hope when my time is out, I shall come and see you."

Sarah yearned to be with her family again, to enjoy a stable homelife with her sister and mother. Yet she felt compelled to maintain her independence. During her apprenticeship, Sarah had spent time at a Congregational church as she began to find a sense of a stability. Sarah asked her mother to facilitate a visit to her sister, Lucretia, in Rhode Island. Catharine Williams examined another letter from Sarah to her sister, a message full of joy.

"I have almost finished my trade, my time will be out in October, and mother is making preparations for our coming to Providence this fall," wrote Sarah in 1820. "Oh shall I behold the face of my beloved sister which I have never seen—or have no recollection of."

It wasn't unusual for female operatives not to see their families for years; travel was hard, and work was demanding. But Sarah and her sister, Lucretia, had also been separated by circumstances; they lived diverging lives. Sarah's mother brought her to Providence in 1822, and the nineteen-year-old seemed overjoyed.

"Her older sister lived there with a relation who had brought her up," wrote Catharine, "and these two sisters, separated for many years, had long desired a reunion."

Lucretia held her sister as they greeted each other. The three women, now together after many years, felt complete. Sarah had worked so hard—there were calluses on her hands from sewing. Her eyes ached from detail work. But she felt at peace, even as she longed for independence.

In November 1822, the sisters happily explored the shopping districts of Providence, which was a larger town than Sarah had grown accustomed to. Restaurants, taverns, and clothing stores dotted the streets. Sarah's eyes beamed at the beautiful dresses in the shop windows. **What must it feel like to own such lovely gowns?** she wondered. Sarah longed to feel pretty after years of slogging to work in proletarian clothing. Catharine documented that this indulgence, so antithetical to the Bible's teachings, was the start of Sarah's descent.

"Those feelings of childish vanity, and love of dress, and show, and ornament, which had been growing upon her for some time, seemed completely to get the mastery," wrote Catharine.

As I began researching this book, it dawned on me that these characters lived lives filled with tiny, seemingly innocent mistakes, like all of us do. But a misstep that would be insignificant today—say, a yearning for a beautiful, expensive dress and the steps one might take to procure it—could prove calamitous two centuries ago, even fatal. Sarah Cornell was tempted by a pretty dress and vowed she'd do whatever it took to have it.

"Lightness and vanity again took possession of her imagination," wrote Catharine. And for that, she would ultimately pay a price.

Sarah was a young, attractive woman who coveted stylish clothing. But on a factory worker's salary, she could afford very little. As she wandered around one store, Sarah knew she wanted these garments. She was determined to take something, yet stealing felt almost impossible because she wasn't a thief by nature. But the draw of the clothes was too much for a woman who had come from much but was left with little. As she thumbed the dresses, she felt nervous. And Sarah apparently **looked** nervous.

"Unused to crime, her manner at the time was so singular and agitated as to excite suspicion in the store," wrote Catharine.

Sarah quickly stashed away a dress. With the clothing hidden, she slipped out of the store and rushed down the road to Lucretia's home with one of the shop owners in pursuit. He soon flung open the front door, demanding to see the stolen goods. When Sarah sheepishly handed them over, he reported her to the police.

"She at length possessed herself of some of them, trifling indeed in amount," wrote Catharine, "but destined to prove her entire destruction in this world as respected character and everything else."

Sarah had stolen clothing worth just a few dollars, seemingly on a whim. The owners were furious, and Sarah was inconsolable. "The grief and agitation of the poor girl vented itself in repeated fits of hysterical laughing and crying at the time, and in the bitterest self-accusation afterwards, when she seemed fully to realize what she had done," wrote Catharine.

Catharine's description about Sarah's impassioned reaction should be noted because it will surface again later in our story. In New England's culture of sedated, smug Congregationalism, such extreme displays were labeled as "crazy" and left onlookers disquieted. In modern times, she would likely be labeled "dramatic," but not unstable. Sarah seemed to understand that she had made a grave mistake.

Sarah fully confessed to the owners and pleaded for leniency, and her friends quickly offered to pay for the goods. But it was no use—the men had made up their minds. This was the story related in Catharine's **Fall River**, but I wanted to verify Catharine's version, just in case she had accidentally misinterpreted something. After reviewing the various trial transcripts and digging deeper into the facts, I realized that Catharine's reporting wasn't entirely accurate.

Sarah had apparently stolen from **two** different stores—she had also visited Charles Hodges's dry goods store several times, each time retiring to the back of the store but leaving with nothing. Finally, she requested silk for a dress, and he allowed her to leave with it on credit. When she didn't return, Hodges pursued Sarah, eventually tracking her down in another town two months later, and she quickly confessed. Like the store owner from earlier, Hodges also found Sarah's reaction curious.

"She would at one moment cry and the next smile," Hodges said. "She bore the character of a thief; that was her general character among our shopkeepers."

Samuel Richmond told a similar story from Providence. He said that Sarah once stole a shawl and bonnet from **his** store, and when she was caught, her friends responded with their own funds.

"Upon being charged with the act, she confessed," said Richmond, "and afterwards restored what she had not used and paid for the rest, and the matter was there settled, by the interposition of the friends of the girl."

In Catharine's version, Sarah's theft was a singular, fleeting indiscretion, but the trial reports indicated that it was a wider pattern. As a result of her actions, Sarah Cornell would be labeled "a thief," a characterization that would follow her for the rest of her life. In the early 1800s, shoplifting was considered a felony and a capital crime—she could have faced the death penalty if any of these shopkeepers had called the local constable. Instead, Sarah was driven out of Providence, away from her mother and sister, in disgrace. She promised to never return, to save her family any more public humiliation. Catharine Williams lamented that the shopkeepers' decision to publicly stigmatize Sarah would cause a ripple effect throughout her life.

"Could those gentlemen have known the effect that disgrace was to have upon her future destiny," concluded Catharine, "doubtless they would have preferred to have lost ten times the amount rather than have exposed her."

That indiscretion and reaction feels like what happened with Hawthorne's Hester Prynne, a misjudgment with serious repercussions. Like Sarah, Prynne was welcomed in the community only when needed, like in a sick house. People discarded them both when they were no longer useful.

"It was only the darkened house that could contain her. When sunshine came again, she was not there. Her shadow had faded across the threshold," wrote Hawthorne. "The helpful inmate had departed, without one backward glance to gather up the meed of gratitude, if any were in the hearts of those whom she had served so zealously."

Like Sarah, Prynne seemed to accept her fate in the opening pages of **The Scarlet Letter** as she stood on the scaffold, prepared to receive public ridicule for her pregnancy. She avoided the judgment of the community.

"Meeting them in the street, she never raised her head to receive their greeting," reads **The Scarlet Letter**. "If they were resolute to accost her, she laid her finger on the scarlet letter, and passed on."

Sarah tried to ingratiate herself to different factory communities by giving donations to churches, offering her needlework, or taking care of sick people, as we'll read about later. But her compassion was rarely returned.

While Catharine's compassion for Sarah's fate might seem admirable, her distortion of these early stories of Sarah's thieving are disheartening. Catharine had hoped to frame her protagonist as an eternal victim—but the author's partial truths undermined our mission to evaluate Sarah's death. Modern critics agree that Catharine Williams was biased.

"Williams establishes virtually a personal relationship. A firm, almost maternal bond with a person who in the ordinary course of things would never have attracted anyone's notice," concluded Patricia Caldwell in her essay titled "In 'Happy America': Discovering Catharine Williams's **Fall River** for the Women Writers Project" in the **South Central Review** in 1994.

That "personal relationship" can be problematic. When journalists grow too close to the victims or the survivors, then the authenticity of their work can become distorted. But Catharine and I agreed that Sarah had tried her best. She had confessed to her family, to her friends, and to the shop owners. She never denied the crimes, even though her agitated reaction was viewed as disturbing by some. Catharine blamed society, to a certain extent, for Sarah's misfortune. Young women of Sarah's generation valued gilded charms over humble items. Innocent, youthful avarice was Sarah's only crime, argued the author. Sarah had no real guidance in life, Catharine believed. Were Sarah **her** daughter, this likely would have never happened. But Sarah had no foundation for stability, thanks to an absent father and a heartless grandfather. She left her family home in shame and rarely returned to visit after, even when her mother and sister left Rhode Island. This event was the beginning of her undoing.

"The seed had fallen on stony ground, where the earth was not of sufficient depth to foster it," wrote Catharine.

CHAPTER THREE

~⁀~

RASH VIOLENCE

CATHARINE WILLIAMS EMPATHIZED with the instability of Sarah Cornell's upbringing, especially the abandonment by Sarah's father. Catharine's life also began with promise. But one poor choice—in Catharine's case, picking a bad spouse, like Lucretia had—adversely affected the author too.

Catharine examined her own alabaster skin in the mirror before bed. She might have been born to a common sea captain in Newport, but she was also the granddaughter of New England royalty. She was born on New Year's Eve 1787, in Providence, Rhode Island, just four years after the official end of the American Revolution. She was descended from the Arnolds of Newport, a respectable and storied family in the area. The family's claim to fame was Catharine's grandfather Oliver Arnold, an esteemed gentleman "who died in 1770, holding the office of Attorney General of Rhode Island, and who, although dying at the early age of thirty-four years, had already acquired the reputation of a profound lawyer and a ripe scholar," wrote Catharine's biographer, Sidney Rider. After her death in 1872, Catharine was considered a significant writer in New England, so much so that she was included posthumously in an 1880 book by Rider titled **Bibliographical Memoirs of Three Rhode Island Authors.**

Oliver Arnold's descendent Alexandra Washburn told me that he had a valued legacy, particularly in her family. I interviewed her over the phone in December 2021.

"He was a boy wonder," said Washburn, who is a former English professor, "and he was the one who might have had some spare legal books that were left behind when he died. And then the generations just pass them on and on, even on scraps of paper."

Oliver Arnold's role as attorney general of the colony of Rhode Island came at a crucial moment during the American Revolution. He was the chief legal advisor of the government and was seen as a stalwart guiding light, helping the colony (and the country) move toward independence during this early, pivotal time. I tried to visit Oliver Arnold's large brick tomb in the historic North Burial Ground in Providence, Rhode Island. His tomb was designed like a small house, complete with a looking window in the door, a shingled roof, and an iron lattice gate with a lock. Washburn told me that her great-aunts once had the key to the tomb, and it was handed down to her by her mother. But it's gone missing amid all the family memorabilia in her house, which is a shame. The day was exceedingly rainy, and I just couldn't find his tomb. I also spent that afternoon fruitlessly searching for Catharine's grave, only to conclude that she likely was interred in her grandfather's tomb too, and rightly so. Oliver Arnold died seventeen years before his granddaughter's 1787 birth, and yet they seemed to share countless traits, including perseverance and moral uprightness.

"His genius was lively and active," read **The Providence Gazette** upon Oliver's death in 1770, "his ideas extensive and beautifully arranged—his conceptions were quick, clear and radiant—his judgement sound. In his writings, his style was mainly pure and correct."

In New England, a strong character and upright pedigree were not simply recommended—they were vital for anyone who wanted to rise above their station in life, or even maintain it. Oliver Arnold's reputation offered his granddaughter a credibility that few women enjoyed in the 1830s.

"The character of Mr. Arnold has been handed down to us, as a lawyer of candor, probity and great uprightness; rejecting those mean and paltry cases which so often disgrace those who espouse them," wrote Sidney Rider in his biography of Catharine.

"But when engaged in a cause which his conscience approved, nothing could turn him in his course, or stay his exertion."

But Catharine's father veered from his own father's path. Oliver Arnold had raised his children with a sense of stability. But Oliver's son Alfred Arnold, Catharine's father, was drawn to a life of adventure, even after starting his own family. Alfred "followed the seas," wrote Rider poetically, as the captain of the privateer ship **Modesty** starting in 1782, five years before she was born. He was often away, even after he took a wife. "He married Amey, daughter of Capt. Oliver Read of Newport, a hero of revolutionary memory," reads an in-depth biography of the Arnold family. So Catharine's family was decorated and respectable on both sides.

Alfred Arnold was an absentee parent, so the burden of raising two daughters and a son rested on Catharine's mother, Amey. But Amey died suddenly at the age of thirty-seven on September 3, 1803, and two months later Catharine's younger brother, Oliver, died at age twelve. Sadly, the cause of both deaths is lost to time. But once Amey passed away, Alfred Arnold did what most single fathers in the nineteenth century would have done: he sent his other children away to be reared by family members. Catharine was just fifteen years old at the time.

Her biographer, Rider, received most of his information about his subject from Catharine herself. I discovered that her autobiographical writings were

housed at Brown University, donated by the family
of her relative and my source, Alexandra Washburn,
years ago; they are Catharine's handwritten notes
penned in the third person, a common style in the
nineteenth century. Her comments are formal and
rather stiffly written, like the "About the Author"
page of a book written today. In them, Catharine
reflected on her childhood as being stable but
stifling.

"Mrs. Williams['s] mother died when she was
young, and she was educated in the family of two
maiden aunts who being ladies of the old school,
[were] strict and dignified in their deportment, as most
of those ancient ladies were," recalled Catharine of
her early life. "Though comfortably provided for in
respects of the things of this life, not yet having a
fortune to keep up formal style, they lived in strict
sentiment and Mrs. W. often makes the remark that
she was brought up a nun."

That remark wasn't a quip—Catharine wasn't
particularly jocular. Her comments seem mournful, and yet the aunts provided her with a strong
religious foundation, more than her parents would
have. They offered her the "love of study and the
sentiments of religion," both of which would serve
her well in the years to come. The pair of older
women were staunch Episcopalians, conservative
socially and committed to every word of the Bible.
Prayers at every meal and church multiple times
a week were compulsory, and Catharine relished

those rituals. But life with the aunts was trying, oftentimes depressing. And then her time with them suddenly ended.

"From this state of seclusion and of partial bondage, Mrs. W. was not released until she was about 23 years of age," Catharine reflected, "when the death of one of her protectors and the unexpected marriage of the other, left her entirely alone, without a protector, launched into the world with as little practical knowledge of it, as they often said, as a child of 5 years old."

The aunt who died left her a small inheritance, for which she was grateful. As Catharine wrote, the bequest "enabled her with industry and economy, to live decently and comfortably"—at least for a time. It wasn't enough to last her for a lifetime, though. Her funds, if not replenished, would soon run out. Naive and isolated, Catharine would need to figure out how to fend for herself. And to a bookish, quiet, introverted young woman, **writing** seemed like the key to her survival. After all, she'd already been doing a bit of it on the side. Catharine's sharp wit and even sharper stories began to impress those around her.

"Some of the productions of her pen had already found their way into the papers of the day," wrote Rider. In fact, "she had already dreamed of the publication of a book," even as a young woman. But in all aspects of her life, Catharine's tendency to do things her way—and to buck convention and common mores—was on full display. Nowhere else was that more evident than in her appearance.

Rider was unsparing in his description of her: she was "short and stout, her face presented a good, healthy color, her eyes were small and piercing." Not a beauty, and not someone who seemed to care a great deal about her appearance, but a solid, healthy type. Catharine herself couldn't be bothered with foolish distractions like following the latest fashions of the day. She sported tacky calico dresses (often criticized by more stylish women) and scuffed low-heeled shoes both as everyday attire and even (as her fame and influence grew over the years) to meetings with influential politicians. Catharine, in an act of self-reflection, reframed her appearance on a trip to Europe as someone who "has rather the appearance of an English woman," lacking "the long face and thin lips of an American."

"In her attire she was somewhat careless," agreed Rider. "In her visits to various celebrated resorts, she was indebted to the kind care of the ladies with whom she boarded, to see that she went into the street in proper condition. She met with many jokes from her negligence in this respect."

Rider recalled one seemingly embarrassing incident when she was mistaken for a server. "Once calling upon a friend at Gadsby's hotel in Washington, she forgot to change her dress, and appeared at the hotel in her morning calico," he wrote. "The porter showed her into the cellar kitchen, and it was not until the fifth servant was called that one was found bold enough to escort her from the cellar kitchen to the ladies' parlor."

This incident would have humbled most public-facing, respectable women, but Catharine didn't seem to care a bit, and her presentation never seemed to prevent her from receiving sought-after invitations. By 1833, as she was embarking on the Sarah Cornell case, she had gained a reputation as a prolific poet and historian, heralded by many but occasionally chided by (mostly male) disingenuous critics.

"She was a woman of great energy of character," contended Rider. "She held an honest, earnest, and sometimes vigorous pen, but her style often lacked elegance. There was yet a truthful sentiment about her books which the people of that day liked."

Despite Rider's lukewarm assessment of her writing, Catharine Williams was a success, starting with a book of poetry published when she was in her early forties.

"It was a small volume, published under the name of Original Poems," wrote Rider in Catharine's biography. "It was printed by Mr. Hugh H. Brown, and appeared in 1828. Its success Mrs. Williams characterized as beyond her utmost expectations."

Catharine had written many of the poems when she was a teenager, before she had really developed her voice, so the success of the book was startling to her—particularly considering the tone. The poems "exhibit a mournful spirit," wrote Rider, "the author seeming to choose melancholy subjects, thus betraying the spirit of her early training." But Catharine's gloomy early life may have been why she gravitated toward Sarah Maria Cornell's story.

Catharine's personality, as unconventional and bracing as it sounds to our twenty-first-century ears, may have come across as a bit eccentric and off-putting to many men. Indeed, if others offended Catharine, she could occasionally be refreshingly combative—"a lively conversationalist, and sometimes quick at repartee," Rider said.

He included an amusing anecdote that framed Catharine's role as a verbal duelist at parties. Her seventh work, a book titled **Biography of Revolutionary Heroes**, focused on a pair of high-ranking soldiers in the Continental army; both happened to be from Rhode Island, her home state. Catharine had promoted the book vigorously when she dined at a hotel with other luminaries, but not everyone was impressed with the subject matter.

"She chanced to be seated at a hotel table with an Englishman who was travelling through the States," wrote Rider.

The man listened to Catharine's pitch about the book, glanced at her, and then sneered, "How can you publish a biography without knowing the genealogy of your hero," adding, "Why, they tell me that even your aristocracy here don't always know who their grandfather was!"

The Englishman was criticizing Catharine's lack of knowledge about the linage of either man in the book, and he was disparaging Americans in general. This slight toward her respected countrymen and, more important, the focus of her book seemed to irritate Catharine. She smirked and replied coldly with her own attack against the English.

"Even then they [the Americans] have the advantage over your aristocrats, for yours often don't know who their **fathers** were."

The Englishman sat back, alarmed by her cheekiness. Catharine's brash insults startled some men but bemused many others.

Catharine Williams has been cemented in literary history as an eloquent, stylistic writer and poet, one worthy of being inducted into the Rhode Island Heritage Hall of Fame in 2002, 130 years after her death. But Catharine's biographer contended that the author was perhaps too forthright. "In addressing persons, she spoke perhaps quickly and with sharpness or decisively," wrote Rider.

Her great-great-great-granddaughter Alexandra Washburn agreed, based on the stories about Catharine from her own family.

"I don't think Catharine Read Williams had too much of a sense of humor, I'm guessing," Washburn told me. "But on the other hand, she was up against so much—I mean, so much more than I can even imagine. She even triumphed, in a world of men."

Catharine also despised boastfulness. While she

was on a book tour in Canada, she stopped one day at a hotel in a rural area.

"The landlord expressed great disappointment that she did not arrive the day before, so as to have seen the Governor General review the troops, drawn by six white horses and a beautiful equipage," wrote Sidney Rider.

Catharine was unimpressed—not by the sheer number of horses, but by the Canadian governor's opulence of parading out too many horses.

"Six, did you say, sir?" Catharine asked.

"Yes, six beautiful white horses," he replied.

Catharine smiled.

"Well, truly, I should have admired to see the Governor of a **single** province with six horses, while the President of the whole United States rides with but two."

Zing. Catharine Williams always seemed to deliver each slight with a sly smile and a nod as she readied to fire off the next tart retort.

———

Catharine Williams was Sarah Cornell's fierce advocate, virtually the only one who published a word defending her. But she wasn't an impartial observer—and she didn't pretend to be. Indeed, the tenets of modern journalism (namely, objectivity) weren't as enshrined in the profession as they are today. So Catharine's blindness, steeped in bias, clouded her journalistic judgment. I can relate. Remaining neutral—even when it seems impossible—is something I've struggled with in my own work.

When I began researching my first book, **Death in the Air**, I was convinced of a convicted murderer's innocence. The story involved Timothy Evans and his wife, Beryl, and one-year-old child, Geraldine, who moved into 10 Rillington Place in London's Notting Hill in the late 1940s. When Beryl and Geraldine were found strangled to death on the property, Tim pointed the finger at his downstairs neighbor, John Reginald Christie—a man who would later be convicted as a serial killer when several other bodies were discovered buried in his flat and outside the home. By the time this gruesome discovery was made, Evans had already been convicted and executed for the murder of his wife and child. Evans, I thought, **must** have been incorrectly accused of a crime that his neighbor Christie had committed. After all, what were the chances that **two** killers could have both lived in the same house at the same time?

But after several years of research, digging into autopsy photos and trial transcripts, I became convinced that Tim Evans **did** murder his wife and child. Beryl's brother agreed—Evans had a history of violence, and my examination of the physical evidence, as well as contemporary experts' forensic and psychological evaluations, convinced me that, in fact, there **had** been two killers living under the same roof in a quiet, postwar London neighborhood, as improbable as it had sounded at first. The facts were indisputable—but the bias remained. And public opinion in support of Tim Evans and against John Reginald Christie (though, again, **both** were murderers!) was led largely by the opinionated newspapers of the day. The press was inherently biased, even if reporters didn't necessarily display those biases to their readership.

The 1800s newspapers were often quite up-front about their prejudices and partialities. Many were explicitly affiliated with a political party and focused on delivering that party's point of view. For a writer like Catharine, there were no real models of journalistic impartiality. She must—was **encouraged to,** in fact— draw her own conclusions and share them freely. She embraced the role of an advocate who leveraged the clues from her investigation, as well as public sympathy, like a weapon. In Sarah Cornell's case, she had already arrived at a decision: Sarah's death was a murder. While the case unfurled, Catharine's prejudices became apparent—and harmful.

———

Early industrial New England offered Sarah Cornell employment and a place to live independently of her family, but it provided her with no real sense of community. A young worker like her might travel from mill town to mill town, seeking new opportunities and fresh adventures. It was an exciting life for a young, carefree woman, to be sure. But also, somehow, lacking in kinship. For that, she turned to the church.

And for a lively and inspiring church service—with charismatic ministers, and racy tent revivals, and scores of other young people just like her—a Methodist church was where many young women in 1830s New England wanted to be. The Methodists were the exciting, alluring newcomers of the emerging religious scene in the fledgling United States—and the bane of New England's prevailing, stodgier Protestant movement, the Congregationalists. While their draw to the younger generation was obvious, the factories weren't as enamored of this emerging sect. After all, the factory owners insisted on piety and respectability in exchange for the protection they extended to their employees. And while the Methodists were many things, "respectable" wasn't always among them.

But to Sarah, "who had for some time given up the idea that she had ever possessed religion," wrote Catharine, the Methodist Church "awakened" something in her. Sarah asked to be baptized and soon joined the Methodist church in Slatersville, Rhode Island, where she had a job. She seemed genuinely happy in Slatersville—in fact, these seemed to be her **most** content years.

"We have the Bible and are taught to read it," Sarah wrote to her sister, Lucretia. "Let it be our daily prayer that God would send more missionaries to the heathen, to spread the gospel to those who know it not."

She stayed in Slatersville for two years, until 1826, when the factory she was working in burned down. Sarah then moved on to a mill close by, but she still traveled to the Methodist church in Slatersville for weekly meetings. As more female factory workers like Sarah joined the Methodists, the largely Congregational church members who were factory owners became alarmed. They had promised the families of conservative New England that their daughters would be guarded from immorality—and staying safe meant quietly praying in the pews of a Congregationalist church, not swooning in a tent, unsupervised, in the woods with the Methodists.

By the time Sarah moved to Fall River, she was entrenched in a denomination that was in the vanguard of America's so-called Second Great Awakening, a revival during the early nineteenth century that spread religion through emotion-laden preaching. All this evangelical frenetic energy, punctuated with impassioned readings of the Bible, distressed many New Englanders who clung to the culture and mores of their Puritan forebears (who had themselves been part of the First Great Awakening).

"I believe there is something in religion that is

durable, it is worth seeking and worth enjoying," Sarah wrote to her sister in 1824. "I feel as though I could enjoy myself in this life while blest with the presence of Jesus, I have found that a form of godliness will never make me happy but I can praise God for the enjoyment of every day's religion."

The citizens of the Fall River factory community perceived the textile mills as mutual aid societies, where the female employees were offered food, shelter, and church as well as access to doctors and social outlets. The women were also tightly controlled before and after their long hours of grueling work. The conservative leaders of New England feared that the Methodists would disregard their traditional churches and the social structure that promoted rectitude . . . and perhaps lure away the most faithful Congregationalists (which they did). **That would be the true sin.**

Methodism, in its original form, was sparked back in 1738, when an English cleric had a crisis of faith. John Wesley was an ordained Church of England priest who had traveled to the American colonies as a missionary to the Native Americans; he fell in love with an affluent woman who eventually rejected him, and he responded by refusing to allow her to take Communion. This cruel knee-jerk reaction resulted in Wesley being drummed out of Georgia.

After this ignoble beginning, Wesley returned to England. Heartbroken and no doubt ashamed, he fretted over many things, including persistent doubts he had about the teachings of the Church of England. When he went to a prayer meeting at a private London residence in 1738, Wesley's life changed. Here's what he recorded in his journal: "In the evening I went very unwillingly to a society in Aldersgate Street, where one was reading Luther's preface to the Epistle to the Romans. About a quarter before nine, while he was describing the change which God works in the heart through faith in Christ, I felt my heart strangely warmed." Wesley said that he and his brother, Charles, had lived by good works, but not by faith. That changed for both when they were converted the same week. Charles Wesley wrote: "Towards ten, my brother was brought in triumph by a troop of our friends, and declared, 'I believe.' We sang the hymn with great joy, and parted with prayer."

John Wesley felt the spirit of Christianity once again renewed—not just renewed but **inspired**. Wesley was now newly determined to preach with unbridled enthusiasm to the masses, to anyone who would listen.

It hardly seems noteworthy today, when zealous, charismatic preaching is the norm in many houses of worship and denominations. But in those stuffy, Congregationalist times, Wesley's approach— that ministers could be devout and yet visibly passionate—was nothing short of revolutionary.

Wesley's enthusiasm at the pulpit distressed the

priests of the Church of England, namely because of who it resonated with: the poorer masses of society. The lower classes had typically been ignored by the elite, including the Church of England priests. The laborers, unable to help financially support the church, were left with little religious support, and the Church of England did little to attract them to services. These masses featured all the "dregs of society," according to the priests; the commoners would make poor parishioners because too many were missing a moral compass.

"The people were brutal, amusements were coarse, law enforcement was barbarous, and jails were cesspools of filth and immorality," wrote Orville C. T. Peterson in his 1969 thesis, "Early Methodist Education." "And drunkenness was more widespread than ever before in English history." A religion that spoke directly to those unwashed masses? Unacceptable. The Church of England quickly made moves to shut down Wesley's populist Methodists.

"The Establishment looked with strong disfavor upon their 'enthusiasm,' that is, their religious fervor," wrote Peterson, "and soon began barring Methodists from Anglican pulpits, as well as penalizing Anglican ministers who fraternized with Methodists."

The Methodists were labeled as "zealots" and cast out of the Anglican churches, but John Wesley was undeterred; he ordered his ardent preachers to spread his message to the rank-and-file of England:

"The world is my parish," he declared. It worked; there was a yearning among the devout to espouse their love of God loudly and passionately. The Methodists offered permission (and encouragement) for vigorously devout Christians, but John Wesley and his cofounders were ostracized by the Church of England.

"They considered themselves good Anglicans, engaged in revitalizing a spiritually moribund state Church to new spiritual vigor and social relevance," wrote Peterson. "Church after church closed its doors to the Methodists. When Wesley returned to Oxford [his alma mater] to preach, he was severely criticised and never invited back."

Methodist ministers preached to the common man, a respite from the stodgy (and wealthy) Congregationalists who cared little about their salvation, only their productivity: "At mines and factories, workers by the thousands flocked to hear the Methodist preachers," wrote Peterson. "Men, women and children of the working classes were converted by the tens of thousands, finding new hope, new meaning, and new dignity for their drab lives."

As Methodist preachers sermonized in the streets and in the fields of England to the lower and middle classes, their churches flourished. Soon, like many cultural and political movements in England did, the Methodists migrated to the United States about thirty years later, starting in Maryland. Along with the preachers arrived the infamous tent revivals. Ministers would gather outdoors to preach to the masses with the liveliness of a modern multiday music festival or a spirited political rally. Like Methodism itself, the origin of these tent revivals centered on John Wesley's time in England in the 1730s. But by the 1830s, a century later, the Methodists of America had become perhaps a more radical and enthusiastic wing of Anglicanism than Wesley's original vision. Some ministers boasted of preaching to thirty thousand parishioners at one time. And there weren't just Methodists under the tents—Presbyterians and Baptists joined them as they traveled across the western frontier of America.

"People came by the thousands on foot, on horseback, by carriage or wagon, to camp for several days, or even three or four weeks," wrote Earl E. Kerstetter in "The Glorious Camp Meetings of the Nineteenth Century." Kerstetter said that one attendee was virtually overwhelmed with the amount of preaching from different denominations.

"[Peter] Cartwright tells about being at camp meetings where ten, twenty, sometimes thirty, preachers of different denominations would preach day and night for four or five days," wrote Kerstetter. "At one camp meeting he heard more than five hundred Christians 'all shouting aloud the high praises of God at once.'"

While parishioners fawned over the litany of itinerant preachers who were fully accessible to them,

Congregationalists were both weary and wary of the fresh denomination from England.

"Methodist preachers were seen to be tempting 'silly' women with their emotional preaching and charismatic personality, leading the women to fawn over ministers with an inordinate level of devotion," wrote Eric Baldwin in his article "'The Devil Begins to Roar': Opposition to Early Methodists in New England." "The irregular nature of Methodist gatherings, lasting into the night or taking place over a number of days, seemed to provide ample opportunity for indecent behavior."

The ministers seemed **too** charming, and many were unmarried and much younger than traditional clerics in Congregational churches. The ministers were **too** passionate about the Bible. Most weren't formally trained in theology. Their spirit not only stirred the hungry crowd but also controlled it. It would be difficult not to be enchanted by a charismatic, emotive Methodist minister. They were very nearly worshipped during these camp meetings and tent revivals—especially by women.

"[Many] supposed that Methodist preachers had some kind of occult power over their audiences," wrote Baldwin.

The Methodist camp meetings were especially concerning because of the ceaseless nature of their format: they lasted for days, causing physical fatigue and emotional exhaustion. "If weekly or nightly Methodist meetings were dangerous, camp meetings were infinitely more so," wrote Baldwin. "The camp meeting, indeed, embodied all of the ills of the Methodist movement as a whole. It was in 'the high pressure of the camp meetings' that religious excitement could be most profoundly stirred up."

Soon, the evangelical Methodists became synonymous with an aggressive style of preaching to the masses; the meetings, whether beneath a tent or in a church, were raucous, spirited celebrations that were reviled by conservative, traditional Christians, like Catharine Williams. Catharine contended that any unaccompanied woman who attended tent revivals would be marked by lascivious predators behind the pulpit, those men craving prey who prayed—a familiar refrain.

"For years it was a common canard against the Methodists that their main fruit was 'camp meeting babies,'" wrote William G. McLoughlin in his essay "Untangling the Tiverton Tragedy." "Who knew what went on in those tents in the woods, or out in the bushes under the summer stars?"

Methodist tent revivals play an important role in this story. A decade earlier, Catharine had gone to one intent on documenting a cultural phenomenon that had seemingly upended religion. In her book **Fall River**, Catharine explains the origin of her reporting.

"So much has been said of late of Camp-Meetings, and such intense curiosity excited on the subject, that the author of these sheets feels called upon to give a history of one of which she was an eye and ear witness," Catharine wrote. "I am fully aware I shall make no friends by an exposure of all I saw and heard there, but I hope no enemies."

Catharine's exposure to Methodist camp meetings had come more than a decade earlier than Sarah Cornell's death, around 1820. Curious to see what they were truly like, to ferret out truth from Congregational gossip, she had located a tent revival in Smithfield, Rhode Island, about 15 miles from Providence. Catharine had felt anxious about her journey. The evangelical Methodists, cloistered deep in the woods, seemed unpredictable to a cautious woman like Catharine. But she prided herself as a poet and a writer with enough varied exposure in life that her books felt authentic to a reader.

Catharine was a stranger at the event—she knew it. She had to be self-aware of her customary grimace during unpleasant encounters; this tent revival, she predicted, would be disastrous. The idea of a minister, flailing behind the pulpit, spittle flying from his mouth as he preached, his fists pounding his chest while the crowd below him swayed and groaned in response . . . that scene terrified her. It was her first experience as an investigative reporter, a job which often requires copious amounts of bravery and (smaller amounts of) stupidity. Catharine noted that, at first glance, the camp meeting seemed almost peaceful. She was surprised.

"A superficial observer, a person who entered and just walked through, or was so fortunate as to be seated in some safe place while listening to a sermon or a prayer, might see no harm in one," she wrote.

But then things quickly shifted, as Eric Baldwin wrote.

"Initially impressed with the stillness and beauty of the place where the gathering was to be held which she regarded as a proper environment for religious inspiration, she gradually became disgusted with the entire affair. In her telling, the meeting degenerated into a riot of sights, sounds, and smells that assaulted the senses and produced a scene of profound disorder and vice."

Catharine Williams proclaimed objectivity as she arrived at the camp meeting, but it was a tall order for a staunch Episcopalian. And despite her self-reassurance, Catharine's repulsion for the Methodist affair devolved into loathing. She stood under the trees quietly studying the scene. Catharine braced herself as a horde of revolting characters swarmed the tent—she described inebriated men and women, stumbling across the grounds, searching for more alcohol and little authentic salvation. Their lives must be plagued by sin, she hissed to herself, like those of gamblers and pickpockets. And then she heard the unmistakable sound of wooden wheels crunching the dry leaves. A load of revelers hopped off a decrepit wagon. There was a rustling in the bushes nearby, a disquieting signal to Catharine of certain sin. She labeled them all as "bad people." Catharine chastised the ministers for a purposeful lack of organization—why were these so-called parishioners not corralled and controlled?

"If it is purposely to call sinners to repentance that these outdoor meetings are held," she contended, "why not have a place assigned them, where they may hear and be profited by the preaching of the word—and kept in sight that people may know what they are about, rather than be driven into the bushes to pollute the place with all sorts of enormities."

Catharine struggled to understand the concept of the camp meeting. Why was it necessary? Why must people travel and gather in groups just to be saved from their vices? If anything, according to Catharine, these camp meetings helped people **acquire** new vices, as they operated unchecked by moral guides. The ministers at these pulpits leaned on passion, not restraint—they were less engaging and more alluring. On the stage stood men and women, both Black and white; these fame-seeking charlatans were the antithesis of the beloved Congregational cleric, who droned on about the Bible from within the safety of Catharine's own church. Catharine longed for his guidance on this day at the camp meeting. The adoration, even worship, of certain men onstage by their female parishioners seemed driven by sex. If they had been in the sanctity—and safety—of conventional churches, these fits of intense passion would be restrained. The ministers would conform to decorum. Catharine watched as worshippers, struck by the spirit, flailed on the ground in a motley tangle of limbs—she mourned for them; their blatant ignorance was horrifying.

"When they go to a campground," she wrote, "they do not know of the dangers that lurk there and menace them at every step. They are told that by going there they may find religion, (a most absurd phrase by the way) as though religion could only be imbibed in certain places and situations."

Finding God was a personal journey, Catharine believed. But it was also a rigidly structured internal pilgrimage that demanded years of traditional worship driven by relentless reverence to traditional clerics . . . as well as blind faith. Publicly proclaiming the word of God in any other way, she believed, was simply heresy. There was no need to convert, to change your relationship with religion within a forest filled with wanderers who had lost all control of their decency. Their detachment from their home responsibilities had led them astray. If they were writhing on the ground, atop one another in the name of God, where were their good works?

Later in her book, Catharine would lay Sarah Cornell's woes and her ultimate downfall at the feet of the Methodist ministers in these camp meetings. If church reflected family, as Catharine believed, then Sarah's church had abused her.

"There can be no doubt that the lives of many delicate females have been sacrificed to the absurd custom of sleeping on the ground, with no covering but a tent to those who have been accustomed to the walls of a house," she wrote. "The want of rest, of sleep, which all who attend these meetings must suffer more or less, must be great."

Catharine detailed how startled she herself had been to hear the ministers demand God to act on their behalf with impunity, without any regard for decency; their privilege and arrogance were both improprieties that she despised.

"And last but not least, the low and dishonoring thoughts of religion which the constant hearing of such familiarity with Deity must unavoidably create," she wrote. "They frequently speak of the Almighty, and speak to him too, as though he were an equal, and even an inferior."

Catharine rushed through the crowd, away from the tent, and escaped to her home in Providence, keenly aware of what she had witnessed: blasphemy.

"She concluded, naturally, that this could not be true religion and that no good was done at these gatherings," wrote Baldwin. "Its effects were uniformly negative, both on the neighborhood where it took place and upon the spiritual and physical health of those who attended."

The Methodists were blatant heretics, Catharine Williams concluded a decade before writing **Fall River**. The camp meeting in Smithfield had confirmed that for her. Catharine was so traumatized by the event that she vowed to never reveal her journal pages filled with offensive details. But in light of Sarah Cornell's case, she felt compelled to draw it from the shadows as a cautionary tale, especially for young women.

"Should it be asked, where has this history been all this time?" wrote Catharine. "I answer, safe locked up in my desk. Why has it never been published before? Because it has never been called for: the occasion which has called it forth has never been so pressing." Her investigation into Sarah Cornell's death—especially now that Methodism and camp revivals were part of the narrative—felt like the right occasion for Catharine to reveal her story.

Catharine's contempt for the Methodists was shared by many New Englanders. The preaching of the itinerant ministers was intentional and intense—and disquieting to the Congregationalists who avowed propriety and constraint. They often reacted harshly to the new denomination, sometimes even violently.

"In the several decades after their arrival in the New England states in the late 1780s, Methodists were the objects of a wide variety of attacks," wrote Baldwin. "Their preachers were accused of being pickpockets, horse thieves, and sexual predators." Methodist preachers were deemed uneducated and unfit to teach the rubes who stumbled onto their chaotic, derelict camp meetings. They used seduction and uncontrolled emotion to gin up business, as well as donations. The ministers reported being threatened, stoned, chased by dogs, even tarred and feathered.

Methodists in England and America were roundly accused of almost any imaginable crime, but the most heinous was the widespread allegation of sexual impropriety.

"A pamphlet from the 1790s charged that a Methodist preacher had 'scandalously deserted his high profession and beguiled two young women' before fleeing the region," wrote Baldwin, "while an early itinerant recalled that some locals suspected that preachers were seducing women behind the closed doors of class meeting."

The verdict of "polite society" was resounding: Methodists were dangerous, corrupt, and downright intolerable for many Americans. And their increasing popularity with the country's youth, particularly its women, was treacherous. Sarah Cornell was certainly entranced by the Methodist Church and its teachings—and that also extended to its captivating preachers. But as she would soon discover, some apostles of faith were false prophets.

———

Catharine and I scoured our notes about Sarah Cornell. We gathered that she was loved by her mother and sister, but she felt untethered from them much of the time. We saw evidence in her writing that she leaned on her unwavering, even fanatical, devotion to Christianity for stability—first with the traditional and strict Congregationalists, and then with the zealous, spirited Methodists. Sarah seemed to thrive in New England's emerging spread of factories, and she relished her independence, but the punishing work of toiling in mills taxed her physically and emotionally. She watched that work break other women. She witnessed suicides, and she saw just how unforgiving it was on others' bodies and souls. Sarah also fretted about the public shaming she had received for what she saw as relatively minor, youthful indiscretions like petty thieving. Sarah's writings revealed a fragility and naïveté, even given her age of thirty.

Sarah Cornell appeared susceptible in a time when it was easy to manipulate a single young woman. Jacksonian America was an era rife with predators of all flavors. When author Nathaniel Hawthorne was strolling around the wax exhibit in 1838, taking note of the display featuring Sarah Cornell and Ephraim Avery, he stood before another display. It centered on the murder of a sex worker named Helen Jewett in a New York City brothel in 1836. The twenty-two-year-old was killed by one of her clients, according to investigators. But he was later acquitted, accused by many of escaping the noose because of powerful connections.

Hawthorne certainly must have also known about two later stories, those of Mary Rogers, also in New York, and that of Maria Buel. Like the tale of Sarah Cornell, the tragic death of Mary Rogers inspired another writer to pen a story about the murder of a vulnerable young woman. The twenty-one-year-old Rogers worked at a cigar store; a stunningly beautiful woman, she was specifically hired to attract male clientele. She turned up murdered in 1841, and her killer was never found, despite circumstantial evidence against a former boarder in her rooming house. Author Edgar Allan Poe had frequented the cigar shop in Manhattan where Rogers once worked. One year after her body was discovered, Poe drew from her death the inspiration for his famous story "The Mystery of Marie Roget," in which he linked the mysterious death of Mary Rogers on the banks of the Hudson River bordering New York City to a botched abortion that was covered up with an attempt to make the unfortunate woman's death look like a rape and murder. For centuries, female murder victims have inspired male authors to reimagine their stories to suit their own audience.

In August 1832, just four months before Sarah Maria Cornell's death, a teenager named Maria Buel was murdered in Trumbull County, Ohio, by her stepfather, whom many suspected of abusing her. He was later hanged. The murders of these girls and women were roundly considered tragedies by the press, though Helen Jewett, because of her history of sex work, was also victim-shamed in the papers. Jacksonian America was horrified by the brutal murders of young, attractive white women, even those who fell from grace. Hawthorne's **Scarlet Letter** echoes those fears on behalf of young, wayward women. Hawthorne knew that laborers like Sarah Cornell and his own Hester Prynne were ripe for predators hovering behind the pulpit.

"Out-of-wedlock pregnancies in the seventeenth and nineteenth centuries often provided their own 'punishment,'" wrote Kristin Boudreau. "The swollen belly and later the infant (as Hester Prynne well knows) served as badges of shame, while the arrival of the child often degraded the woman's economic status. In Cornell's case . . . the woman was an uneducated mill worker from a poor family in Connecticut; living far away from her natural family, she became easy prey for an eloquent and charismatic minister."

But during her life, Sarah Cornell's prayers for an ascent to heaven never wavered; her singular aspiration was for redemption in God's eyes. At her own desk in 1833, Catharine transcribed a particularly painful passage from one of Sarah's letters after her troubles began.

"My heart is hard, and I am as prone to sin as the sparks that fly upwards," wrote Sarah in 1820, when she was seventeen. "Oh my sister pray for me, that

God in his infinite mercy pour the sweet refreshing of his grace on my soul."

Sarah Cornell gazed at a parade of charismatic preachers over the years, each espousing the Bible. They seemed passionate, charming, so alive. But she never seemed to cast doubt about their intentions to guide her to salvation . . . until she learned that some men of God were simply sinners.

———

On Friday, December 21, 1832, John Durfee hovered over Sarah Maria Cornell's body, lying on the ground near the haystack pole. He was accompanied by Dr. Thomas Wilbur, the woman's physician prior to her death. Dr. Wilbur silently touched Sarah's abdomen.

Dr. Wilbur had kept a terrible secret for months. He not only had been concerned for his patient's mental stability, but he also feared for her life. Now he looked down at her corpse. He turned to the men and solemnly explained the truth that had been shameful in life and was now even more damning in death.

Sarah Cornell, his patient, had been pregnant when she died.

This revelation seemed to shock the group. Dr. Wilbur nodded and unfurled the sad circumstances. Sarah, who had been under his care for several months, was destined to be a single mother, likely with no financial support from the father. Her dire situation had depressed her greatly—she was already an outcast because of the thefts years before, and she knew all too well the sad fate that awaited a woman who was pregnant out of wedlock and away from the protections of a family.

Sarah at times felt hopeless, she had admitted to Dr. Wilbur. What's more, she seemed to grow increasingly unstable. The circumstances seemed clear to Dr. Wilbur: Sarah had likely taken her own life the night before. The crowd that stood around her body all whispered that this was a certain suicide. There could be no other explanation. About an hour after the body was discovered, John Durfee turned to the coroner, an elderly man named Elihu Hicks, and requested that Sarah be transported to his farmhouse. She had been found on his land. He felt a sense of duty to be sure she was cared for from this point forward.

"She was carried in a horse wagon," recalled Durfee. "First laid in a blanket, hay placed under her, and carried as slow as the horse could go. The road is smooth." Durfee was explaining that the ride to his house would not have jostled or further damaged Sarah's body; the trip was gentle. Any marks upon her person would have been inflicted prior to her discovery. This was an important disclosure for later.

"The coroner had summoned a jury," recalled Durfee, "and when she was removed to my house they proceeded to their duty."

Throughout much of American history, coroner's juries had been used to rule a cause of death. There might have been just a few appointed jurors or more than a dozen, depending on which citizens were available. They might have visited the crime scene, examined the body, interviewed witnesses, and even named suspects. Most members of coroner's juries in the 1800s had little to no medical knowledge, just good standing. Even coroners didn't need to have a medical degree, because many times they were elected, not appointed. You can see how haphazard the makeup of the coroner's jury could be. These panels issued verdicts—not on guilt or innocence of a suspect, but on how, where, and perhaps when the person died. If the jurists suspected murder, their verdict would likely lead to charges. Prosecutors could accept the guidance of a coroner's jury or ignore it.

Catharine Williams wasn't impressed with the coroner's jury in Sarah Maria Cornell's death. She called the assemblage "hasty and irregular"; nonetheless, a coroner's jury would respond to a surprising or suspicious death like that of Sarah Cornell. Catharine called them "irregular" for several reasons. The group of six men, which included John Durfee's father, immediately refused to examine Sarah's body without her clothes, out of propriety; suicide was the likely cause of death, they had quickly determined, mostly based on Dr. Wilbur's disclosures about her pregnancy. But the coroner asked them to meet early the next morning, Saturday, for a final verdict. This was the day after her body was discovered. The men nodded, saddened by the end of a promising young life.

But first, a group of matrons was ordered to do an abhorrent but necessary task: preparing the body for burial. Catharine wrote that Sarah "was then delivered into the hands of five or six of some of the most respectable matrons of the village who had volunteered to perform this office of benevolence towards the hapless stranger." This happened on the day her body was discovered.

The women lamented Sarah Cornell's decision to take her own life—she would certainly not go to heaven now, they agreed, because suicide was a sin and an act of blasphemy. "They commenced this work with mournful reflections upon the subject of self-murder, and some expressions of pity towards her whose hard fortune some way or other must have driven her to so rash and daring an act," Catharine wrote, "for that she died otherwise than by her own hand never entered the heads of either of the good women."

But as they removed Sarah's cloak, as well as her dress and her undergarments, they gasped.

"There were bad bruises on the back," the matrons later told Catharine Williams, "and the knees scratched and stained with grass as though they had been on the ground during some struggle."

It had been a terrible discovery—signs of struggle

that went undetected by all the men at the scene
because probing her body would have been improper—
yet the jurors had missed physical evidence. One
matron quietly turned to another.

"'Oh' said one of the oldest of the ladies who they
called Aunt Hannah, 'what has been done?'" wrote
Catharine.

A woman turned to Aunt Hannah and replied:
"Rash violence."

CHAPTER FOUR

~⌣~

BODY OF EVIDENCE

IN MOST CRIMINAL TRIALS TODAY, juries are asked to evaluate complicated digital evidence that is often argued to be indisputable: phone records, internet history, financial statements, CCTV footage, GPS coordinates, even Fitbit data. These clues seem straightforward.

But there's often additional evidence that requires interpretation from a forensic expert, such as a toxicologist, a DNA analyst, or a forensic pathologist, for example. We didn't have that kind of expert interpretation available in Sarah Cornell's case from 1832, of course. But we did have a lot of eyewitness testimony and physical descriptions—crucial evidence that put us close to the scene of the crime and the moment of Sarah's death. In this respect, I was relying almost exclusively on the contemporaneous records and notes that Catharine Williams had recorded almost two centuries before. I was going to have to lean on my coauthor more than ever.

But sometimes, if clues are evaluated incorrectly, they are less helpful and more harmful to an investigation. That was my fear as I read Catharine's account of what the "experts" who arrived at the Durfee farm discovered that December morning.

But first, I reviewed our study of Sarah's life before her death. Who was our victim before she died? What was important to her, and what led her to that field that night? What I started to see was the portrait of a woman who, in the last years of her life, was drawn back to her family—only to find her path was blocked. She went years without seeing her siblings and endured months without letters. Sarah was hopelessly lonely yet surrounded by so many people.

"I want to see Mother and if any of you desire to see me—write and let me know and I will try to come and spend a few days with you before long," Sarah wrote to her sister, Lucretia, in 1824. "But whether I ever see you again or not, I want you should forgive me and bury what is past in oblivion and I hope my future good conduct may reward you."

Since her banishment from Providence the year before for thieving, Sarah had been distanced from her sister and her mother—her dubious reputation left her vulnerable. Now it was time for Catharine and me to research Sarah's social circle; her friends and coworkers might have been able to illuminate

her mental health struggles, her past romantic relationships, and her encounters with potential predators. What about her fellow parishioners at the
Methodist church, which provided the community
and family she was otherwise so distanced from?
And what about the farmer who had discovered her
body on his land, John Durfee? Would Catharine
consider him a suspect?

We've also discussed crime scene investigation:
Sarah died at a rural farm in Tiverton, a spot that
was secluded under the cloak of darkness yet accessible to anyone. The Durfees had neighbors not
far from their property, and several would become
"ear witnesses" to what they believed was a crime.
John Durfee, the man who discovered Sarah's body,
had claimed, "There are no intervening objects to
obstruct the view of the hay-stack from my house."
Why didn't he see something that night?

All this in sum meant that if this **were** a murder,
then the suspect list could be endless. Sarah Cornell
wasn't socially isolated, as a farm wife might have
been in rural New England—she was exposed,
almost constantly, to people as she moved from job
to job and church to church. We'll examine our
witnesses in a later chapter.

First, it's important to evaluate the physical evidence on the Durfee property, as well as the forensic
clues left behind on Sarah Cornell's body. Today,
the coroner, or the medical examiner, is usually
the first investigator to gather that sort of evidence

during an in-depth postmortem exam that includes photographs, tests, and sample collection. But the coroner in 1833, Dr. Elihu Hicks, was a peripheral character in Sarah's case when she was first discovered, because the men at the scene, the coroner's jury who would decide her cause of death, all presumed that she died by suicide.

Sarah's body was then delivered to the matrons, who prepared it for burial. These women evaluated Sarah, and their examination of her body created a narrative that they would soon pass on to John Durfee. Nathaniel Hawthorne mirrors this theme, in many ways, during the opening scene of **The Scarlet Letter**. A pregnant Hester Prynne is forced to stand on a scaffold for three hours, enduring public ridicule as her punishment for adultery. Some of the most vicious criticism comes from women.

"'What do we talk of marks and brands, whether on the bodice of her gown or the flesh of her forehead?' cried another female, the ugliest as well as the most pitiless of these self-constituted judges," wrote Hawthorne. "'This woman has brought shame upon us all and ought to die. Is there no law for it?'"

These women have created a narrative that ultimately damns Prynne to a life of isolation. While the women in **The Scarlet Letter** condemn Prynne, it was the female villagers in Fall River who emerged as some of the heroes for Sarah Cornell; they were the first to become alarmed, the first to suspect murder. Social mores had stopped the male coroner and his all-male jury from closely examining Sarah's body, except for her throat, where the cord had become deeply embedded. But the matrons, including two of John Durfee's sisters, were now some of Catharine's most important witnesses. And what they reported startled them all: there was significant bruising on Sarah Cornell's body.

Did bruising on her body mean Sarah had been shoved or even beaten prior to her death? "Yeah, that gives me concern," said forensic investigator Paul Holes, when looking at the facts of this case alongside me through a contemporary lens. When there's bruising on a body that is seemingly not explained by other factors, Holes said, "the manner of death should be left undetermined" pending further investigation. I asked him, what could be one possible interpretation of these bruises? He replied, "I'm a little bit concerned that maybe she had been in a struggle prior to being hanged."

Women in the 1830s were not immune to violence; they were often accustomed to it. Domestic abuse frequently went unreported. In fact, men had the legal right to beat their wives throughout the 1800s—certainly some of the matrons were likely victims themselves. And several of the women became fearful when they recognized evidence of a struggle. It was a sign that there might be more to this case than the suicide of a pregnant woman.

To find out more, Catharine Williams requested an interview with the group of women who prepared

the body for burial in 1833, right around the same
time she talked with farm owner John Durfee. The
women had the difficult task of recounting a terrible discovery—one they made while conducting a
usually banal and all-too-common domestic task:
preparing another woman's body for burial.

"Before the late 1800s in the United States, it was
almost unthinkable for a man to prepare a body for
burial," wrote Briony D. Zlomke in "Death Became
Them: The Defeminization of the American Death
Culture, 1609–1899." "As death primarily occurred
in the home, preparations surrounding the body
were designated as a female duty." As foreign as
it seems to us today, this practice was "viewed as
an extension of birthing children and nursing the
ailing," Zlomke continued. "The responsibility of
preparing the dead fell upon women."

The matrons properly dressed Sarah after cleaning her body and observing the bruises, making her
presentable for viewing and a quick burial. They
were ordered to have her body prepared by the next
day, Saturday, for a speedy funeral service and inter-
ment. It all seemed rushed to both Catharine and
me, but nineteenth-century customs would have
required that the body be buried before it began
rapidly decomposing. And the matrons knew that
Sarah was pregnant, so that might have increased
their urgency.

Yet, there were others who slowly, quietly wondered
over the weekend about the initial verdict of suicide.

Sarah's face itself had revealed some curious clues; she had suffered visible injuries that should have alerted any coroner. And while Dr. Hicks seemed to dismiss any concerns, Sarah's physician, Dr. Wilbur, seemed increasingly upset. He would become one of Catharine's most important witnesses and one of Sarah's few advocates right after her disovery.

Because Dr. Wilbur had seen her several times as a patient, his description would prove to be invaluable. He noted that her short dark hair had fallen over her face, and it was frozen to her skin—remember, it had been 29 degrees that cold December morning. The cord wrapped around her neck was embedded in the folds of her throat by nearly half an inch. Dr. Wilbur described her as "livid and pale," as if all the blood had been drained out of her. **What about her face? Her mouth?** The author pressed the physician for more details as she took notes.

"Her tongue protruded through her teeth," Dr. Wilbur replied, "pushed out her under lip, that was very much swollen as though it had received some hard blow or had been severely bit in anguish."

Dr. Wilbur continued: "[It] gave a dreadful expression of agony, while a deep indentation on the cheek looked as though that too must have been pressed by some hard substance." Perhaps Dr. Wilbur was insinuating that Sarah's face was marked during a struggle, as a blow threw her back against the haystack pole? Or her face was pushed against a rock on the ground? No matter what had caused the injuries, they were certainly the result of a physical assault, concluded Dr. Wilbur.

But investigator Paul Holes disagreed. "If she committed suicide, this type of hanging, it's not like she's doing a long drop," he said. "She's swinging, she's bumping into things, which could possibly cause bruising." Holes meant that Sarah didn't experience the same type of hanging as a condemned prisoner, standing high above the ground on the gallows.

The bruises could have also been caused by her struggling during a suicide. But her face, Dr. Wilbur insisted, wore a twisted expression that Catharine interpreted vividly. "Her countenance was exceedingly distorted, and there was not only an expression of anguish upon it, but one of horror and affright, combined with an angry frown," she wrote. "'That terrible look,' said the doctor, 'was present with me for months, and often in the dead of night has appeared to my imagination with such force as to awake me, and I can scarcely think of it now without a chill.'"

Dr. Wilbur paused—he told Catharine that he had never seen that look on someone's face who had **not** died violently. Sarah had suffered, he was sure of it, and Catharine believed him. But we know that you can't interpret how someone died based solely on their facial expression.

Catharine reviewed her notes from the handful of matrons tasked with preparing Sarah's body. She had died of "strangulation" via rope. There was no debating that. The author squinted at her writing through her spectacles as she detailed their description of Sarah's injuries to help piece together **why** the young woman died—and Catharine was already certain that it wasn't "self-murder," as suicide was once called.

"Just above each hip were marks of hands, the bruises of which were very bad, so that the spots of the thumb inwards," Catharine wrote, "and the fingers outside were distinctly visible, they were those of a large hand."

The markings concerned the matrons, but they didn't note their shade or color; those can be clues as to when the injury was received. It was important to establish whether they were old or new bruises— the women described them only as "dark" or "bad." During the healing process, a bruise evolves. It's usually red at first because fresh, oxygen-rich blood has newly pooled underneath the skin. After a day or two, the blood at the bruise begins to lose oxygen, so it will often change to blue, purple, or even black. In less than a week, several compounds break down the hemoglobin and the bruise will become yellow or green. Eventually, after about two weeks, the bruise fades. Might these dark spots have been the normal process for a natural death?

Another caveat: cold weather can accelerate the healing process. Cold exposure causes something called "vasoconstriction," which narrows blood vessels and helps them close faster, which is why doctors recommend using an ice pack when you're newly injured. The bruises found on Sarah might have been new . . . or old. The frigid weather made it almost impossible to tell. But because there were other signs of trauma, they needed to be considered.

When they spotted the large bruises in the shape of two hands above Sarah's hips, the matrons conducted an experiment with their own hands. "The marks just fayed [fitted] to my fingers," said Penelope Borden. "The marks on the thumb on the lower part of the belly, and of the fingers opposite on the loins, just behind, were on both sides."

Mrs. Borden then demonstrated how Sarah's hands were specifically positioned. "Her right hand raised up thus [to the breast]," she explained, "and the hand twisted round so [the palm turned outward from the person] and was very stiff."

Catharine wrote: "One or two of the women applied theirs and they were not large enough to cover the marks. One only, the person they called Aunt Hannah, found her hand to fit."

Catharine didn't interpret the results for her readers, but clearly the matrons assumed that a man, not a woman, had inflicted the injuries. The women carefully turned Sarah on her side and then on her stomach. They discovered more bruises on her back, as we said earlier. Again, we don't know if these were recent, perhaps from the night before, or older bruises. We know that blood can coagulate in the body in different areas. The women turned Sarah back over and looked closely at her pale legs. There was more evidence of violence.

"The knees scratched and stained with grass as though they had been on the ground during some struggle," wrote Catharine. "Spots below the knee where the skin was rubbed off."

Some of the matrons weighed in. "The knees were so bent, that we had to use warm water to get them down," said Penelope Borden. "I first formed an opinion that she had been violated."

"Violated" was one nineteenth-century term for "sexually assaulted," as were "molested" and "ravished." Borden detailed to Catharine that Sarah's abdomen was bruised, her undergarments were bloodied, and there was fecal matter embedded in them. Another matron, Dorcas Ford, said, "There was froth tinged with blood, which had proceeded from the mouth and nose."

The froth comes when fluids flow into the airway; even after death, gases escape from the lungs, causing the bubbles. Paul Holes told me that these bubbles don't dissipate, like those in the head of a beer. They're more rigid and stay for quite a while after death if they aren't disturbed. So this froth was normal for a hanging.

Ford said that Sarah had been "dreadfully bruised." It seemed to Catharine as if Sarah had fought with an offender, who had dragged her down to the ground, perhaps onto her knees.

These were all crucial observations. How had Sarah's body become so battered? And when? If the struggle had occurred well before her death (as some would later claim), why didn't Sarah wash the grass stains from her skin immediately?

As part of their review of Sarah's body, the matrons hoped to examine her arms more closely, but there was a problem: rigor mortis had set in. Rigor is the stiffening of the limbs and joints that happens about two hours after death; today it's a key method for checking time of death, even more accurate than a liver temperature test, though both are problematic, depending on the condition of the body. All muscles are immediately affected by rigor, but smaller muscles, like those in the neck and jaw, are impacted first. The matrons looked closely at Sarah's arm—it looked so odd.

"The right arm was bent up and the hand turned back," wrote Catharine, "and it was with much difficulty the females could bring it down."

They couldn't bury her like that. The women loosened the tightening of her arm muscle by soaking it in warm water. But then something terrible happened.

"And when they succeeded in bending it down," said Catharine, "it snapt so that they thought it must have been broken." The matrons were appalled.

Over the past thirty years, I've often reported on the murders of women, many times at the hands of men. Their bodies before burial are often exposed for hours while their corpses are examined, photographed, dissected, probed, and then sewn shut. They're then clothed, and sometimes put on display for gawkers during high-profile criminal cases. Thank goodness, I thought, Sarah had these women to care for her in the end. Very soon, Sarah Maria Cornell would receive more attention in death than she ever did in life.

Catharine listened to the matrons—she had reviewed her notes from Dr. Wilbur's interview beforehand. She hoped that the women could corroborate the physician's description of the damage on Sarah's face, that she had been hit in the mouth before her death. But this is a good time to remind the reader that just because Sarah suffered violence at the hands of someone else before she died, it doesn't mean she was murdered. Right now, our edict is to prove or disprove murder, which was also the duty of the coroner's jury. And then we will weigh the evidence under the rules of law, like a jury in a criminal case—it doesn't matter what we believe; it only matters what can be proved in court.

———

Back on that Friday morning in December, hours after Sarah's body had been discovered, and as the matrons examined the brutality evident on it, they began to whisper among themselves. Sarah's body seemed too traumatized to be a result of suicide. But they stayed muted when the men arrived to place her in a coffin. And then about three hours later, something changed.

As the coroner and his jurors stood inside the farmhouse, assessing Sarah's cause of death but before their final verdict, the matrons asked John Durfee to locate proper burial clothes for Sarah, as well as letters to friends or family who needed to be notified about her death. The farmer nodded, sat on his horse-drawn wagon, cracked the whip, and soon arrived at Sarah's boardinghouse in Fall River. He called to Sarah's landlady, Mrs. Harriet Hathaway, and requested the young woman's belongings.

"She delivered it to me, and a bandbox, saying the key of the trunk was probably in the girl's pocket, as she generally carried it with her," said John Durfee.

Sure enough, when Durfee walked back into his home, one of the matrons, Ruth Cook, handed him a small key that had been found in Sarah's pocket. It fit in the keyhole of her trunk—turned the lock. When Durfee lifted the lid, he stared down at several envelopes.

Sarah had been a prolific letter writer, and at the bottom of the trunk, the farmer retrieved four letters that were of interest: one written on yellow paper, one on pink paper, and two on white. One of the white letters was written by Sarah to Reverend Ira Bidwell, the pastor at her Methodist church; he was also the cleric who had attested to Sarah's good character when her body was discovered.

"The other three were anonymous, but directed on the outside to Sarah M. Connell, Fall River," wrote Catharine.

Durfee thumbed the three letters, all unsigned. They seemed to be requesting a rendezvous at a previously discussed location, but none signaling a meeting specifically at John Durfee's farm. One mentioned two different days, depending on the weather. A different letter ended with "Write soon— say nothing to no one." None was threatening or mentioned a pregnancy. Despite the curious nature of the anonymous letters, Durfee stayed quiet.

Some of this evidence is suspicious, but none of it points definitively to murder. There was more to be found, though, in that trunk that John Durfee had retrieved from Sarah's room. He reexamined it and found a vial of an unusual liquid inside—something called tansy oil. Catharine and I had never heard of it; in 1833, she asked Dr. Wilbur about its use.

"The drug referred to was the Oil of Tansy," wrote Catharine, "one of the most violent things ever used, and never given except in very small quantities, and under the direction of a physician."

Dr. Wilbur denied prescribing the oil of tansy to Sarah Cornell. **Why was it in her trunk?** both Catharine and I wanted to know. I asked a poison expert and fellow author, Dr. Neil Bradbury, to do some research on tansy. He's a professor of physiology and biophysics at the Rosalind Franklin University of Medicine and Science in Chicago.

"The principal active ingredient in tansy oil seems to be a chemical called thujone," Dr. Bradbury told me, "which can affect the nervous system and lead to convulsions, causing kidney failure and marked nausea and vomiting."

Oil of tansy could have been used for suicide, like arsenic had been—though it would have been a painful death. In the 1800s, it was also used to terminate a pregnancy, though tansy was tricky. It wouldn't take a very large amount to accidentally overdose the patient. But tansy was also used as a medicine, principally for digestive tract problems, such as stomach and intestinal ulcers. It also seemed to help with joint pain, almost like a numbing agent. I asked Dr. Bradbury if it might have been used recreationally. Yes, he replied.

"As I am sure you know," wrote Dr. Bradbury, "another source of thujone is the plant wormwood, which was used in the making of absinthe. This likely led to the prohibition against absinthe, and its supposed relation to killing its drinkers, or turning them into killers."

We still don't know why Sarah Cornell had oil of tansy in her trunk, but it certainly might have been medicinal. Or it could have been recreational. Or it might have been used for suicide or to terminate her pregnancy. Without the advent of toxicology, we don't know if there were drugs, like tansy, in her system. Toxicology wouldn't appear in a courtroom until 1840 in France. It certainly would have been helpful in this case. John Durfee examined the vial of liquid, but still stayed quiet.

Catharine reviewed her notes from witnesses who recalled details of the day Sarah was discovered hanging by her neck from a haystack pole. She looked over her writing during her interview with Sarah's personal physician, Dr. Wilbur. He had publicly agreed that her death was certainly suicide due to her pregnancy, but privately he had doubts.

"The truth struggled hard in the breast of the doctor," wrote Catharine. "He had felt himself bound to secrecy."

Another secret? What was Dr. Wilbur keeping to himself? He'd already confirmed Sarah's pregnancy to the coroner's jury, after all.

Back in the stackyard that Friday, the physician turned to the Methodist minister, Ira Bidwell, who had declared that he knew Sarah to be a devoted, respectable member of his flock. Reverend Bidwell sighed, declaring that her death was a sad affair— his parishioners would mourn her. John Durfee wondered aloud about Sarah's burial. **Would the Methodists help one of their devout parishioners if no one else came forward?**

According to Catharine, Bidwell "replied that he did not exactly know their rules in such cases, but he would go and consult them and return soon." With that, Bidwell turned on his heel and began walking toward the main road.

Dr. Wilbur's heart pounded—he grew nervous.

He chased after Bidwell, grabbed the minister by the arm, and told him a quiet truth about Sarah's supposed suicide.

"The awful manner of it impelled him to reveal what he believed to be the cause. Stepping after the clergyman, he related the confession of the unhappy girl to him," wrote Catharine, specifically: "what she had said respecting his [Bidwell's] brother."

"Brother" in this case meant Reverend Bidwell's fellow Methodist minister. It was this man, Reverend Ephraim Avery, who had made Sarah Cornell unhappy, Dr. Wilbur explained to Bidwell. Bidwell's eyes widened at the mention of one of his most favored disciples. Sarah Cornell, Dr. Wilbur continued, was lying lifeless today because Avery had been manipulative and cruel. Reverend Bidwell turned and left briskly, promising to return with information about burial funds. But Dr. Wilbur saw a flash of fear from Reverend Bidwell—something was wrong.

"A storm was gathering which was destined not only to call forth the dead from her grave," wrote Catharine, "but to shake the society to which she belonged to its centre—a storm whose effects have continued to be felt ever since."

———

Sarah and Catharine's America was rapidly changing. In March 1833, Andrew Jackson had been

sworn in as president for a second term after winning
on a platform of representing the mass of voters,
the everyman. Meanwhile, the still-young country
was expanding at a ferocious pace. Railroads were
spreading into western territories, and Jackson was
the first president to ride a train. But the societal
upheaval caused by this rapid growth was expanding as well.

For one thing, industry was growing rapidly—
and nowhere was this more evident than in the
emerging rural/urban divide. Workers were shift-
ing from toiling in the fields to grinding gears in
factories. "In 1830, most New Englanders lived on
farms and grew much of the food they ate," wrote
Peter Temin in his paper "The Industrialization
of New England: 1830–1880." "By 1880, most
New Englanders lived in cities, worked for wages,
and bought their food." Cities like New York and
Boston swelled as more people were drawn from the
countryside to urban areas.

At the same time, America's world view and politics were still rooted in its Puritanical founding ide-
als, based not just in New England but in England
itself, despite the country's independence about fifty
years earlier. These "New Englanders" adhered to a
sense of individualism that intersected with social
responsibility. Congregationalists placed their
unflappable commitment to God above all else.

"Men not only placed themselves under a rigorous
self-examination to determine whether or not they

were among the saved," wrote Frederick Jackson Turner in his essay "New England, 1830–1850," "but they also felt the community sense of responsibility for sin . . . that man was his brother's keeper."

That responsibility translated to harsh judgment leveled at anyone who dared to step out of line. New Englanders were morally upright, they told themselves, and they expected their neighbors to fear God as they did. "Businessmen as well as statesmen and ministers took frequent stock, in their diaries, of their moral condition and were mindful of death and the final reckoning," wrote Turner. The classic New Englander of the early nineteenth century was reserved, as the Puritans had been. Even humor was expected to be respectful. Overzealous amounts of joy were frowned upon. The fastidious nature of New England was stifling to many, particularly to women.

That seems like a precarious concept: a society that held itself responsible for policing abject avarice and secret desires, and parishioners who were eyed if they showed an interest in exploring other religions. The vision of an idealistic New England clashed with its reality. Women were cloistered emotionally, and spiritual growth was specific: it must be done in the church, led by capable, steady, and properly trained Congregationalist ministers. Author Nathaniel Hawthorne was clear in his novel **The Scarlet Letter** that the rules established by the Puritans were expected to be stringently followed, especially by women. Any deviation was considered . . . sinful. The public rebuke was swift, particularly from **other** women.

In Hawthorne's novel, a group of matrons complain about the treatment of Hester Prynne for her sin. They accuse her of escaping a swifter, more appropriate justice: "At the very least, they should have put the brand of a hot iron on Hester Prynne's forehead," says one woman in **The Scarlet Letter**. "Madame Hester would have winced at that, I warrant me. But she—the naughty baggage—little will she care what they put upon the bodice of her gown! Why, look you, she may cover it with a brooch, or such like heathenish adornment, and so walk the streets as brave as ever!"

They describe Prynne as a "living sermon against sin." In our story, Sarah Cornell would experience similar judgment. Catharine Williams wrote, in disgust: "Some were almost ready to exclaim, 'No matter who killed her—such a person [like Sarah] were better out of the world than in it—they have certainly done society a good service.'" These types of quotes littered the pages of New England newspapers, and Hawthorne certainly read them.

Congregationalists dominated the religious ideology of the early 1800s—the church's parishioners were New England's titans of industry. They developed the whaling industry, which created immense wealth for a select group of families. Congregationalists propelled the shoe industry, while New England fields were harvested to feed their families. But agriculture was changing because farmers were able to purchase items, thanks to flourishing factories. It was less expensive to buy clothing than to pay women in the countryside to spin cotton for household goods.

"The daughters, released from the spinning wheel and loom, flocked to the factories, became 'hired help,' or schoolteachers, or sewed the shoes, plaited the straw hats, and made the ready-to-wear garments, parceled out by the neighboring manufacturers," wrote Turner.

Women were leaving the safety of the farms, sparking a feminist movement that made Congregationalists uneasy. As women gained new independence, the idea of feminism and their autonomy developed, to the dismay of many men. Again, we see echoes of Sarah Cornell's journey through the mills of New England intersect with Hawthorne's Hester Prynne. "Although Hawthorne does not make his townspeople comment on the dangers of Hester's economic independence," wrote Kristin Boudreau, "we can see in her chosen work echoes of the anxieties about factory work for women that arose in the debates about the Cornell murder."

Prynne's career as an independent seamstress threatens the patriarchal power of the New England community.

"Her needlework liberates her from the economic control of a husband who is (like Cornell's own parents) singularly unable to provide guidance for the woman in his charge," said Boudreau. "Hawthorne conflates her economic and sexual independence, thereby rehearsing the debates about factory work for New England women."

Both Hester Prynne and Sarah Cornell were avatars for independence and vulnerability. They didn't need men to survive, and this was troubling for many New Englanders.

Along with women's self-reliance came self-reflection, and doubts about their spiritual paths emerged—the restrictions of the traditional Congregationalist church were suffocating to a woman now accustomed to having agency over her life. Then came the Methodists: liberated, jubilant, unmoored from Puritan tradition—it became a study in contrasts. Many Congregationalists were initially wary of the Methodists, and then suspicious.

———

On John Durfee's farm, Dr. Wilbur stood near the farmer and waited for Reverend Bidwell's return. Dr. Wilbur had been certain that Sarah had taken her own life after years of suffering. He told the coroner's jury his suspicions: a married man (he left unnamed) had sexually assaulted Sarah, humiliated her, and then left her destitute—and that, ashamed, Sarah had died by suicide. But she deserved a proper Christian burial, he believed. The other men nodded.

Then Dr. Wilbur watched Reverend Bidwell scurry back up the road toward Durfee's property. Wilbur and John Durfee greeted him, anxious to hear the news about Sarah's burial. Bidwell seemed much less congenial, less solemn during this second visit.

"Very shortly he returned to the house of Mr. Durfee, and said that 'the deceased was a bad character and the meeting would have nothing to do with burying her,'" wrote Catharine. "Of course Mr. Durfee's astonishment was very great, having just before heard the Rev. gentleman say she was a respectable woman and a member of their society."

What happened? wondered John Durfee. **What changed? And what had Sarah Cornell done that was so egregious?**

Durfee's brow furrowed. He didn't like this turn of events. But Reverend Bidwell was steadfast—the Methodists would have nothing to do with Sarah Cornell. Durfee quickly made a decision, announcing it that day.

"Nothing influenced the honest and benevolent farmer to omit his own duty, and deny the right of burial to the poor unhappy girl whose remains Providence seemed in a peculiar manner to have confided to his care," wrote Catharine.

"She shall have a burial place in my grounds," Durfee told the group, "near my family, and as respectable a funeral as anybody, and as respectable a clergyman as any other to make the prayer, and everything that is necessary and decent shall be attended to."

John Durfee then ordered one of his farmhands to dig a grave on his property as Sarah Cornell lay in his home. She would be buried the following afternoon, Saturday, at 1:00 p.m., after the coroner's jury issued their official verdict about her cause of death. The matrons were pleased that the plans were moving along. But later that day, they made another disturbing discovery, one that changed the course of so many lives. Two of John Durfee's sisters, Susannah and Meribah, stood over the trunk that had contained Sarah Maria Cornell's personal (and mysterious) letters. They had hoped to contact **anyone** who could come to the services the next afternoon, people close to the tragic young woman. They rummaged through the trunk, sifting through innocuous papers, when they lifted a bandbox, a circular box used for carrying hats. They told Catharine about their discovery, a tiny clue that turned the attention of investigators.

"Near the middle of the bandbox lay a small piece of soiled paper and a lead pencil," wrote Catharine. "Mr. Durfee did not open the little piece of paper or think of its being of any consequence whatever."

Durfee had not noticed it—or he probably thought it was rubbish. But when the two women unfolded the four-inch-long paper and looked closely, it appeared to be a note, written in pencil.

Their eyes widened, and one of the two ran to find John Durfee. The other matron squinted at the tiny paper with beautiful, slanted lettering written on it, signed "S.M.C."

"It contained these words," wrote Catharine. "'If I am missing enquire of the Rev. E. K. Avery.'"

CHAPTER FIVE

~⌒~

"IF I AM MISSING"

"IF I AM MISSING ENQUIRE of the Rev. E. K. Avery." What could this possibly mean?

"Missing" sounded ominous to the women. **Why would Sarah Cornell go missing? And who is Reverend Ephraim Avery?** Dr. Thomas Wilbur had explained to the coroner's jury that Sarah had confided in him that she had been somehow involved with an unnamed married man. She had been pregnant and in despair when he last saw her. Now this note, tucked away in the dead woman's trunk, cast a pall on her already sad circumstances. The matrons fretted about what to do. The funeral was scheduled for the next day, as was the final verdict of the coroner's jury. John Durfee's sister Susannah had to tell her brother about this solemn discovery. However, for some reason she reportedly didn't do so right away, according to Catharine, who chalked up the delay to the general upheaval Sarah's death and discovery had brought to the Durfee farm.

"There were a great many persons in the house," wrote Catharine about the day Sarah was discovered, "and constantly going and coming, and although the women talked much about it and shew it to others in the house . . . it was not seen by the master of the house until next morning."

On Saturday, December 22, 1832, the day after Sarah's body had been discovered, the coroner's jury reconvened, preparing to issue a verdict on the woman's death. The letters found in Sarah's locked trunk were read into evidence.

One was penned on November 13, 1832, a little more than a month before her death: "I have just received your letter with no small surprise, and will say, I will do all you ask, only keep your secrets. I wish you to write me as soon as you get this, naming some time and place where I shall see you, and then look for answer before I come; and will say whether convenient or not, and will say the time. I will keep your letters till I see you, and wish you to keep mine, and have them with you there at the time. Write soon—say nothing to no one. Yours in haste."

Sarah Cornell, the coroner's jury surmised, had perhaps met with the man and then faced rejection. She later ventured to Richard Durfee's property that night and had decided that her life was too trying; she couldn't bear the shame of being a single mother. She had hanged herself. They couldn't fathom any other explanation. Soon, the jury presented their decision on Sarah's cause of death to the coroner.

"Sarah M. Cornell committed suicide by hanging herself upon a stake in said stackyard and was influenced to commit the crime by the wicked conduct of a married man," read the verdict, "which we gather from Dr. Wilbur together with the contents of three letters found in the trunk of the said Sarah M. Cornell."

Her cause of death was finalized: suicide. The jury still did not suspect murder. They didn't know about the ominous slip of paper. And now the funeral service was just a few hours away. Orin Fowler, a minister with the First Congregational Church of Fall River, was preparing his sermon as mourners from Tiverton and Fall River arrived that day. But all the while, Susannah Borden, John Durfee's sister, was in angst over the note she and her sister had discovered in the bandbox. After much debate, she handed the slip of paper to her brother, just hours before Sarah's burial.

Durfee examined it, reading it multiple times for context. He was confused by the grim message— and then he became anxious. And yet, he stayed quiet. A crowd of local mill workers gathered at his house that morning, and Reverend Fowler offered a prayer.

No Methodist leaders were seen on the Durfee property that day. Reverend Ira Bidwell, the Methodist minister who had been among the men who discovered Sarah's body the day before, was on his own journey—to notify the reverend mentioned in Sarah's note, Reverend Avery, that his relationship with a dead woman was under suspicion.

Numerous people from Fall River formed a procession that led Sarah Cornell to her final resting spot on the Durfee property. Dr. Wilbur stood near her grave, and men lowered the coffin. Reverend Fowler murmured a series of prayers, and she was covered with dirt.

Catharine Williams, writing about this scene in the years that followed, marked Sarah's burial as the impetus for an oncoming storm—Sarah was not destined to rest in peace. Her spirit was meant "to shake the society to which she belonged to its centre," Catharine believed. "[It] has embittered former friends against each other," wrote Catharine, "created many heart-burnings, assailed the peace of families, hindered the Christian missionary in the exercise of his pious duties, caused the name of Christ to be blasphemed, and in some places almost depopulated churches."

Sarah Cornell's case would reverberate throughout history, throughout literature—a fallen woman murdered by a man lionized by his church.

But that was all in the future. As Sarah Cornell lay deep in a grave, down the hill from John Durfee's house, the farmer fretted. He tossed in his bed. On Sunday morning, December 23, 1832, the day after Sarah's funeral and two days after her discovery, Durfee stretched after a dreadful night's sleep.

"Although consigned to her grave, the image of the murdered maid (for murdered he now no longer doubted she was) continued to haunt the pillow of Mr. Durfee, and he rose on the following day determined to investigate the dark mystery which hung over her fate," wrote Catharine.

Durfee encountered his first witness later that day. Fall River resident Thomas Hart was strolling near the farm when he spotted something on the ground less than 500 feet from where Sarah had died—a broken comb. Because of the circumstances, and the rumors swirling around Sarah's death, Hart quickly handed the comb to Durfee. The farmer looked at the accessory and seemed concerned. It matched a piece of a comb found not far from the haystack on the day she was discovered. Durfee jumped onto his horse and cart and swiftly returned to the boarding-house where Sarah had lived.

Durfee knocked on the door and Mrs. Hathaway answered. "Do you recognize this comb?" he asked. The woman nodded. It was her former tenant Sarah's comb—and in fact, she had just paid for it to be repaired. She pointed in the direction of the jeweler whom Sarah had hired. The jeweler immediately recognized it because it had unusual beading. **What was Sarah's broken comb doing in the middle of John Durfee's field?**

If this were modern times, then investigators could have tested the comb for DNA or dusted for fingerprints to determine if the would-be murderer had touched it. But the first known use of fingerprinting as identification in the United States came about fifty years later, in 1882, when American geologist Gilbert Thompson in New Mexico used his own thumbprint on a document to prevent forgery. A print would not be helpful in this case. And DNA technology wasn't even a glimmer in an investigator's eye.

A bunched-up handkerchief had also been found near Sarah's body; Catharine confirmed that it was Sarah's personal handkerchief, and it was unusually wet. Catharine was convinced that it had been soaked by saliva—as if it had "been used to stop her mouth by some person who murdered her," she concluded. The wet handkerchief was another piece of evidence for the author that supported her theory of murder.

She lamented that investigators should have soaked the handkerchief in water to determine if the wet substance was dew, snow, or saliva. Saliva is 99 percent water, but 1 percent is a mixture of electrolytes, mucus, enzymes, and antibacterial compounds. Could you really determine the difference between rain and saliva by pouring water on it? No, according to forensic investigator Paul Holes.

"These are water-based fluids," he said. "I would not expect any type of difference in terms of observable physical characteristics. That doesn't make any sense to me." So Catharine's experiment (though creative given the limited resources at her disposal) would have been invalid. But I must confess: I'm also not sure how a soaking-wet handkerchief would get inside someone's mouth while they were being strangled—wouldn't it have been frozen by morning? And the weather was below freezing that December evening, 29 degrees. I asked Holes about whether a wet handkerchief would freeze overnight.

"I would expect that handkerchief would have been stiff at that temperature," Holes said. "Is it possible that that was something that was in her mouth, and for some reason it ended up on the ground in a reasonably short period of time, prior to it actually being recovered? Yes. But it was likely frozen if it had liquid on it."

Catharine said nothing about the handkerchief being frozen, which seems like a careless (at best) or misleading (at worst) piece of "evidence" from Catharine. She continued to frame Sarah as the consummate victim of murder. Was she letting her own assumptions and biases lead her to a conclusion?

Catharine continued gathering evidence leading to questionable suppositions. Dr. Wilbur reported to Catharine that Sarah's face and cloak had nasal discharge on them, as well as what he perceived to be tears. Of course, without testing, it's impossible to know if they were tears—and if they were, whether those tears resulted from self-torment (leading to suicide) or external pain (resulting from murder). But Catharine's insinuation was clear: Sarah was in agony, a pitiful creature turned helpless victim. The physician prayed that the tears were ones of penitence "when she found the fangs of the murderer were upon her, and she was about to appear in the presence of her God."

Other pieces of evidence that Catharine cited in her notes related to Sarah's clothing. John Durfee had said, "Her outside dress was a cloak, hooked together nearly the whole length, except for one hook a little below the chest." Sarah was wearing her cloak, and her hands were underneath it. Catharine seemed to think that someone who had tied a rope around their own neck would not have left a bulky cloak on (even in the December chill) and then calmly concealed their hands beneath the cloak as they were being strangled by the noose. And one of the witnesses described Sarah's hand position as "both hands were under her cloak." Did this point to her already being dead when someone tied the cord around her neck? That's what Catharine seemed to believe. However, there's conflicting testimony on this point as well. Another witness, Seth Darling, said that the right arm was raised up to her breast, and the left was down by her side, just as the matrons had reported.

Other items of Sarah's clothing that Catharine scrutinized for meaning: her hat and shoes. Durfee said Sarah was wearing a black calash bonnet, which was a winter accessory in early 1800s New England. That style of bonnet offered significant coverage of the wearer's hair and face and was meant to protect from both inclement weather and societal impropriety. According to the Metropolitan Museum of Art's Costume Institute: "The name 'calash' is derived from 'calèche,' the hood of a 'French carriage,' because the material was ruched along a collapsible cane support structure, much like the hood of a carriage. Many calashes were treated to be water-proof."

Durfee reported that the right side of Sarah's bonnet had been bent so far back that her right cheek was resting against the haystack pole. She had been wearing the bonnet when she died. And her shoes were nearby, "lying about 18 inches from her," said Durfee, "and one of them had mud on it."

Why would she remove her footwear and set it neatly near her? wondered Catharine.

Regarding the mud on her shoe: the ground was muddy throughout the property; even walking gingerly across the grass would have resulted in a tarnished shoe.

Now let's talk about **how** she was hanging. She was only a few inches off the ground: "her feet were close together as if they had been tied, and her toes on the ground; her knees bent forward nearly to the ground," as described by John Durfee. Catharine explained further: the cord around Sarah's neck was preventing her knees from touching the earth, but "her knees [were] within four inches of the ground."

Later, farmer John Durfee would demonstrate the way that he found Sarah's body, saying it was more like six inches. A court reporter recorded his response during the trial with yet another distance: "Witness descended from the stand and showed the distance to be eight or nine inches, by placing himself in a similar position."

Was that enough height off the ground to facilitate a suicide? Yes, according to forensic investigator Paul Holes. "Many hanging suicides are not where somebody climbs all the way up into a tree," said Holes. Rather, they're done from a lower height—surprisingly low, in some cases. "Could she have done that herself, at least from her height relative to the pole height? That, absolutely, is entirely possible. But it doesn't eliminate the possibility that an offender would have done that." More inconclusive facts, and here are some more questionable assumptions from Catharine:

"It was known that when the neck is not broken by hanging . . . there is a great struggle in death, and there was not on the ground beneath the least signs of any."

Holes contends that Catharine was wrong; he told me that it can take as few as ten seconds for a person to go unconscious during strangulation; in the case of a suicide, there might be no struggle at all.

"It's actually not a painful death," said Holes. "And if you watch UFC fighters, when they will put a guillotine hold on their opponents, and how rapidly their opponent will lose consciousness—it happens very quickly. Our brains need a constant supply of oxygen. And when that supply is cut, generally ten seconds and you're out."

Another witness described the ground that morning as "boggy grass," and confirmed that it had not been disturbed underneath her feet. But "there was no appearance of a struggle either in the stack yard or near it," reported witness Seth Darling. Curious. Yet Sarah's body showed signs of struggle. **Was it suicide or murder?**

To Catharine, some of the most damning evidence was found on Sarah's gloves . . . or rather the **absence** of evidence on her gloves, which were "on her hands, without any marks of a rope or anything of the kind upon them." Was it possible for a pair of gloves to remain unmarked, even amid all this violence and struggle? Or even as she tied the cord around her neck during a suicide?

Once again, I did my own experiment with a pair

of gloves and some marline twine, the same sort reported to have been found around Sarah Cornell's throat. The twine had been deeply embedded in the skin of her neck, over the strings of her calash bonnet. John Durfee's older brother, Williams, had helped unwind the cord when they cut down Sarah's body.

"We were compelled to cut the cord," said Williams Durfee, "and when we had picked out the ends, we gradually passed it round the neck till it was unwound; the calash strings were under it. It was a kind of string which sailors call marline."

Marline is a double-stranded twine, usually twisted loosely. Mariners used it to wind around ropes or cables to help prevent them from fraying. When I wore a pair of thin gloves and I greatly tightened the twine, no residue transferred onto the gloves. In the 1800s, the twine might have been covered with a thin layer of tar, which could leave behind residue. But, Paul Holes told me, maybe not. He'd want to experiment with the exact type of twine, which is not possible, of course.

"If you're dealing with tar that's embedded in this marline twine, and you're dealing with 29-degree temperatures? Well, that tar is also going to be very hard and then soften as it warms up," said Holes. "I could see both arguments."

On Sunday, the farmer considered the evidence that he had gathered, with help from well-meaning townspeople: the broken pieces of Sarah's comb, the extensive bruising on Sarah's body, and the troubling, conflicting evidence at the haystack pole that seemed to point away from suicide. But it was really the cryptic note, "If I am missing," in Sarah's personal trunk that tormented Durfee.

In addition, Reverend Ira Bidwell, Sarah's minister in the Methodist church, had suddenly besmirched her character and then vanished quickly after Dr. Wilbur expressed private concerns with Sarah's involvement with a different Methodist minister. Was this minister the man that Sarah had mentioned in the note, the Reverend Ephraim Avery?

And there was one other thing that gnawed at the farmer: the report from a witness he had encountered the night before he discovered Sarah's body, about a few minutes before sunset. Durfee told Catharine that he was close to his home, herding his cattle to feed, when he spotted a man about a quarter mile away, down the hill, and about 300 feet from the haystack pole.

"I could not see his face," said Durfee, "but he was a tall man, wearing a surtout coat of a dark color, and a hat with a broader brim and higher crown than normal."

Two other witnesses recalled also seeing the man around the same time at the same location. Benjamin Manchester and Abner Davis were laboring on land nearby, determined to blast apart a massive rock. They placed quite a large charge of powder on the stone, ignited it, and then briskly walked away to avoid the blast. A tall man wearing a dark brown frock coat and a wide-brimmed black hat had been sitting on a nearby wall holding the tails of the jacket. Before the blast, the mysterious man hopped down and inadvertently walked toward the burning powder as Manchester and Davis called out to him to retreat.

"He canted his head a little to avoid the falling stones," said Manchester. "His height was rather above the common standard, but I had no opportunity to see his features."

The man walked briskly back across the meadow and vanished. When Manchester and Davis returned to the land they had been working, they both glanced at some burlap sacks they had used as seats as they drilled sitting on the ground. The man had been near them before leaving. Manchester noted that some cord was missing.

"These bags were sewn up with such cord as that round the stake."

The bags had been tied with marline twine—a common accessory in a laborer's toolkit, and the same sort of rope that had been found tied around Sarah's neck. Durfee was alarmed by all this new information, but Sarah Cornell was now buried, resting in eternity on his own property. But after earnest conversations with his wife, his sisters, and his father, Richard, John Durfee made a critical decision.

"The case seemed to call loudly for examination," Catharine wrote.

On Sunday, Durfee approached the coroner, Dr. Elihu Hicks, about his suspicions, including the slip of paper indicating that Sarah had not traveled alone to his stackyard. Durfee suggested to the coroner that Sarah Cornell's corpse be disinterred and reexamined more closely by experienced physicians as well as a second coroner's jury. **This was not suicide**, Durfee insisted, **this might be murder**.

Fall River's elderly coroner was nearly deaf, certainly ornery, and many times combative—but Durfee and this new evidence had convinced Dr. Hicks. In fact, he had already been nervous about his jury's verdict. Something didn't seem right to the coroner either. When Durfee presented him with the evidence, Dr. Hicks agreed to the odious and arduous task of digging up Sarah Cornell's body on Monday, when she had scarcely been at rest for two days. For God-fearing people, this was a monumental decision, but the evidence **against** suicide seemed to be overwhelming.

Dr. Hicks told the farmer that he needed to gather more information from someone: Dr. Thomas Wilbur. After greeting Durfee at his door, Dr. Wilbur sadly recounted his visits with his patient concerning her angst over the minister's manipulation. He also agreed to conduct an autopsy— Dr. Wilbur was steadily growing more and more concerned that Sarah Cornell had been murdered; he believed that she deserved justice.

The day of the funeral, the rumor mill in Fall River churned, despite John Durfee's pleas for silence. The residents asked authorities about the investigation into Sarah Cornell's death: **Who was this Methodist minister?** "All day, little knots of citizens were seen gathering at the corners of the streets, and even at the meeting-house doors, discussing the subject of the murder, though in an under tone of voice," wrote Catharine. "No active measures were, however, taken until morning when a few citizens met in the street, and agreed upon having a meeting at the Lyceum Hall."

On Sunday afternoon, three days after Sarah's death, a boy strolled the streets, loudly ringing a bell, to summon Fall River citizens to the meetinghouse later that day. Quickly a citizens' committee of five men was formed that would attend the second examination of a new coroner's jury first thing on Monday morning. At nine o'clock the next morning, several men with shovels unearthed Sarah's coffin from the freshly dug grave and slowly opened the wooden lid; they carefully carried her rigid body nearby to one of Durfee's barns, where a cadre of men had gathered. The farmer stayed behind in his home—no need to see her corpse for a second time.

Dr. Thomas Wilbur and Dr. Foster Hooper,

holding scalpels and other tools, stood nearby as the same coroner's jury hovered near Sarah Cornell. Two of the original jurors were replaced because they had been disqualified (they were required to own land, and they didn't). This new panel, with fresh eyes, was likely to return a verdict of murder at the hands of Methodist minister Ephraim Avery. Sarah's ominous note, naming him, had seemingly damned him. This time, propriety was not an option—they had missed so much during the first viewing, even ignoring the visible trauma to her face. Soon Sarah was stripped of her funeral garb as gas lamps were lit.

The group of men discussed the purpose of the exam: they would document any signs of additional trauma, both external and internal. They would determine if she had been sexually assaulted and then murdered. They would assess if she had been, in fact, pregnant—as she had claimed to Dr. Wilbur. Or had she been assaulted, been abandoned at the farm, and then in shame and despair taken her own life? Or was she, as Dr. Hicks assumed earlier, a victim of depression that led to her suicide?

Dr. Hooper was a new addition—a local physician in Fall River, he had not been there on Friday afternoon for the initial exam. Perhaps if he had, Sarah might not have been buried at all. He seemed young at age twenty-seven, but competent. Dr. Hooper began taking notes as he bent over Sarah's body, noting that she had been dead for almost four days at the time of the autopsy (and had spent two of them buried)—both important points.

This is pertinent because in 1832, coroners had not started using embalming fluid—that method of body preservation would not become prevalent until the Civil War era, some thirty years later. When a corpse is buried sans embalming fluid, decomposition accelerates quickly, within a day. With embalming fluid in a sturdy coffin, five to ten years is a more typical decomposition timeline. After that, only the bones will be present.

At the start of his examination, Dr. Hooper's descriptions of Sarah's injuries tallied with the observations of John Durfee, the matrons, and Dr. Wilbur from just a few days before. There was a horizontal indentation around her neck about half an inch deep, which had turned a reddish, almost black color from decomposition. He confirmed the scratches, cuts, and wounds on her legs and knees, along with the grass stains, which had been noted by the matrons.

"There were a few scratches on the left leg below the knee," said Dr. Hooper, "and at two places skin was knocked off about the size of a fourpenny piece."

These abrasions were about half an inch deep, but he was unsure if they had been inflicted hours before her death or even **days** earlier. Her neck had not been broken—she had been strangled to death, either inflicted alone or by someone else. Sarah seemed to have struggled on the ground at some point—but not directly below where her body was discovered hanging. Catharine Williams found that to be suspicious. "The rope must have been drawn with great strength by two hands before it was tied to the stake," she wrote.

Is that true? I wondered. Would this mean that someone with a lot of strength must have strangled her, because the twine was so deeply embedded in her skin? Absolutely not, said forensic investigator Paul Holes.

"As the tissues compress, if they've been there for a period of time, that the noose itself is embedded within the neck is pretty significant," he said. "You're dealing with, let's say, conservatively, seventy pounds of pressure."

The deeply embedded rope doesn't necessarily mean it was pulled tight around Sarah's neck by a strong pair of hands. Rather, that sort of pressure could have been created by the load of Sarah's own body weight. Catharine's assertions couldn't always be trusted, I was concluding.

Dr. Hooper and Dr. Wilbur examined Sarah's body for more injuries.

"On the right cheek and temple there were irregular indentations, perfectly colorless, as though occasioned by pressure against some hard substance after circulation had ceased," reported Dr. Hooper.

The physician seemed to believe that Sarah's body

had been pressed against something very hard for a long period of time after she died. Was that the haystack pole? He wasn't sure. Dr. Hooper made several incisions to her stomach and then her lungs.

"The stomach appeared perfectly healthy," he reported, "but the lungs were engorged with black venous blood."

Black venous blood in the lungs after death, Catharine wondered. **What does that mean?** It just meant that the blood had been deprived of oxygen, because of Sarah's death.

"Venous blood is pushed from the right ventricle of the heart to the lungs to get oxygenated, then back to the heart and ultimately pushed out to the body by the left ventricle," Paul Holes told me. "Venous blood in the lungs means that the circulation has been interrupted or stalled. It's a very generic observation."

So that observation wasn't helpful in determining what caused the hanging. Dr. Hooper insisted that he couldn't predict whether her death was murder or suicide, based on that finding.

"The engorged state of the lungs might have been the same whether she died of strangulation or of hanging," insisted Dr. Hooper.

But Catharine Williams omitted Dr. Hooper's opinion, stating instead: "Three of the principal physicians and surgeons of the place examined the person of the deceased. . . . From the state of the lungs it appeared she died of suffocation, and from the mark of the rope around her neck, that she could not have died by hanging, but by the drawing of the cord, which had been drawn tight as to strangle, and must have been so before suspension from the stake."

This conclusion was not just misleading—it was false from a medical standpoint. The physicians had been clear: Sarah could have been murdered **or** she might have taken her own life. **Why would Catharine deceive her readers?** I wondered. She felt compelled to convince readers to sympathize with Sarah, as Nathaniel Hawthorne did decades later with Hester Prynne in **The Scarlet Letter**.

"Thus the young and pure would be taught to look at her, with the scarlet letter flaming on her breast," wrote Hawthorne, "at her, the child of honorable parents,—at her, the mother of a babe, that would hereafter be a woman,—at her, who had once been innocent,—as the figure, the body, the reality of sin."

But Catharine's work was presented as factual, not fanciful—as nonfiction. And her discrepancies began to frame her, to me, as an unreliable narrator. Yet much of her reporting was accurate, like the details about the scene the morning Sarah was found. Which information could I trust? Much of it had to be verified.

As Dr. Hooper continued his autopsy, he reported that the right side of Sarah's abdomen was severely discolored, but he attributed it to decomposition, not a bruise from trauma. That didn't seem to be the case for the left side of her abdomen, because just above her hip, Dr. Hooper discovered a large contusion. He gingerly sliced open her uterus, which was slightly distended. He was especially careful because of Dr. Wilbur's disclosure: Sarah was pregnant. Was she lying to her physician? No.

"We discovered a fetus, which at first appeared to be about half grown," he said, "but it required a minute inspection to ascertain its sex, which proved to be female."

Next, they tried to determine how far along Sarah was when she died.

"We measured and weighed the fetus as accurately as possible," explained Dr. Hooper, "and found its length to be 8 inches, and its weight 5 ounces. The umbilical cord attached to it was an inch and a half in length."

In modern times, of course, experts would use an ultrasound image to establish gestational age. According to perinatology.com, the average seventeen-week fetus is about 8 inches long and weighs 6 ounces, making Sarah's unborn child almost four months old; their measurements in 1832 were surprisingly accurate.

Dr. Hooper had estimated the fetus to be about four months old—it had been conceived in late August 1832, exactly when Sarah had told Dr. Wilbur that she had been alone with Ephraim

Avery. Dr. Hooper and the other men looked sadly at the tiny remains.

And yet, despite this stark evidence, propriety kept the men from further investigation of Sarah's body. "We did not at this time examine the lowest parts of the abdomen," explained Dr. Hooper, "for some of the jury objected to the removal of the cloth with which they were covered." Out of "respectability," once again, a proper and thorough exam was thwarted because the men were uncomfortable. Drs. Hooper and Wilbur whispered and then turned to the coroner and the committee of men, standing in Durfee's barn.

"I am convinced that violence was exercised upon Sarah M. Cornell before her death," concluded Dr. Hooper.

The elderly physician, Dr. Wilbur, stood nearby and gazed down at his former patient. Her eyes were closed, her face was pale. Sarah had confided in him fewer than two months earlier.

"I had seen the deceased several times before her death, for she had consulted me about her health, and wished to know whether she was in a state of pregnancy," said Dr. Wilbur. "I could not form a decided opinion the first visit, but afterwards told her she was undoubtably so. This was seven or eight weeks prior to her death." Now he feared that this was the result: murder.

"When I first saw the body, the day after her

death," recalled Dr. Wilbur, "the tightness of the string around her neck, her cloak being hooked throughout and her arms and hands under it with gloves on were circumstances which looked like homicide, and caused a doubt on my mind which I could not dispose of."

Dr. Wilbur, Dr. Hooper, and the coroner's jury spent time in John Durfee's barn discussing Sarah's injuries as they examined her body while the small citizens' group stood by. **Why would she be injured like this?** the jurors wondered. Dr. Wilbur was searching for specific signs of something deemed taboo in the early 1800s: the termination of a pregnancy. In the early 1800s, abortions weren't illegal, but the drugs used during the procedure were against the law. In an article for **The Atlantic**, reporter Katha Pollitt detailed the history of abortion in America. She wrote that until the late 1800s the termination of a pregnancy was illegal in every state after a period that's called "quickening," which is when a pregnant woman starts to feel her baby's movement, like flutters. Quickening can happen between weeks sixteen and twenty, or even sooner. But during colonial times, women had at-home remedies for unwanted pregnancies.

"Colonial home medical guides gave recipes for 'bringing on the menses' with herbs that could be grown in one's garden or easily found in the woods," said Pollitt. "Unfortunately, these drugs were often fatal."

Pollitt wrote that the first statutes regulating abortion were poison-control laws passed in the 1820s and 1830s. But the restrictive rules didn't seem to reduce the number of abortions.

"By the 1840s the abortion business—including the sale of illegal drugs, which were widely advertised in the popular press—was booming," wrote Pollitt. The primary patients in the nineteenth century were middle- or upper-class white women. In fact, voluntarily ending a pregnancy wasn't labeled as "abortion"—it was called a miscarriage.

Perhaps Sarah Cornell had been seeking to terminate the pregnancy, the jury wondered. A young, single, pregnant woman would have been publicly chastised, like Hester Prynne in **The Scarlet Letter**.

"No," replied Dr. Wilbur. Sarah Maria Cornell **didn't** want an abortion—she wanted to keep the baby. Dr. Wilbur confirmed Sarah's decision to Catharine Williams during her interview with him. As the physician sat with the author months later, he disclosed a sad tale about a distraught woman who felt grief over her life but was hopeful that being a mother would help. Catharine jotted down notes as the doctor detailed his meetings with Sarah.

But a caveat: Catharine's recollection of this conversation is the single acknowledged instance, referenced earlier, of embellishment in her book **Fall River**:

"With respect to embellishment in this book," wrote Catharine, "no person acquainted with the facts, who has seen it, pretends to say there is any, **except in the first interview between the physician and the unfortunate heroine of the tale; where it is said the phraseology is improved without altering the facts**. If the error is on the side of delicacy we hope to be pardoned" (emphasis mine).

Accuracy matters in nonfiction narratives, despite the claim that they're meant to only mirror the dramatic flair of fiction. Catharine had adjusted facts earlier about Sarah's reputation as a thief, as well as some of the physical evidence. She was indulging in speculation during part of her investigation. Now she was fabricating conversations. It was all starting to feel slightly manipulative—Catharine felt an urgency to convince the readers of **something**. What were her motives?

Subsequent writers and scholars investigating true crime narratives have asked this question of Catharine as well. As Leslie Rowen wrote in "True Crime as a Literature of Advocacy," Dr. Wilbur's reaction "acts as an example for the reader. . . . This is how Williams desires the public to react, too, not with disgust or disdain but with sympathy and disbelief. Controlling the narrative gives Williams ownership of these events—true or not—and how the public perceives them."

Good writers move readers or persuade them; they don't manipulate them. Catharine promised that her embellishments would happen just once, with Dr. Wilbur's interview. Was it really the only instance of this in **Fall River**? I'm not so sure. But this is the story—whatever its truth is—that Catharine relays to us:

Two months before Sarah's death, in early October 1832, the thirty-year-old had stood in the parlor of Dr. Wilbur's office for the first time. He observed Sarah: attractive, fit, and seemingly respectable. Sarah had initially complained that she hadn't felt well for quite a while, and she needed a diagnosis. Sarah felt nauseated, exhausted, even a bit depressed. She told Dr. Wilbur that she had worked as a weaver in a nearby mill. **Perhaps the work is too trying for you?** Dr. Wilbur wondered aloud. **No**, Sarah replied, **I've been laboring at this rate for years**. The physician was quiet and then paced his office.

"Are you married, madam?" he asked Sarah.

"No," she replied meekly.

Dr. Wilbur felt flushed and sighed. He gingerly suggested that she might be pregnant, certainly the victim of seduction. He feared that she would be shunned by their society.

"Your evident distress bespeaks you to have been the prey of a villain."

Sarah was silent as Dr. Wilbur began with more pointed questions.

"Has not the person who has thus entailed misfortune upon you, the power to take you from the hardships of a factory and place you in a comfortable situation, until you can again resume your employment with safety to yourself?" asked Dr. Wilbur.

"I am afraid he would not be willing to do so," Sarah replied.

"Not be willing! Then he must be a very base man. It certainly is in his place to do so. Who is he?"

Sarah wept.

"Can you not tell me his name?" insisted Dr. Wilbur.

"I cannot, I dare not," Sarah replied before weeping more.

But Dr. Wilbur continued to press Sarah for the name of the baby's father, the man who had defiled her. She refused. He asked her about friends in the area; she had none, she replied, except for those in the local Methodist church.

"It was not until many apparent struggles with herself, much persuasion, solemn injunctions to secrecy and finally a promise on the part of the doctor not to expose the name, that she at length reluctantly disclosed it—the Methodist minister Ephraim Avery," wrote Catharine.

"'Monstrous!' said the appalled physician."

She was determined to keep the baby, Sarah insisted to both Dr. Wilbur and her own family, according to Catharine Williams.

But there's a problem with Catharine's story. The author's retelling of Dr. Wilbur's recollections differs from the official record. We know this because the physician would eventually testify in court. Under oath, Dr. Wilbur revealed that Sarah had, in fact, considered terminating the pregnancy early on.

"She called on me the latter part of October," said Dr. Wilbur on the stand. "She said 'will it be safe for me to take the Oil of Tansy to procure abortion?' I told her, by no means—it could endanger her life, or if she lived through it, would destroy her health. She replied, 'then I will not take it, for I'd rather have my child and do the best I can, than to endanger my life.'"

In her letters to her family, Sarah said she would work hard to support her child. But, according to Dr. Wilbur, if termination had been a safe option, Sarah might have considered it. That's a very different angle than the storyline Catharine Williams had proposed, that of a woman determined to rear her child from the start. For almost two centuries, critics have assailed Catharine for those embellishments.

"Her narrative tends to slide between argument from material data (paper, handwriting, dates and times), and interpretations of the letters' contents and the correspondents' written exchanges with each other," wrote Judith Barbour in her essay "Letters of the Law: The Trial of E. K. Avery for the Murder of Sarah M. Cornell." "So despite her access to the original court exhibits, which allowed her to read for herself in full . . . she retains the privilege over her readers of silently amending, conflating, and occluding parts of the documents at her disposal." Catharine, Barbour explains, often interprets—even tweaks—facts to fit the narrative she has in her head about the case.

But does this mean that Catharine's reporting should be dismissed? Of course not, but I decided to proceed with caution.

In December 1832, standing over his former patient's body, Dr. Wilbur had realized that an unwanted child could have been a motive for murder. He knew that Ephraim Avery, a married minister, would never have married Sarah. What if Avery had arranged for Sarah to meet him at John Durfee's farm, late that night, to talk her into terminating the pregnancy, perhaps using the oil of tansy? What if, Dr. Wilbur wondered, he tried to force her to drink it, but she fought back, which would explain her abrasions and bruises? What if . . . he murdered her? Dr. Wilbur's angst seemed to build as he considered the scenarios.

But there was another very viable possibility that we should consider. What if Sarah had been so distressed by the termination attempt, and their subsequent struggle, that after Reverend Avery left the farm, she hanged herself on the haystack pole? We must reserve the idea that it might have also been a suicide—that she had taken her life out of despair. But on Monday, December 24, the second coroner's jury arrived at a different conclusion: Sarah Maria Cornell had been murdered.

"Sarah M. Cornell came by her death by having a cord or a hemp line drawn around her neck and strangled until she was dead," their verdict read, "and they also believe, and from strong circumstantial evidence, that Ephraim K. Avery, of Bristol, in the County of Bristol, and State of &c. was principal or accessory in her death."

CHAPTER SIX

~⌒~

THE SINNERS

EPHRAIM AVERY HAD BEEN NAMED as a suspect in the murder of his former parishioner Sarah Maria Cornell—and now his situation was dire. But first, the Methodist minister had to be hunted down.

Investigators needed more information about the married man at the center of Sarah Cornell's death. **Who is he? Where is he?** A small municipality like Fall River would not have had a formal police force to investigate a crime like murder. Instead, a larger citizens' committee of investigation formed to investigate Ephraim Avery. Fall River and its taxpaying citizens would foot the bill.

"It was resolved that the truth should, if possible, be elicited in this search," wrote Catharine, "and that they should report everything of a favourable nature respecting the accused, as well as that which should appear unfavourable."

One would think that the first step in finding Reverend Avery would be to ask his fellow Methodist minister (and Sarah Cornell's beloved pastor) Reverend Bidwell. You'll remember that he was also among the men who found Sarah's body. But Bidwell quickly betrayed Sarah.

Bidwell had once called her a devout, respectable parishioner, a faithful Christian who had written him heartfelt letters about her love of the church. But now Bidwell told a different story, about an unhinged young lady placed on probation at his church. She had been desperate to be loved, Bidwell claimed, but she was too troubled to keep as a member. What was the truth?

When Bidwell had quickly left John Durfee's farm on the day Sarah had been discovered, he'd had a secret meeting with Ephraim Avery. **Her doctor says that you two were involved**, Bidwell told the minister, **and now she's dead**. Avery quickly, vehemently replied with a denial. Bidwell returned to John Durfee and the other men on the farm.

"The reverend listener [Bidwell] was at once roused to defend him, and express his full belief that his brother was perfectly innocent," reported Catharine, "and finally asserted 'that the deceased was a very bad character, and that Avery had told him so, and warned him against her.'"

The Methodists had refused to bury her because Sarah was, in their eyes, an immoral creature. But Avery realized that he needed proof of Sarah's depravity—and after Reverend Bidwell left, Avery apparently stewed. The following day, Avery hired a stagecoach driver in Bristol to pass on a message to Bidwell.

"He called on me at Bristol on Sunday, the 23d December, and desired me to call on Mr. Bidwell at Fall River," recounted Stephen Bartlett, the stage-coach driver, who would later offer this story on the witness stand, "and ask him whether it would not be advisable to go to Lowell and obtain information respecting the bad character of the girl."

Ephraim Avery was clearly unsettled, and Catharine quickly learned why. Many of Sarah Cornell's problems started when she lived in Lowell, Massachusetts, in 1828, four years before her death. Yes, she had con-fessed to theft as a teenager, but her time in Lowell had cemented her poor reputation. This is when her relationship with Ephraim Avery began, at the start of his assignment as a Methodist minister.

Catharine Williams did little investigating into Avery's character, though she did dabble in quite a lot of speculation.

"We are sorry to say we have so little account of the early years of a man who has made so much noise in the world," she wrote, "but from the time we can get anything of his history, there seems to be something in almost every place that goes to prove him a bad tempered, daring and unprincipled man."

As she learned about his relationship with Sarah, Catharine Williams felt nothing but repulsion for Ephraim Avery, which is evidenced by her description of his physical appearance.

"[He had] a pair of very thick lips, and a most unpleasant stare of the eyes," wrote Catharine. "However it was agreed on all hands that notwithstanding these blemishes, he would almost anywhere pass for a tolerable good looking man."

In criminal cases set in the early 1800s, it's difficult to gather an accurate physical description because oftentimes there were no portraits of the victim or the offender. We have no photos of Sarah Maria Cornell, just crude drawings frequently showing a scared, dark-haired woman in a cloak hanging from a pole. Incidentally, one drawing features a rail-thin John Durfee, wearing a top hat and tails, with a horrified expression as he discovers Sarah's body. That's our only real description of him.

Ephraim Avery is depicted in illustrations donning stylish colored glasses (called shades) covering his small, beady eyes; he's wearing a high-collared jacket, with slicked-back dark hair, and displaying a slight smirk, giving him a mysterious, almost sinister likeness. Avery's relatives offered me one photograph of the minister and his wife, Sophia, but there's little to add to Catharine's description. He was tall with dark brown hair, and he had a thin frame. But he was not middle-aged in 1832, as Catharine declared; at the time he became a suspect, Avery was just thirty-three years old (although many men lived only into their sixties, so perhaps he **was** considered middle-aged). Avery's birthday was four days before Sarah's death.

I've gathered most of this information from Avery's descendent Ray Avery in Ohio, whose mother discovered the story as she was mining the family papers for a short history on the Averys. Ephraim Avery's sister was Ray Avery's third great-grandmother.

Ephraim Kingsbury Avery was born in Coventry, Connecticut, on December 18, 1799, one of eight children, the son of Amos and Abigail Avery. "Ephraim did not wish to become a farmer, which was his father's occupation," according to the Avery family book. "He studied to be a doctor but did not complete his education. He then worked at a General Store—became a schoolteacher—went into the ministry and became a Methodist minister preaching at Camp Meetings and in homes."

Avery began preaching at age twenty-two in 1821 and married Sophia the next year. By the time of Sarah's death, Avery had two daughters and two sons, and his wife was pregnant with a third daughter. Catharine described Avery's journey as a preacher in Duxbury, Massachusetts, in 1827, where he led the Methodist society. There are no pleasantries about Avery's promise as a preacher; rather,

Catharine quickly offers a harrowing story about an unsavory encounter with a female parishioner that framed Avery as a vicious slanderer.

It began with a forty-five-year-old woman named Fanny Winsor, who had been an established member of Avery's church, someone dependable and even cherished for her compassion. Avery, according to Catharine, became jealous of Winsor's influence.

"The new minister took a terrible dislike to her from the very first," wrote Catharine. "He thought 'the people put too much confidence in her,' and averred 'that he would see she was not made a goddess of.'"

Catharine described how Winsor privately disparaged Avery to fellow churchgoers—she'd heard him making a cruel remark about a recent widower, and it just didn't sit well with her. When Avery discovered her criticism, he unleashed a torrent of public accusations, all asserting that Winsor was ungodly, unseemly, and deceitful. She tried to apologize for overstepping, but Avery ignored her. Catharine wrote:

"His hatred had now broken out into acts of hostility, and he commenced writing letters to various persons in Duxbury and elsewhere, to try to get her expelled from the church."

His ploy failed and it infuriated Avery. Fanny Winsor was not expelled, much to the minister's frustration, and in fact, she received a certificate of good standing from the head of the church in 1831.

This was a letter from the head of the area's church stating that a parishioner was worthy of joining any Methodist church as a full member. A parishioner who wished to move to a new city could use the certificate as proof of their virtue. Winsor's certificate read: "This may certify that Fanny Winsor, the bearer, is a member of the Methodist Episcopal Church in Duxbury, and is recommended as such by me, the subscriber." It was signed "Enoch Mudge, minister in charge of said church." While Fanny Winsor was ultimately exonerated, she and other parishioners were furious that Avery himself had not been expelled from the church for launching false allegations against a respected member.

In a different episode, Avery allegedly slandered another Methodist minister, this time in Saugus, Massachusetts. Catharine explains that Avery joined the Reverend Thomas Norris as they both preached to the same congregation. One Sunday, Avery stood up and accused Reverend Norris of thievery as well as an array of other sins.

"His hearers who relate the story remark, that, 'all this time his [Avery's] face was violent red, and he appeared to be in a great passion,'" wrote Catharine. Norris immediately accused Avery of slander; he took him to court and after two trials, Avery was ordered to pay a fine.

These stories are concerning, but they're also hearsay. Catharine interviewed both Fanny Winsor and Thomas Norris, as well as witnesses who corroborated their stories, for her book research. But neither Winsor nor Norris was called by investigators in the case, and they were never asked to testify. Those stories in Catharine's book effectively impugned Avery's character, and he never disputed them. The allegations spoke to Avery's vitriol toward women and his penchant for revenge. But these accusations would not be allowed in a criminal trial today, nor were they permissible in 1833. Forensic investigator Paul Holes told me that there's a good reason for that.

"Fundamentally, you have the crime at hand. And you have to prove beyond a reasonable doubt that the defendant is responsible for the crime that they've been charged with," said Holes. Other details and cases—even if they seem to speak to a defendant's character—are not generally admissible, as they "can prejudice the jury and they can be swayed to convict, when in fact, the facts aren't there. That's really one of the safeguards within our justice system."

But even if these details weren't admissible in an official court proceeding, Catharine would argue (and I'd agree), they were crucial to create a profile of Ephraim Avery. Was he a killer or just a deeply unpleasant man? Did he cover up a crime—and if so, what crime was it? And could Catharine Williams—given her obvious distrust and dislike of the man—be trusted to collect the evidence for me?

———

The Methodist Church had labeled Sarah as "troubled" shortly after the shoplifting incident in her youth. The ministers welcomed her donations but refused to make her a member. After shopkeepers caught Sarah stealing from their stores in Providence, Rhode Island, in 1822, the clothes were returned and paid for. Sarah and her family prayed that the matter would remain in her past. It did not. Sarah's unsavory reputation trailed her from state to state.

After her time in Providence, Sarah had moved to Connecticut, where she worked in the weaving room of a mill, but she was always viewed with suspicion because of the theft in Providence, and soon she was fired. She then lived with the family of a merchant tailor as a seamstress. Sarah settled into a routine, and she seemed pleased with the work. Soon, a single young man came into the shop and would sit with her, whispering stories to her as they laughed. One night, he asked her to take an evening walk, and as they left the shop, they were spotted together and serious rumors about indecency began.

"This circumstance, as he was a young and unengaged man, and she very pretty, would probably of itself have caused no suspicion, had not the saying that she had been talked about been so often repeated," wrote Catharine. Sarah was now labeled both a thief **and** a harlot.

The merchant tailor's wife fired Sarah the next day, giving her just enough time to board a stage-coach to another town. Later, Catharine would interview the woman, and here's what she said:

"To this day, my conscience reproaches me for the harshness with which I spoke to her, when memory recalls the tears she shed, and her meek, forbearing manners, and I must say, that she had the meekest temper, and one of the mildest and sweetest disposi-tions I ever met with."

The merchant tailor's wife told Catharine that Sarah had requested to stay the night so she could board a stagecoach. The woman agreed and then was startled by Sarah's unexpected act of kindness. The merchant had a very ill relative staying with them, and they needed someone to watch over her throughout the night. The family had researched the community, and no one was available. Despite being fired hours before, Sarah volunteered.

"Though they were ashamed to accept of her ser-vices, they were constrained to," wrote Catharine. "She was so kind and attentive to the sick, that the woman after her recovery often enquired after her, saying, 'she was the kindest and best person to the sick, she ever saw.'"

Nathaniel Hawthorne mirrors this episode of Sarah's incredible kindness in **The Scarlet Letter** when Hester Prynne also attends to the sick. The townspeople consider her charity a gift, a series of redemptive acts. The humbling of the scarlet letter has allowed Hester to think of others first, they claim.

"'Do you see that woman with the embroidered badge?' they would say to strangers," wrote Hawthorne. "'It is our Hester,—the town's own Hester—who is so kind to the poor, so helpful to the sick, so comfortable to the afflicted!'"

Eventually, many people, like the merchant's wife, would regret their reproach of a weeping Sarah Cornell and their view of her behavior. She would become martyred, like Hester Prynne.

As the case against Ephraim Avery was building, the gossip against the minister began to center not on Sarah's sordid reputation but on his suspected crime. He was the criminal.

"Fictionalized representations portrayed her in the manner of conventional sentimental heroines," wrote Kristin Boudreau, "praising not only her physical beauty but also her charity, industry, and integrity."

Out-of-wedlock pregnancies, like those of Sarah and Hester, were badges of shame. But in both cases, the societies found extenuating circumstances to rescue the women's reputations.

"The woman was an uneducated mill worker from a poor family in Connecticut; living far away from her natural family," wrote Boudreau. "She became easy prey for an eloquent and charismatic minister."

Soon after her expulsion from the merchant's home, Sarah Cornell arrived in Rhode Island, where

192 KATE WINKLER DAWSON

she became entrenched in the local Methodist church as she toiled as a weaver in a factory for two years. Sarah's brother visited her in Slatersville, and he privately chatted with her host family. **How is she doing?** he asked.

"Very well indeed," they replied, according to Catharine, "and very much engaged in religion . . . and set a very good example."

But that good opinion of Sarah was brief. Soon Sarah was admonished by her Methodist church in Slatersville for "lewd behavior." The circumstances were vague, and though Sarah would never confess to sleeping with a man, Catharine admitted that Sarah did encounter many men as she traversed New England throughout her twenties.

"During the time of her sojourn in the towns already mentioned, at several different times she received attentions from some young man, who she thought and others thought wished to marry her," Catharine wrote. "Many young men make a practice it is well known of amusing themselves at the expense of young women who are apparently without friends and natural protectors to call them to account for such baseness and compel them to act honorably. S. M. Cornell had the curse of beauty, and she was not without admirers."

It was not uncommon for men to promise marriage to women in the 1800s so that they could sleep with them, and then abandon the engagement. This likely happened to Sarah Cornell, Catharine admitted, but that couldn't be confirmed. Yet that didn't stop the cascade of rumors, and Sarah was ejected from several Methodist churches for fornication and lying. In Lowell, Massachusetts, she allegedly had a relationship with a mill clerk that ended with more rumors of lewd behavior. Catharine lamented Sarah's doomed future, driven by a lack of family ties: "How different her fate would have been could she have been settled in life and tied to the duties of a wife and mother, we cannot now say," wrote Catharine, "but the probability is she would have made a very respectable figure in society."

It was in Lowell that Sarah Cornell met Reverend Ephraim Avery, and her life path was irrevocably altered. One of the letters discovered inside her trunk was directed to Reverend Bidwell, the minister in Fall River who later deemed her as an unsavory character. The letter was unopened and undated; she had never posted it, but it was certainly written just months before her death.

"I take this opportunity to inform you that for reasons known to God and my own soul I wish no longer to be connected with the Methodist Society," wrote Sarah to Reverend Bidwell. "When I came to this place, I thought I should enjoy myself among them but as I do not enjoy any religion at all, I have not seen a well nor a happy day since I left Thompson campground."

This was the crux of the controversy around Sarah Cornell's death—what happened at the Thompson camp meeting at the end of August? Sarah Cornell made a terrible admission to her family and her doctor, one that would put Ephraim Avery squarely in the crosshairs of the committee of investigation.

———

In August 1832, four months before her fateful journey to John Durfee's farm, Sarah Cornell's already troubled life had taken another awful turn, and Ephraim Avery would soon be accused of covering up something unspeakable that had happened during a camp meeting.

As Catharine gathered more information from her sources, her resentment toward Ephraim Kingsbury Avery deepened. Sarah's family described how she had once admired Avery as her spiritual guide, but he had done some things that made him untrustworthy. Sarah's family disclosed that the minister was manipulative and dangerous. Catharine would record it all in her book **Fall River**.

Despite her strong sense of propriety, Catharine was probably the perfect person to dive into this dark, seedy story and investigate it unflinchingly. She did not find Sarah's story shocking. Sad, yes, but not surprising. After all, she had been disappointed in men for much of her life.

Catharine crafted a narrative about Sarah Cornell, her life and death, that was both moving and harrowing. David Kasserman concluded in **Fall River**

Outrage that Catharine Williams, who exposed the world to Sarah Cornell's plight, was a unique author. As a woman in the upper-class echelon of high society in New England, Catharine was expected to pity Sarah, even chastise her actions, not defend her. But Catharine's turn in life, her struggles, would shape her attitude toward working women. Unlike her female contemporaries, Catharine had developed a deep well of empathy, thanks in part to learning more about Sarah Cornell over the course of this investigation.

"To say that **Fall River** is a feminist writing would be inaccurate but, as a divorced, single parent, who took up writing for survival, it seems only fitting that Williams be 'sympathetic to the plight of the poor working girl,'" Kasserman wrote. "Williams clearly reflects the changing and contradictory social roles for women, especially single, working women in the early nineteenth century."

Catharine Williams was a single mother, like Sarah Cornell. Some of her caution originated from her only marriage—one ill fated almost from the start. Catharine married at age thirty-seven, which was unusually late in that era. She admitted that she had made a poor choice, showing "the least judgment in that of any action of her life," likely influenced in part by her sheltered childhood in the church and growing up with her God-fearing aunts.

Catharine contended that God intended to humble intelligent, ambitious women by steering challenging men into their paths. That was certainly the case with her husband, Horatio Williams, whom she met through friends. They initially bonded over their mutual desire to move west for a new life.

Horatio's family was indeed illustrious; his relative Roger Williams was a New England Puritan who founded Rhode Island—"an unquestionable family," wrote Catharine. The union of an Arnold and a Williams would shine a positive light on both venerable New England families. But the marriage did not go well. They rushed into the relationship, marrying after a two-month courtship during a small ceremony at a bishop's home in New York on September 28, 1824. Catharine despised showy weddings, and her husband was anxious to retreat to the West immediately. During her ceremony, there appeared a harbinger of things to come in the marriage.

"The Bishop had just returned from a funeral service as the wedding party came in," wrote Catharine's biographer, Sidney Rider. "He had still on his mourning scarf, which he was about to remove, when Miss Arnold interposed, saying there was no necessity for his disrobing, and the ceremony proceeded, the Bishop appearing in the habiliments of mourning."

Catharine might have regretted not heeding the warning. She asked her new husband to take her to Michigan, and initially he agreed. But when she became pregnant with their daughter, Amey,

Horatio seemed to change. Her husband quickly reneged on his promise to begin anew in the West and isolated Catharine and Amey in western New York. Her recounting reminded me of how Sarah's mother must have felt trapped by her own husband before he abandoned her and their three children in Connecticut. Rider's story about Horatio suddenly ended with the separation, and omitted some more uncomfortable details that the writer likely found to be too unseemly to publish in his own book. But Catharine expanded a bit on her doomed marriage in her own handwritten notes.

"The marriage proved a most unfortunate one," Catharine wrote. "She found herself deceived and . . . she had no domestic happiness to look forward to."

Catharine soon became alarmed by the unsavory companions her husband chose.

"His social character was fast deteriorating notwithstanding the efforting of his wife," she wrote in her memoir. "Although he never was implicated in the commission of any crime."

She didn't expand on his illegal activities, but Horatio alarmed both Catharine and his mother. In fewer than two years, she had divorced him, and she had taken their nine-month-old daughter, Amey, with her. Her marriage must have been terrible, because divorce in 1820s New England was unusual and problematic for a woman of Catharine Williams's social stature—it had surely resulted in public humiliation. But divorces in America were on the rise. In the United States, the escalation of divorce came in the wake of the American Revolution, said Steven Mintz, a historian at the University of Texas at Austin.

"Just like you could break a union of countries, by analogy, you should have been able to break a union of couples," Mintz said. "The revolution ideology had a real effect on divorce in the 1820s and 1830s."

Much like Sarah Cornell, Catharine was on her own, but there was a bright moment when she discovered her talent for writing. It seems to have pulled her from a dark place. Catharine said she discovered her craft "after years of affliction when the trials of life had driven her into the world and compelled her to seek from within the means of supporting herself and child."

Catharine had gained self-confidence as well as some hubris, which is unusual and refreshing to read in a memoir from a woman in the mid-nineteenth century.

"And it was then that the latent energies of her character became aroused," Catharine wrote about herself, "and the pain and mortification that would have killed some women served in her but to display a fortitude and energy almost unsurpassed."

With the encouragement of friends, Catharine began publishing books of poetry with success. By the time Amey was eight, Catharine was solely reliant on her writing career to support them in

Providence, Rhode Island—rare circumstances for a woman of Catharine's social standing in the 1830s.

"Until recently, most of the women writers from the Puritan migration to the early republic were similarly dismissed and rarely recognized or received 'upstairs' in the American literary," wrote Patricia Caldwell in "In 'Happy America.'" "She seems not to have belonged to any literary group or coterie or to have enjoyed any important literary friendships, but she published eight books, succeeding well enough to live comfortably on her earnings as a writer."

Catharine rarely felt at ease with her daughter even when the girl was small but vowed to raise Amey with the Christian values she treasured. After her divorce, Catharine opened a school to educate teenagers, but her health soon gave out, and she closed its doors. In 1828, at the urging of her friends, she offered a publisher a small volume of poems, many written when she was a teenager. They were melancholy and reflective—there were no young loves to pine over, just sadness over the absence of parents and a deference to her beloved Christianity. America loved her poetry. H. H. Brown, Market Square, published her book entitled **Original Poems, on Various Subjects**. One poem spoke of her mother, who died when Catharine was a girl.

> **Here in sweet peace and soft repose,**
> **Releas'd from sorrow and from care,**

Dismiss'd too from a world of woes,
From dangers and unnumber'd snares,
Oft on thy bosom gently laid,
My infant cries were hushed to rest,
And when beside thee I have play'd,
I thought myself supremely blest.

Catharine collected public accolades beginning with that book, and she continued to write over the next five years. She penned a book of prose called **Religion at Home**, which had three editions printed, a startling achievement in 1829. Catharine was proud of her success, and looking back later in her career, she regretted not leaving her husband and starting her writing career much earlier, acknowledging that she "might have soon realized an independent fortune, and her after history of struggles might have been very different."

But Catharine did support Amey, very well. They lived in a large house in Providence, a gift from her deceased aunt. Amey went to private school and didn't seem to want for anything. Despite Catharine's frumpy appearance, she hobnobbed with some of Rhode Island's elite, though she preferred to remain at home reading or praying at church. Now, with the Sarah Cornell case, Catharine was determined to right a wrong, to discover just how terrible, duplicitous, and murderous Ephraim Avery might be.

By late December 1832, investigators were

building their own profile of a would-be killer, beginning with the forensic evidence left behind. Who would know how to terminate a pregnancy? In the 1800s, someone with medical knowledge certainly would. Ephraim Avery had studied to be a physician before becoming a minister.

There was also that bottle of oil of tansy that John Durfee had discovered in Sarah Cornell's trunk. Was it an innocuous clue? Maybe. Tansy was a common medical remedy for many different things, but it was also used in performing abortions, as noted earlier. Durfee wondered: **Was it really Sarah's bottle?** A fledgling doctor would have known how much tansy could be used to cause a miscarriage. But so would many women who asked their personal doctors for advice.

There was more physical evidence to consider. The committee of investigation would examine the knot used to tie the noose that strangled Sarah. It was curious, a clove hitch knot, one not commonly used by laborers. Did Sarah Cornell know how to tie it? Or did Ephraim Avery? The clove hitch might offer investigators in 1833, and us today, a clue to Sarah's fate. But as I would soon discover, the importance of the knot was also very misleading.

CHAPTER SEVEN

~◡~

THE CLOVE HITCH

CATHARINE WILLIAMS LACKED patience. She was restless as she sat in the frigid parlor before a heavyset woman who was digging through various bags.

Catharine watched the middle-aged artist in front of her drag her easel into position; the woman adjusted her oil paints and smiled occasionally. Susanna Paine was an American portrait artist in New England, as well as a poet, like Catharine. The author and the painter shared life experiences: both had fathers who were mariners, though Susanna's father had been lost at sea. Both women had escaped abusive husbands. Both were single mothers. And both struggled to find national recognition in the art community. To help support herself and her young daughter, Paine accepted commissions for personal portraits as she traveled across the Northeast.

Catharine fidgeted in the chair. She had paid $8 for the sitting, almost $300 today—a steal for a large oil painting in a wooden frame.

Susanna's brush slid across the canvas as cream-colored paint swirled behind it. She had warned Catharine that Susanna would have to return multiple times to complete the piece; it would turn out to be a beautiful painting that would cement Catharine's role as an esteemed author. Her dark, almost raven hair is swept into an updo. Her cheeks bear heavy rouge while earrings featuring black stones dangle from her lobes. Catharine offers her characteristic smirk, but her brown eyes seem tired. Her pale skin glows on the canvas; her right hand grips a white quill pen, as she covers several unfinished lines on parchment. Her fingertips rest on the outer edge of the page; Catharine still wears her petite gold wedding ring, despite being divorced from Horatio Williams for many years.

After Catharine's death in 1872, her portrait would be offered to the Rhode Island Historical Society. The painting exemplifies Catharine's grace, her natural beauty, and her self-confidence. This portrait, she believed, was worthy of her image. While Catharine Read Arnold Williams would be remembered in her era for her remarkable defense of a defenseless woman, the victim, Sarah Cornell, would mostly vanish from history books—until now. Catharine and I will detail the story behind the story of Sarah Cornell and Ephraim Avery's tangled relationship, one rooted in blind devotion, abject abuse, and persistent manipulation.

———

In 1828, Sarah Cornell felt desperate when she knocked on the minister's front door. She was living in Lowell, Massachusetts, unable to escape the rumors that seemed to trail her across New England.

Catharine Williams argued that the gossip was slander, except for the shoplifting charges in Providence years earlier. But it's likely that Sarah had dabbled with romance throughout her travels, as many women did. The vernacular of the 1800s makes interpreting Sarah's various conversations about her life a little murky. One of her former friends, Lucy Davol, reported that Sarah had admitted being "bad" since she was fifteen. While there was no elaboration on what "bad" meant, Davol framed it as a confession to sexual dalliances. A former landlord named Timothy Paul claimed that Sarah had confessed to three affairs with men while in Lowell. There were rumors that she had terminated at least one pregnancy. She had been reportedly treated for a venereal disease by several different doctors. One physician in Somersworth, New Hampshire, described his visit with her.

"In January, 1831, a person who gave me her name as Sarah Maria Connell [sic] came to my shop to get a prescription for a complaint which proved to be chronic gonorrhea, apparently of long standing," said Dr. Noah Martin. "She went into particulars of her contracting the disease; she said a young merchant in Lowell had paid her attention, and invited her to ride out with him on a Sunday afternoon; that they represented themselves, where they put us, as man and wife; that they slept in the same bed, and that her disease was the result of their cohabitation."

Later Sarah would deny all this, but the scandalous stories escalated. Her former coworker Sarah Worthing claimed that Sarah had made several confessions to her.

"She said she had been led on strangely," claimed Worthing. "That she was guilty and had unlawful intercourse with three [men]. . . . She said she had the disease, though she did not know it at the time. . . . I considered her a very vile girl."

But there were also stories written about Avery's mercurial character, his penchant for control, and his flirtations with women. Gossip, both in the press and around the community, would become a crucial part of Sarah Cornell's story, as it is in Hester Prynne's narrative in **The Scarlet Letter**.

"Hawthorne observed in the Fall River case and reproduced in his own novel the ongoing, quasi-institutional power of gossip both to punish and to forgive," wrote Kristin Boudreau. "Although the Boston townspeople, unlike the Fall River community, have no access to the printing press, their public utterances operate in strikingly similar ways. What we see in the vindictive statements of Hawthorne's matrons is an effort to wield communal power even in the absence of access to the press."

Gossip is very powerful. Catharine Williams set out to use her book to repair Sarah's reputation, despite Sarah's supposed confessions to various people about interactions with men. Catharine insisted that the witnesses were lying because they were Methodists. They were motivated to lie to protect the minister, Ephraim Avery. These were the types of stories that Avery wanted to gather when he asked Reverend Bidwell if he should seek out scandalous information about Sarah. Half-truths and lies are still used in murder cases, even almost two hundred years later. But now there are strict rules about whether they are admissible in court.

Sharon Vinick is a managing partner with Levy Vinick Burrell Hyams in Oakland, California, who specializes in representing sexual harassment victims in civil court. I asked her to read a few documents relating to the case.

"It seems totally familiar to me. It brought to mind some of the things that they said in the witch trials," said Vinick. "A woman was guilty until proven innocent because that's exactly what they're doing in this case. They were saying that she was promiscuous, that she did all this stuff, and she can't defend herself. She's dead."

Vinick said that none of the statements would be used in a criminal or civil court today.

"The federal rape shield law is a bar against the use of evidence of other sexual behavior in a rape case," said Vinick. "So for example, in a sexual harassment case in California, if you are representing the alleged harasser, you cannot bring in that this woman has had affairs with five people at the company, that she engages in rough sex. They're not supposed to talk about what kind of clothing she was wearing, that she was asking for it."

Vinick told me that we've come a long way, but not far enough.

"They still blame the victim," said Vinick. "They do within whatever subtle ways they can suggest that somehow she brought it on herself."

Sarah's family was weathering a blatant attack on her character. Catharine wrote that Sarah's sister, Lucretia, and Lucretia's husband believed that Sarah had been honest with them about her sexual history, about what happened with Ephraim Avery.

"She did not attempt to deceive them, and they knew of no other instance of the kind of her offending," wrote Catharine. "They knew by the same means, viz. her own confessions, of her intercourse with Avery, and they know of no other person with whom they believe her to have been criminal."

Between the heresy on one side and Catharine's determination to frame Sarah Cornell as the "sympathetic victim" on the other, the truth seems lost to time. Sarah had often publicly denied the charges against her during her life, particularly those accusing her of lascivious behavior, though in her letters to her family, she often called herself a sinner.

"I was a great sinner but I found a great Savior," Sarah told her sister in 1829. But that sentiment would not be uncommon for a devout Christian, and she was never specific about her "sin." The possibilities could range from extramarital sex to envy.

One thing that seems clear to both Catharine and me was that Sarah Cornell seemed to abhor suicide because it was certainly a sin. This is a crucial part of victimology: Was the victim likely to take her own life? Months earlier, Sarah had written to her mother while she was still in Dorchester.

"There has been several shocking cases of suicide within a few months here," Sarah wrote on March 2, 1828, "one of which a man about 30, cut his throat yesterday a few rods from me, he is to be buried this afternoon, he was intoxicated."

Sarah told her mother that a month earlier, another young man shot himself as she looked out the window in horror: "He tied himself to a tree and placed the gun to his breast," Sarah said, "and before anyone could get to him he made away with himself."

Sarah said that another young woman had jumped into the river to drown. "After remaining two days in the water she was found, the most awful sight I ever beheld," wrote Sarah. "How short and uncertain life is; it vanishes like the early cloud and the morning dew. It is time to go to meeting and I must close. Adieu, I am your affectionate though unworthy child. Maria Cornell."

Would Sarah **really** have taken her own life? Perhaps not. But what's clear is that she was a lonely, traumatized, and sometimes persecuted young woman, without protectors and with deep vulnerabilities, much like Hawthorne's Hester Prynne. Catharine saw that as she spoke with those around Sarah. And when Sarah crossed paths with Reverend Ephraim Avery in 1830, he would surely have seen it as well.

———————

Two years earlier, Sarah arrived in Lowell, Massachusetts, looking for a fresh start. In 1830, she heard a particularly charismatic minister preach, and his gospel moved her deeply.

"She sat under his daily and nightly ministrations," wrote Catharine. "She heard him at Great Falls and in other places in the neighborhood of Boston. . . . She seemed to contrive to be somewhere within the range of his preaching from the first of her acquaintance with him."

The character of Ephraim Avery, of course, is one of the most striking parallels between **The Scarlet Letter** and what happened to Sarah Maria

Cornell—the persona of the charismatic, and seductive, minister.

"In **Fall River**, as in **The Scarlet Letter**, the minister who has traveled to a new location in a small town near the Atlantic Ocean seems to be guilty of extra-marital impregnation," wrote Shirley Samuels in **Reading the American Novel, 1780–1865**. "The association between the misadventures of unwed pregnancy and the misaligned identification with wayward ministers thus has a long lineage in the culture of the United States."

More specifically, Hawthorne's Reverend Arthur Dimmesdale and Fall River's Reverend Ephraim Avery were both charming, both handsome, both pious, and both outwardly trustworthy. But when their sins were exposed, both were unmasked for their false piety and ostracized by their communities.

"No man, for any considerable period, can wear one face to himself, and another to the multitude, without finally getting bewildered as to which may be the true," declares the narrator of **The Scarlet Letter** regarding Reverend Dimmesdale. Hester Prynne is redeemable, as was Sarah Cornell, in the eyes of their judgmental societies—the men, not so much.

"The woman's transgressions paled by comparison to the man's, and the full elaboration and discussion of Avery's crimes effectively diminished the significance of his victim's," wrote Kristin Boudreau. "The social violation represented by Cornell's pregnancy became insignificant in light of her apparent seduction and murder at Avery's hands."

Two years before her death, Sarah Cornell yearned for salvation, but she required work. As she stood before the door of Reverend Avery in July 1830, she hoped for employment with the captivating young minister. We know these details not because Avery offered them to investigators, but because of a sheriff looking for information about Avery in Lowell. For the record, Avery denied ever hiring her, despite anecdotal evidence provided by witnesses to the sheriff. These witnesses were never requested in court—they were considered immaterial to the case. Avery never had to address the accusation that he had hired her, because the story was inadmissible. His wife and children never testified.

Avery said that Sarah had asked for employment one day, but that his wife, Sophia, didn't like the way she looked; perhaps Sophia deemed her too attractive to be around her husband. Avery claims that he refused her a job. He denies that she ever even stepped foot in the house. But Sarah and various witnesses indicated that she had been with the Averys for about a week. And now you'll learn **why** Avery was anxious to deny that Sarah had lived with him.

According to Sarah, she looked up at the tall, imposing minister and quietly requested a position with the family. His wife, Sophia, looked at the young beauty and reluctantly agreed. She and her husband had their son, Edwin, and their daughter, Elizabeth, by 1830—they had been married only six years. Sophia needed assistance with the home. Avery traipsed from town to town, Bible in hand, preaching the Word and collecting devout followers. Sarah attended all his meetings; she marveled at his magnetism, his deep knowledge and intense passion for God. During the day, she dutifully traversed around his house, flitting around his suspicious wife and their children to do laundry or change linens. She listened intently as she sat at dinner with the family while he espoused his devotion to Methodism. But Sarah's opinion of Avery started to slowly shift over time.

"He was in the habit of keeping very late hours, being out without his wife," wrote Catharine, "and giving no satisfactory account of himself, not even to the family in the house, whose rest he often disturbed, by obliging them to sit up for him, as they did not feel safe to retire and leave the front door unfastened."

Catharine detailed for readers several events meant to illustrate Avery's selfish nature, all delivered to her by the sheriff when he interviewed neighbors. Before Sarah Cornell moved in, Avery was renting rooms in a larger home—the landlord lived in one section, and Avery and his family in another. One night, Avery's wife and children went to bed around nine o'clock. They waited for Avery to return for two hours and then, exhausted from the long day, the family retired with the door locked. When he returned home, Avery created chaos.

"He behaved with most unbecoming passion, beating and banging the door as though he would stave it in," wrote Catharine, "and that the owner of the house hurried to let him in as quick as possible, and then retreated; when Avery entered, flung the door too, and snatching the key from the lock, carried it to his chamber."

The landlord followed Avery into his room and forced him to return the key. The owner soon sold the house to another landlord and quickly moved out, perturbed by his mercurial renter. But Catharine admitted that not all the chatter circling Ephraim Avery was true.

"Of course, much was said respecting this man which was false," Catharine wrote. "There is no one so base but may, after all, be slandered. For instance, the story of the mysterious and sudden death of his first wife must have been altogether false, for we cannot find that he ever had but one wife. Nothing of this sort is credited by the author, or mentioned, without sufficient proof."

But she insisted that her **own** reporting was accurate, and beyond reproach. She detailed a story about Avery's abuse of a horse, a tale she found particularly horrifying. The reverend's young son, Edwin, said that "the horse kicked his father." And then Avery retaliated cruelly.

"He drove two spikes into the floor and tied his heels down, and kept him there two days without anything to eat or drink," reported Catharine. No notes from Catharine on her source for that story but, if we believe her integrity, then she had a **good** source.

Avery was often absent, and when he was home, he was often private. "It was customary for him to be shut in his study with some young woman or other almost every day; sometimes several, in the course of the day," witnesses told Catharine. "Very seldom any of these were seen by his wife."

Avery had invited a stream of women into his house for meetings, perhaps private ministering, though that would have been unusual, even improper, for the early 1800s. Catharine and the witnesses were suspicious.

"[There were] frequent closetings with young women in the study," she wrote, "which stood at the head of the stairs and contained a bed and was rather remote from the sitting room and lodging room of his wife, having to pass through the front entry and front room, and a passageway, to get to the kitchen."

Catharine said that Avery's wife was at the other end of the house from the study much of the time. And then Avery began to knock on Sarah's door.

"He used to come out of her room after ten o'clock at night," wrote Catharine; "the family, on being questioned upon the subject, gave as a reason 'that she was ill, and sent for him to come in and pray with her.'"

We don't know what happened during those nights. Sarah conceded nothing to her family about her time in his home. Remember that Avery refused to admit that Sarah was even in the house. Catharine was conflicted over the information from the witnesses because social mores required that the author issue a level of judgment against Sarah Cornell that seemed almost cruel.

"If it was indeed true she used to send for him at that hour of the night to come to her room and pray with her, she courted destruction and might almost be said to deserve the fate it is supposed she met with at his hands," wrote Catharine. "If, on the contrary, he stole into her room, without an invitation, the case might be a little different. That he was there, I suppose to be a fact."

But to convince readers that Avery had murdered Sarah, Catharine had to expunge all Sarah's sexual transgressions, real or imagined. If Catharine were to admit that Sarah had sinned, then her readers might dismiss Sarah as an unsympathetic victim. Sarah Cornell, Catharine felt, had fallen prey to the reverend's charms. Indeed, one of the more damning pieces of evidence that the sheriff had disclosed to Catharine involved Avery's young son, who reported something upsetting: "It appears the little boy of Avery, after having accompanied him on one of his rides, said on his return, 'Pa kissed Sarah Maria Cornell on the road.'"

Witnesses told the sheriff that Sophia Avery was enraged.

"His wife, though habitually a mild, forbearing woman, on this occasion rose, and positively declared 'she would not have the girl in the house any longer,'" Catharine wrote.

Avery's wife appeared distraught over her young son's accusation, and she seemed to blame Sarah.

"That unfortunate woman was often seen with eyes red and swollen, as though she had recently been in tears," wrote Catharine, "and though used to speak mildly, she never mentioned the name of S. M. Cornell but with evident resentment and bitterness of feeling, even after she had gone from there."

Catharine was insinuating that Sophia Avery was aware of her husband's liberties and indiscretions with other women; she had cast out Sarah to save her marriage. Sarah left the Avery house and continued searching for work in Lowell. This had not been the first time that Sarah had been the subject of perhaps unwanted advances. Catharine interviewed a witness who relayed a disturbing story involving two brothers from her past who were both married.

"There is one anecdote, which has been related to the writer of this, which proves she could not have been the abandoned creature represented previous to this," wrote Catharine.

She means that Sarah had not abandoned her morals, as so many people had represented, solidifying her sordid reputation.

"S. M. Cornell, at one of the places where she lived, worked in the employ of two older brothers, partners in an establishment," wrote Catharine. "Something had been said in their hearing about her not being prudent; and the oldest formed the resolution to find out how far her imprudence extended."

Catharine's witness was a man who worked in the tailor shop, someone who personally verified the story. The brother first flirted with Sarah and then soon pressed her to sleep with him. She steadfastly reproached him, retorting that he had insulted a respectable woman.

"The older confided the affair to the younger," wrote Catharine, "who felt piqued to try himself."

The younger brother was persistent with his advances, harassing Sarah relentlessly as she tried to work. Each time he was met with dismissal.

"But in the moment when he thought himself sure of success," Catharine reported, "[he was] met with a still more severe repulse than his brother. Upon comparing notes, they agreed it was only because they were married men."

Sarah Cornell had spurned both brothers, so unsurprisingly they concluded that it was best to fire her. When a male employee asked the men where Sarah had gone, they replied that "she was rather too fond of young men."

Catharine pressed her witness on those details—had the brothers **really** seen Sarah being lascivious?

"He did not know what proof they had of her being fond of **young men**," wrote Catharine, "except that she did not like **old ones**."

From there, a series of mistakes or misunderstandings continued to plague Sarah Cornell. She was ejected from a camp meeting on Cape Cod when she briefly disappeared, potentially with a man. She returned to Lowell to seek advice from Reverend Avery, despite being banished by his wife from their home.

She had been fired from a weaving room for allowing her loom to be damaged. She was suspected of theft in other mills, but no one seemed to be able to produce evidence. And, as we talked about earlier, Catharine found conflicting opinions about Sarah's character from other men. While there were complaints from some about odd, erratic behavior, others found her to be kind and stable.

Dejected and fearful that she would never be allowed at another Methodist church, she begged Reverend Avery for a certificate of good standing, like the one given to Fanny Winsor by another minister. Avery agreed, but he had ordered her from Lowell, likely to keep her away from his wife. Despite his orders, Sarah stayed—she enjoyed her work there too much to leave. Soon, Avery retaliated. And just as with the thefts years earlier in Providence, the decision to defy Ephraim Avery would haunt Sarah Cornell for the remainder of her life.

———

Sarah had secured a mill job in Lowell, this time at another textile mill that made high-quality cloth, but the overseer (who was Methodist) confronted her with the rumors of her promiscuous behavior. It never seemed to end. Sarah was exhausted from defending herself.

She wept and admitted to an illicit relationship with a mill clerk but claimed that she had reformed. The overseer agreed to let Sarah keep her job, but there was a caveat. She must return to Ephraim Avery, her minister, and confess her sins. Sarah sobbed. She nodded and soon knocked on Avery's door, offering an apology and a request to listen to her transgressions so she could keep her job.

Rather than offering forgiveness, Avery initiated a church trial against Sarah—he had trapped her. Her confessions to Avery would assure that she would be expelled again from Avery's church for fornication. She might have been able to defend herself at the church, but when the trial occurred Sarah was missing. Sarah had left to attend a camp meeting on Cape Cod, at Avery's encouragement.

"It seems S. M. Cornell was expelled while absent at a Camp Meeting on Cape Cod," wrote Catharine with disgust. "He advised her to go away while the process was going on against her."

Avery had convinced Sarah that she was a sinner, though she adamantly denied that she had fornicated. Then she admitted it. And then she denied it again. Catharine believed that Sarah admitted that she had slept with men so that she could repent and stay in Ephraim Avery's church in Lowell—Sarah Cornell was desperate and hopeless.

"For it was upon those conditions she offered it," wrote Catharine, "as though to be out of the pale of the church was to be excluded from salvation."

Sarah wrote to Ephraim Avery, begging for his forgiveness and for a certificate of good standing. **I'll do better**, she assured him. She needed Avery's help, his protection.

"I will confess all, if I can only be continued in the church," Sarah wrote to Avery.

Catharine listened to the whispers in Fall River.

"She was willing to endure any disgrace, and would have signed anything but her death warrant," wrote Catharine.

Before her church trial ended, Sarah fled to New Hampshire, got another mill job, and attempted to join a Methodist church there. Meantime, in Lowell, a physician named Dr. William Graves went to Reverend Avery to ask about Sarah's whereabouts. Dr. Graves claimed that on August 30, 1830, she had visited him, giving her name as "Maria S.

Connell" and needing treatment for a sexually transmitted infection. He was happy to help, but now she needed to pay her bill. **Where is she?** Dr. Graves asked Avery.

But Sarah had offered friends a different story, a harrowing tale of attempted sexual assault. She had accused Dr. Graves of trying to rape her in his office in Lowell when she went there to be treated for a cold. There were rumors that this was something he had done often—that he attacked patients. When Sarah refused, Dr. Graves threatened to raise the amount of her bill and then tell people about the supposed disease she had.

"She said that Dr. Graves had slandered her," said a landlord in Great Falls. "That being sick, she had called on him for advice, and he had closed the door, insulted her, threatening to report that she had the foul disease, unless she complied with his importunities."

For context, Dr. Graves's involvement in this case was not what he was known for. In 1837, five years after Sarah's death, Dr. Graves killed one of his clients, widow Mary Anne Wilson, during an attempted pregnancy termination. Dr. Graves was certainly an unreliable witness.

When the minister of the Dover, New Hampshire, church, where Sarah was, wrote to Reverend Avery as her character reference, Avery told him that Sarah was guilty of fornication, theft, and lying; Avery told him about the "foul disease" she had. His letter ended: "Now if you want her in your church, you may have her."

She was rejected once again by another Methodist church, and Ephraim Avery was to blame. Inexplicably, Sarah sent several more desperate letters to Avery confessing her sins and asking forgiveness, as a last-ditch effort to seek his reassurance. The truest proof of perfection is persecution first, she thought. If Sarah could survive the onslaught of judgment against her, she would be closer to God. She believed that. Avery offered no response to her earnest confessions. Finally, Sarah went to Lowell and confronted Avery in person, and he agreed to sign a certificate of forgiveness that would allow her to join a church in New Hampshire. But this was more manipulation, because the day after giving Sarah the certificate, he wrote to the minister in New Hampshire revoking it.

"We should all of us here be opposed to her joining anywhere," Avery wrote. "Alas! Alas!! Alas!!! This morning direct information was brought that she had told a known willful falsehood."

Sarah Cornell was humiliated. By 1832, she had been banned from Methodist churches across New England, and the blame fell squarely on Ephraim Avery. The thirty-year-old left New Hampshire, and after a few stops in Massachusetts, she went to live with her sister and brother-in-law in Woodstock,

Connecticut. She stayed connected to the Methodists by attending academic classes at the church, but she wasn't a member.

Still, Sarah felt like she needed to meet with Ephraim Avery one final time to repair her reputation, to demand the return of her letters of confession. She was ingenuous, thought Catharine Williams, and she sincerely wished to begin a new life.

"If she could have rested content without another interview with Avery, it is probable this last final work of destruction might have been avoided," the author wrote, with shades of victim-blaming.

Sarah and Avery would talk in the late summer of 1832 at a camp meeting in Thompson, Connecticut, the fateful event that Sarah spoke about in her letter to Reverend Bidwell. At this camp meeting, hundreds of people slept in tents and shuttled between four days of prayer and services. Sarah told her family that she saw Reverend Avery and several other Methodist ministers she had known in Lowell—by this time, Avery and his family had moved from Lowell to Bristol, Rhode Island. Sarah told her sister, Lucretia, in a letter that at the tent revival camp meeting, she had approached Avery with a request to return her shameful letters of confession. She had been concerned that he might once again use her "sins" against her, so she demanded the return of the letters.

"They sat down; some conversation followed about Avery having burned the letters," Grindall Rawson,

Lucretia's husband, said. "He said he had not. . . . At that time he took hold of her hands and put one [of his] onto her bosom or something like it."

Sarah told her sister that she tried to get away from Avery, but he was too strong.

"She said he then had intercourse with her, and they returned to the camp," said Catharine. "He promised to destroy the letters, on his return to Bristol."

Ephraim Avery had raped Sarah Cornell. This was the story that Dr. Wilbur had been keeping a secret in despair for months until he revealed it when her body was discovered. This is why she never admitted to having sex with a man—she had never had **consensual** sex. It was difficult for everyone, including men in the 1800s, to discuss anything related to sex, especially sexual assault. Dr. Wilbur grappled with recalling his conversation with Sarah to Catharine.

"He had felt himself bound to secrecy in case the girl had lived," wrote Catharine, "respecting the name of her betrayer, but her death and the awful manner of it impelled him to reveal what he believed to be the cause."

We know now that Sarah had refused to expose Avery because she feared consequences; she would likely have been shunned by society for being a "liar" and a saboteur of his marriage, a slanderer who was targeting a respected minister with terrible allegations of rape. **Who would believe her?**

It was clear to Catharine Williams that Ephraim Avery had a motive to murder Sarah Cornell—he had raped her, even if no one had accused him of it.

"How the intimacy commenced, and whether it was of a criminal nature previous to the Camp-Meeting at Thompson, we believe no one has taken upon themselves positively to say," wrote Catharine, "but from what is related of the circumstances of their intimacy, everyone can judge." Catharine went on to add, "That fatal tenderness too, doubtless betrayed her at the campground."

Catharine often referred to her own experience at a Methodist camp revival years earlier. As Catharine had prepared to leave that camp meeting, she observed a young woman in distress, vulnerable and naive.

"The first object that met our eyes upon coming within the barrier was a young woman of extreme beauty, who was staggering through the Camp, with her clothes torn and her locks disheveled, wringing her hands and mourning that the people were not more engaged," wrote Catharine. "She appeared to excite great attention wherever she moved through the crowd. We observed, as she passed along, that the young men exchanged winks and jogged each other's elbows. We subsequently saw the same young woman lying in a tent, apparently insensible, i. e. in a perfect state of happiness, as they assured us."

Her description was a stinging retribution of the camp's lascivious nature.

———

Sarah Cornell was in misery after the rape. She had not only been assaulted but, it was soon clear, was also pregnant.

"Gone was the look of cheerfulness she was wont to wear; it was evident something pressed heavy on her heart," Catharine wrote.

But now Sarah was determined to begin a new life . . . as a mother. She wanted to keep the baby. Once again, the intersection between Sarah Cornell and Hawthorne's Hester Prynne is clear: both were mothers, determined to use their skills to raise their children without fathers. Sarah visited her sister, Lucretia, and her brother-in-law in Connecticut, and she disclosed her pregnancy. Lucretia and Grindall were shaken, but supportive.

"The brother finally resolved to ask counsel of his pastor, and subsequently of another friend, an attorney in the neighbourhood," wrote Catharine. "They advised her immediate removal into the State of Rhode-Island where Avery resided."

The lawyer suggested that Sarah could sue Avery for child support if she moved nearby. **You must exercise your rights**, the lawyer said. In October, Sarah moved to Fall River, Massachusetts, on the Rhode Island border—not far from the town of Bristol—where she knew she could get factory work.

"Here she lived for about two months without reproach or suspicion, being perfectly correct, as everyone supposed who saw her, in her conduct," wrote Catharine.

Sarah rented a room in a boardinghouse and lived with numerous women, who all considered her kind and generous. On October 8, she knocked on Dr. Wilbur's office door for the first time, and that was when he confirmed what she already knew: she was pregnant.

"Have you no connexions in this place, young woman?" demanded the doctor.

"None, sir, except religious connexions."

"Then you are a member of some religious society—of which?"

"Of the Methodist, sir."

Soon, she had revealed that the father was a Methodist minister.

"Monstrous!" said the appalled physician, "and does he preach now?"

"Yes sir, in Bristol, next town to this."

Dr. Wilbur asked where they had met for their tryst, which he referred to as an "interview." Sarah quickly replied.

"Our interview, sir, was at the late Camp Meeting in Thompson, Ct. It was unsought by me for any such purpose, but I trusted myself with him in a lonely place, and he acted a treacherous part."

"Amazing," exclaimed the doctor, "under the mask of religion too!"

Dr. Wilbur advised her to unmask the minister as a cad, a man who attacked her during a camp meeting when she was begging for his help. He told Sarah that it was in her best interest.

"Such a man deserves to be exposed, it is a duty you owe not only to yourself but to the public to expose the man," Dr. Wilbur told her. "I would therefore if I were you boldly go forward and expose him to the world."

Sarah seemed startled by the physician's strong suggestion.

"Oh, I cannot, I cannot sir, indeed," said the young woman, with a shudder. "I cannot consent to bring such disgrace and trouble upon the church and upon his innocent family too. He has a worthy woman for a wife, and she and all his innocent children must be disgraced if he is exposed."

Dr. Wilbur paused and pondered her response. He told Sarah that if she refused to make his assault on her public, that she must threaten him with exposure if he didn't support her.

"You must at all events be provided for before long, and the best way is in case you do not expose him, to threaten to do so unless he settles handsomely with you, and enables you to leave the factory until after the termination of this unhappy affair."

Sarah nodded her head in shame and left Dr. Wilbur's office with the promise that she would write to Ephraim Avery. Then Sarah left and, not long after, returned to Dr. Wilbur's office once again.

"She had recently received a letter from Mr. Avery requesting her to come to Bristol and see him there," reported Catharine, "that he had appointed a time and place and seemed anxious for the interview."

Dr. Wilbur seemed suspicious—why was Avery so eager for the meeting? Surely, he realized that Sarah would demand something—marriage, child support, a public declaration? The doctor suggested that she request $300 so she could leave her factory work until the baby was born. Sarah gasped.

"He is not able to give such a sum," she told him. "The Methodist ministers are poor—all poor. They are very illy paid for their services, and I doubt his power to make up such a sum, besides I should not dare to name so much for fear he would think I had told someone."

Catharine believed that Avery, according to Sarah, was fearful that she had told someone about her pregnancy. Sarah said this would be their **second** meeting about the baby.

"She then informed the doctor that she had a short interview with him at Fall River, where she met him on the meeting-house steps," Catharine wrote, "and walked away with him, and that he wished her to take a medicine that he recommended, in order to prevent future trouble and expense, and at once obliterate the effects of their connexion."

Dr. Wilbur was silent for a moment; Avery had suggested that Sarah take a concoction that would terminate a pregnancy—the oil of tansy. It was the liquid found by the matrons of Fall River when they had searched Sarah's trunk. They had wondered why she had it—now Catharine understood.

"Mrs. Nancy Durfee testified to the author that she was the first person who saw it in the trunk, where it lay with a teaspoon beside it," she wrote. "We believe there is one person who knows who sold this vial [Avery]. We have ascertained she did not procure it herself at Fall River, nor carry it there with her."

How much did he want you to take? asked Dr. Wilbur.

Thirty drops, Sarah replied. Dr. Wilbur was horrified. "Four drops is considered a large dose," Catharine explained. Oil of tansy was "one of the most violent things ever used, and never given except in very small quantities, and under the direction of a physician," she concluded.

And Ephraim Avery, the former medical student, would have known that.

Avery had tried to kill her.

"The girl seemed shocked," Catharine wrote, "but could not seem to believe her betrayer had designs on her life."

If you want to terminate the pregnancy, you'll need to see another doctor, Dr. Wilbur told her. But that wasn't Sarah's wish—she would keep the baby despite the personal shame and public disgrace it would cause her "and take care of her child as well as she was able."

Dr. Wilbur felt no sympathy for Ephraim Avery—
he was troubled by his patient's insistence on propriety. The reverend did not deserve Sarah's tolerance
or kindness, the physician concluded. **Please don't
meet him alone**, Dr. Wilbur begged.

Sarah dried her eyes with a handkerchief.

"Thanking him for his kindness she withdrew,"
Catharine wrote, "leaving an impression of pity and
admiration upon the mind of the good physician."

The next time Dr. Wilbur would see Sarah Maria
Cornell, several weeks later, she was hanging from
a haystack pole.

———

Forensic experts are crucial to a murder trial. They
offer the jury or the judge guidance grounded in
experience and education—sometimes. Some fields
of forensics don't require a deep understanding of a
discipline for the so-called experts to be allowed on
the stand. This was the case with the investigation
into Sarah Cornell's death.

In 1833, the breadth of knowledge of forensics
was limited. The field of toxicology hadn't been
developed yet. Fingerprint analysis was not used in
criminal cases (that would come fifty years later).
The analysis of shoe-print impressions, however, was
useful to investigators starting in the late 1700s.

"The origin of the principles used in the forensic
analysis of footwear and tire impression evidence

dates back to when man began hunting animals," according to the U.S. Department of Justice. "At that time, hunters realized that different animals made different tracks and they used this information to identify the type of animal. Using this same premise, investigators began associating patterns observed in impressions at the crime scene with features on the suspects' footwear and tires."

Medical evidence provided experts with some of the most reliable testimony by 1833, but as with most clues, its veracity often came down to the expertise of the experts. The day after Sarah's body was discovered in December 1832, the coroner examined her exhumed corpse on Durfee's farm; joining him was the second coroner's jury, as well as several physicians. They discovered bruising on Sarah's abdomen, suggesting that a pregnancy termination may have been attempted, perhaps by kicking or punching her in the stomach. Sometimes doctors used probes. But they pointed to the cord that was wrapped around Sarah Cornell's neck and still insisted on suicide.

Then a man from the crowd stepped forward: John Durfee's brother, Williams. A retired mariner, Williams Durfee had experience with knots, specifically this one: the clove hitch. That knot would be the crux of the case for murder. Remember: the loop of marline cord was so tight, the cord could not be cut off without cutting her skin; it was embedded nearly half an inch into her.

"On turning her head I discovered a little knot, near the right ear," said Williams Durfee. "The cord was taken round the neck twice, two half hitches as the farmers call it, or a clove hitch as we sailors used to call it."

He described it as two loops passed, one under and one over, and it was doubled, making four strands. Williams Durfee then made a bold statement.

"To draw a clove hitch you must draw it at both ends to tighten it," said Durfee. "If placed over a standing stake, it must be drawn at both ends horizontally to tighten it. If drawn up with both ends together it will not tighten at all."

Durfee insisted that Sarah Cornell could not have drawn the clove hitch knot herself. Specifically, he claimed that a clove hitch would not have pulled tightly if Sarah had tied it herself. Unlike a hangman's noose, a clove hitch wouldn't have been tight enough to strangle her.

The fact that a clove hitch knot had been used, Durfee claimed, meant that Sarah Cornell had been murdered.

A multitude of evidence had been presented to convince the committee, the physicians, the coroner, and Catharine that Sarah had definitively been murdered, including Dr. Wilbur's disclosures, the mysterious letters, and Sarah's ominous note. But Williams Durfee's insistence that Sarah **could not** have tied that clove hitch herself was the linchpin.

This was murder, they declared. **She was strangled, not hanged.**

The men examining Sarah's body determined that a slip knot would have been the simplest choice for suicide—why use a clove hitch, a knot with a reputation of slipping? Someone attempting to take their own life wouldn't have bothered with a knot like that. The only conclusion was murder, and the clove hitch knot theory was the primary evidence.

But after consulting with forensic investigator Paul Holes, I discovered that investigators in 1832 might have been wrong—it **would have been** physically possible for Sarah to have tied the clove hitch herself, resulting in her death.

"All you have to do is go take a look at inmate suicides, where they hang themselves with bedsheets from the bed frame inside their cell," Holes explained to me. "As long as there is weight compressing the front of the neck, that's sufficient to kill."

Holes told me about a case he had in Colorado concerning the clove hitch knot.

"A woman was completely suspended over a balcony. And the noose was merely a clove hitch, but it was sufficient to hold her up," said Holes. "And she was a petite woman—she weighed one hundred to one hundred and ten pounds, somewhere in there. The clove hitch will tighten up; it is completely sufficient."

And that was Ephraim Avery's claim—Sarah had taken her own life. But did that make sense?

———

When Reverend Ira Bidwell met his fellow Methodist minister Ephraim Avery after the murder accusations surfaced, Avery seemed panicked. He offered Bidwell a string of denials: Avery had never hired Sarah to work in his home, he had never raped her, he had never tried to induce an abortion, and he was not the father of the baby.

Then why is this happening? asked Bidwell.

Revenge. Sarah Cornell had framed him, Avery claimed. She was furious over being expelled from his church, he said, so she'd tried to frame him for causing so much sorrow in her life.

"He thought if he could get the facts of her being a common prostitute, it would satisfy the people at Fall River he was not guilty of the things they charged him with," reported Stephen Bartlett, the stagecoach driver who had talked with Avery that day.

Avery and Bidwell both claimed that Sarah Cornell took her own life to set up the preacher for murder. It might seem ludicrous, but there are examples of this in history—a person in despair resorting to death by suicide while framing someone for murder. One of my previous books, **American**

Sherlock, is about forensic scientist Edward Oscar Heinrich, who investigated the 1928 murder of Cora Van Ness Mead, a wealthy married woman. She had called the police claiming that her husband was threatening to shoot her in the kitchen. When police arrived, she was sitting in a chair, dead from a shotgun blast to the head. Her husband, a serial philanderer, was arrested, and Heinrich was called in by investigators. Using trigonometry and the angle of the gun's trajectory, Heinrich proved that Mead had shot herself to frame her husband for her murder. He had also found a small stick that she used to pull the trigger with her feet. Heinrich's evidence freed the husband and he eventually remarried . . . only to be killed later in the kitchen with a gun by his second wife.

Did Sarah Cornell frame Ephraim Avery? There were three anonymous letters written by someone who anxiously wanted to meet with Sarah on the night she died. Who wrote those? Was Sarah a scorned, calculating woman, bent on revenge, even if it meant taking her own life in despair?

No, her family and friends replied. Catharine Williams did some further investigating on this point, starting with the night Sarah Cornell allegedly met Ephraim Avery at John Durfee's farm, December 20, 1832.

"The persons who worked next to her in the factory, deposed that she went out about six in the evening," Catharine wrote, "went in good spirits, and was exceedingly anxious to get leave to go out at the hour of six."

Catharine was told that Sarah had spoken to the daughter of her landlady about a mysterious appointment. Catharine wrote:

"[She] said she 'did not care how many days it rained, if it was only fair on that day,' 20th of December."

Sarah showed the woman two letters: a pink and a yellow note, found later in her trunk. In one of these letters were Sarah's instructions for that evening: she was excited to keep an important meeting, but with whom?

As Catharine Williams pondered the fate of the young woman, she, too, wondered about Sarah's accusation of rape.

"It was strange indeed, if she had suffered the injury she complained of, at the Camp Meeting, without manifesting any resentment afterwards, she should, on the contrary, uniformly speak of him and his family with tenderness, and above all things seem not to desire to expose him," Catharine reflected. "It may be enquired, if this were the case, why did she leave that little bit of paper to direct, if she was missing to enquire of him?"

Why did she go, was she not scared? Catharine wondered. If her accusation against Avery was true, that he had raped her and then tried to murder her with poison, why ignore Dr. Wilbur's pleas and agree to see the reverend secretly? Attorney Sharon Vinick said that it didn't surprise her, based on her years of working with sexual harassment victims. She explained that a victim will often exhibit counter-intuitive behavior when they are raped or assaulted by someone who is already in their life. Even if they fear that person, they might be reluctant to cut that person out of their life, and "often they are more reluctant to come forward or to accuse that person."

"It was neither fair nor honourable in the first place, to ask a female to go to that cold, lonely place on a dark evening," opined Catharine. "She knew, probably, it was a fearful thing under such circumstances, or indeed under any, to go there to an assignation."

Catharine scoffed at the idea that Sarah wanted to die that night. After all, there were easier ways to die than by ingesting poison or hanging oneself.

"The dark deep waters of Mount Hope Bay rolled below," she wrote, "and it could have been easy to give one plunge there, as to have poured down a dose of tansy oil."

We see more shades of **The Scarlet Letter** in the supposed meeting places of Sarah Cornell and Ephraim Avery: a farm by the bay and the woods where she accused him of sexually assaulting her.

"This meeting place of river, bay, and ocean, this insistence on water as the marker of place and, further, as the place of momentous assignation, may, by extension, suggest the water of the stream where

Arthur Dimmesdale meets Hester Prynne," wrote Shirley Samuels.

Hawthorne compares Prynne to the ocean, because of her spirit: "But the sea, in those old times, heaved, swelled, and foamed, very much at its own will, or subject only to the tempestuous wind, with hardly any attempts at regulation by human law," he wrote in **The Scarlet Letter.**

Arthur Dimmesdale also meets Prynne in the woods, as Sarah Cornell did Ephraim Avery during the camp meeting at which she contends that he sexually assaulted her. The Puritans in **The Scarlet Letter** considered the forest wild and dangerous—a place where bad things happen. But Hawthorne takes that narrative and shifts it, converting the forest to a rendezvous point where Dimmesdale and Prynne meet to escape judgment. Yet Sarah was not safe in the woods alone with Avery. They offered privacy, and danger.

In 1833, Catharine needed to interview more witnesses; she wanted to question the people closest to Sarah Cornell—the two sisters who lived with her at the factory's boardinghouse in Fall River. **How did she seem that night before leaving? Was she suicidal? No,** insisted her coworkers, she was very, very cheerful. And they provided Catharine with a crucial explanation for that short, seemingly ominous note.

"She came out of the mill early and changed her clothes," the sisters told Catharine, "and then probably wrote that little strip of paper, 'If I am missing enquire of Rev. E. K. Avery.'"

But while questions remained, the coroner's second jury's opinion coalesced around one belief: that Sarah Cornell had been murdered and Ephraim Avery was her killer.

Things progressed quickly. Ephraim Avery was scooped up, and on Christmas Day, he was arrested for murder and presented to a panel of justices for a probable cause hearing.

"Avery appeared in the Bristol Courthouse and, keeping to a carefully prepared text, painted an unsavory, promiscuous, dissipated young woman while simultaneously painting himself as a model of Christian solicitude," wrote Ian C. Pilarczyk in "The Terrible Haystack Murder."

As he stood before the judges, Ephraim Avery offered little explanation for the accusations against him—he simply produced a series of counteraccusations, framing Sarah as an unsavory, dodgy, promiscuous woman who took advantage of the generosity of the Methodists. Meanwhile, the prosecutor did little to convince the justices that there was solid evidence against the reverend. On Sunday, January 6, the justices ruled that there was not enough to say that Ephraim Avery killed Sarah Maria Cornell, and he was free to go.

This, of course, enraged the people of Fall River and throughout New England. One newspaper called him "Rev. Criminal." The verdict from the justices in Bristol, where Avery had lived, seemed like a farce. But then, the prosecutor found a legal loophole. Sarah's body had been found in **Tiverton**, not Bristol, therefore Avery should have been tried elsewhere. Soon, a deputy sheriff held an arrest warrant in his hand for Ephraim Avery to appear on murder charges before the Supreme Court of Rhode Island in Newport. Now the officer just needed to find him.

In January 1833, Reverend Ira Bidwell seemed frenzied. He knew that another arrest of Ephraim Avery was imminent. Bidwell rushed to Bristol to meet with the reverend. Soon, Avery hired the stagecoach driver Stephen Bartlett to travel to Fall River for an update.

"In the meantime, Avery kept his house, walking it, as was said, in a state of very great agitation," wrote Catharine Williams. "He did no preaching that day."

Bartlett had hoped to find Dr. Wilbur to discover more details about what was to happen next. **Would Avery be arrested?** After Bartlett found the physician, who was visiting a patient, the two walked toward the physician's house and discovered John Durfee and the deputy sheriff waiting. Dr. Wilbur showed Bartlett into the parlor and then requested privacy. He needed to speak with John Durfee and the deputy alone.

"Aiding Bartlett into the parlour, he went out to see them," wrote Catharine. "It had been decided to apprehend Avery."

The deputy had a warrant for the minister's arrest on the charge of murder. Dr. Wilbur fretted, then sighed and turned to Durfee. **Go quickly**, he urged him. Catharine pressed the doctor to remember his own precise words to John Durfee that day: **Why is an arrest so urgent?**

"If he is not apprehended soon, he will be off," replied Dr. Wilbur.

CHAPTER EIGHT

❧

THE TOTALITY OF TALES

IN JANUARY 1833, JOHN DURFEE and a deputy sheriff stood with Dr. Thomas Wilbur at his home. The physician warned them to leave **now** if they wanted to capture Ephraim Avery—the reverend had many friends in the Methodist Church who would hide him.

Wilbur nodded toward the parlor, where stagecoach driver Stephen Bartlett sat, eager for news. The men suspected that Bartlett had traveled to Fall River at Avery's request to probe for information. Dr. Wilbur urged Durfee to start their search for Avery immediately. After the first indictment was vacated in Bristol, Avery must have thought that he had escaped suspicion. That was obviously not the case, and Avery would soon learn the news.

"Here is Bartlett in the other room now, come to see how the business stands," whispered Dr. Wilbur.

The doctor suspected that if the stagecoach driver made it back to Avery with news of his new indictment before they found him, Avery would never be seen again.

Durfee seemed panicked. The men begged Dr. Wilbur to keep the stagecoach driver occupied as long as possible while they got a head start. The elderly physician agreed. Soon he greeted Mr. Bartlett in his parlor and told him, **I need to talk with you, but I must have dinner first.** Bartlett nodded politely, apparently not realizing that Dr. Wilbur was stalling. After the physician had finished his meal, Bartlett asked about Sarah Maria Cornell; he wondered about her death and why Ephraim Avery was being scrutinized. Dr. Wilbur slowly recounted his conversation with Sarah in the fall; she had accused Avery of sexually assaulting her, maligning her character, and then driving her out of the Methodist Church. He had violated her in numerous ways. Bartlett seemed surprised.

"And do you know that he is suspected of the murder too?" Dr. Wilbur asked Bartlett.

"No!" the driver replied in shock.

Dr. Wilbur described the clove hitch knot, the timing of Sarah's pregnancy, and the three anonymous notes that left more questions than answers. Bartlett seemed anxious and then resigned. He hopped up, snatched his hat, and rushed through Dr. Wilbur's parlor, jumping on his coach and racing off. But by the time he reached Bristol, the citizens' committee of investigation had already been to Avery's house . . . and found it without a master. The minister had vanished. Perhaps Dr. Wilbur's warning was right—after days filled with denials, the Methodist minister had panicked. In mid-January 1833, Ephraim Avery disappeared from Rhode Island. This made his critics even more wary, and even some of his supporters.

"Those who believed him innocent," wrote Catharine, "had thought he would court a trial in order to free himself from the odium attached to him."

If Avery had simply disappeared, hoping to begin a new life, he was misled. Only a criminal trial would remove the stain of the accusations from his pulpit, Catharine contended. If he were acquitted, he might be allowed to preach the gospel in public again. But if he avoided a trial, then his career in the ministry would be finished. His supporters insisted to the committee that his disappearance was not a sign of guilt. Wrote Catharine, "They were confounded, but for the most part wise enough to keep still."

The sheriff in Bristol turned to one of the men standing by the reverend's house: Colonel Harvey Harnden, his deputy sheriff and a member of the committee of investigation appointed by the people of Fall River. Harnden would take the lead in hunting Ephraim Avery. But the thirty-eight-year-old was at a loss because Avery had simply vanished;

Harnden suspected that the minister had help, and while he was concerned about justice, Harnden was nervous that a vigilante group would form soon in Fall River to search for the minister on its own.

The Fall River citizenry was incensed over the rumors that a Methodist minister had murdered a young, pregnant mill worker. "But the indefatigable Col. Harnden was not to be daunted or disheartened in the cause he had undertaken," wrote Catharine. He had ample resources at his disposal; the committee had authorized Harnden to spend whatever was needed to track down their runaway. They had pressured the Rhode Island legislature to declare Avery a fugitive, which would allow anyone to detain him and deliver him for examination in Rhode Island.

Harnden boarded a stagecoach and then a train, traversing three different states over hundreds of miles. He was eventually drawn to New Hampshire, where Avery had connections to a fellow Methodist minister who lived there with his family. Harnden arrived in New Hampshire around January 23, 1833, about one month after Sarah Cornell's death. Harnden entered a local bakery, and a young employee asked why he was in the state. The deputy sheriff explained the story—he was there to arrest a Methodist minister named Ephraim Avery for murder.

Do you know him? asked Harnden. The baker's boy thought for a moment. He replied that he once went to a local Methodist meeting and a woman he called "Mrs. Mayo" had been accused of doing something egregious; we don't know what that might have been. Her husband called to Ephraim Avery, a minister who was there at the time. Catharine wrote that whatever the problem was, Avery fixed it and Mrs. Mayo wasn't ejected from the church. The boy in the bakery wondered if Avery might have asked the Mayos for a favor in return.

"The lad's thinking was . . . [that] he was concealed at that house," wrote Catharine.

The Mayos lived in a large two-story house in rural Rindge, New Hampshire, about 100 miles from Fall River. Warrant in hand, Harnden ordered Captain Mayo and his wife to step aside and allow Harnden and a deputy, named Mr. Foster, from another town to wander through the rambling home. The other men stood watch outside the home's exits.

"I went through the house into the room in which the family lived," said Harnden. And then he watched Mrs. Mayo disappear into a small, dark room with a light in hand.

"Mr. Harnden followed her," wrote Catharine, "and found Avery hid, pale and trembling behind the door of a chamber, evidently fitted up for his concealment, having the windows completely darkened, with lights and firewood laid in."

"I discovered Mr. Avery," said Harnden. "He stood quite motionless, and, from his appearance, was more agitated than any person I ever saw. I presented my hand to him, and said, 'Mr. Avery, how do you do?'"

Avery tried to speak, but he said nothing—he appeared terrified. Harnden tried to reassure him.

"I then took him by the hand and said, 'do endeavor to suppress this agitation; you need fear no personal violence; you shall be kindly treated.'"

Avery stepped into the light and quickly informed the deputy sheriff that he was told by his attorney that only the governor could compel him to leave New Hampshire. His life was in danger, he believed. **Not true**, said Harnden, **this warrant is legal**. Avery reluctantly agreed to leave his friend's home. As the men stepped on the porch, the minister touched his beard. **I'd love a shave**, he mentioned to the deputy sheriff. Since disappearing several weeks earlier, Avery had grown facial hair and his beard needed trimming.

"We left Captain Mayo's between eleven and twelve, and went up to the tavern in Rindge, where Mr. Avery shaved, having previously expressed a wish to do so," said Harnden. "His face then appeared as it had done at Bristol."

Clean-shaven, Ephraim Avery traveled to Newport, Rhode Island, with Harnden through Boston. Despite the heinous charges, the minister enjoyed an incredible amount of support from the Methodists along the way, all proclaiming publicly his innocence, "giving him the right hand of fellowship" and "having several 'comfortable seasons of prayer'"—all,

Catharine marveled, "with a man then laboring under the strongest presumption of being both an adulterer and murderer."

In Newport, Avery sat in jail as his followers and his fellow Methodist leaders gathered their financial resources—they feared, rightly so, that he would stand trial. And he would sit behind bars, perhaps for months, awaiting his trial. There was no bail offered for people charged with murder. Meanwhile, the committee of investigation in Fall River, bolstered financially in part by the Congregationalist mill owners, worked to gather more evidence for the state's attorney general.

Rumors spread across New England about everyone involved in the case. There was gossip that the judges in Bristol who threw out the charges against Avery were members of the secret, fraternal organization the Freemasons—and that Avery was a member too. They whispered that Avery had been a pirate in the Caribbean, that he had murdered his first wife, whom no one had ever heard of. Neither Catharine nor I found any evidence that he had been married before Sophia, and the other chatter was unfounded. But still, the gossip continued.

By the time the minister returned to Rhode Island, a rumor was widely circulated "that Sarah Cornell's arm had been broken, thus rendering her unable to hang herself and indicating a violent struggle," wrote David Kasserman in **Fall River Outrage**. "Hoping the story might be true so it would quash any attempt to prove suicide, the selectmen of Tiverton (probably Charles and John Durfee) commissioned Foster Hooper and Thomas Wilbur to do another autopsy."

On a frigid evening in late January 1833, Sarah's body was lifted from her grave on John Durfee's farm for a second time while the pair of physicians examined it once again. This time, it was at the request not of the coroner but of the magistrate, Charles Durfee. Drs. Hooper and Wilbur took note of extensive discoloration; they attributed it to the decomposition of a body that had been buried for more than a month.

"On the 26th of January, I again examined the body, when disinterred," said Dr. Hooper. "The face was covered with a white mould, where the flesh had been touched with frost. The body was in a good state of preservation except where incisions had been made."

They found no broken arm—even if they had, they knew it could have been caused by any number of factors. Remember, the women who had prepared Sarah's body for her burial had soaked her arm in warm water so it could be bent when it was placed in the coffin. They thought they had snapped it accidentally.

The next morning, John Durfee returned Sarah Cornell to her grave, and within days Ephraim Avery appeared in a brief examination in Tiverton,

Rhode Island, before two judges, one of whom was a member of the Durfee clan (which seems prejudicial, but no one seemed to have objected). A jury quickly decided that Avery should be remanded for trial in the Rhode Island Supreme Court in the spring. Visibly dismayed, Avery found out he would spend several months in a dreary jail cell in Newport.

"It is not possible, I am confident, to conceive the feelings I experienced upon being conducted to my dismal abode," complained Avery later. "I was placed in the criminal's cell, my ears assailed with the grating sounds of bars of iron and the turning of keys, and the retiring footsteps of the jailer died away on my ear."

Avery complained bitterly of the cold weather, but his Methodist brothers provided a bed, blankets, a stove, and a Bible for him, which he read constantly. His wife and young son slept on a mattress nearby for some nights. Avery's righteous indignation over his imprisonment and the Methodists' loud condemnation over the State of Rhode Island's case only seemed to enrage the Congregationalist factory society of nearby Fall River. The pews of their churches filled with discontent parishioners, all sounding off against the Methodists and their lascivious minister. Here was a man who was once hallowed by congregants across New England, and now the Methodists were providing a murderer with praise bordering on idolatry, Catharine declared. And now she demanded that the reader witness the shameful result.

"The absurd custom of crowding round some handsome preacher on every occasion, in order to share his smiles, and be distinguished by his gracious gallantries, has justly excited the ridicule of a large part of the community," Catharine crowed. "Ministers are mortal men and with good intentions, sometimes persons of weak minds and it requires a very strong mind to resist continual flattery."

Ephraim Avery's ministry engendered credibility for more and more parishioners across the country, but Catharine refused to be bewitched. There were Methodist ministers, she jeered, slithering around the northern states, who deserved nothing but contempt and ridicule.

"Some of them too are ignorant persons, people, who, if they had their proper places in society, would be hewers of wood and drawers of water, rather than teachers," she wrote.

This was the sentiment for many in New England; Ephraim Avery was the devil incarnate, a wicked creature preying on pathetic female followers, preaching at a hollow pulpit. Again, we see how Hawthorne was influenced by the growing contempt for Avery and his kind—and it's epitomized in **The Scarlet Letter** in the character of Reverend Arthur Dimmesdale.

"It is the unspeakable misery of a life so false as

his [Dimmesdale's]," wrote Hawthorne, "that it steals the pith and substance out of whatever realities there are around us, and which were meant by Heaven to be the spirit's joy and nutriment."

Dimmesdale very closely resembles Avery, "who is hated as much for his shallow acts of inauthentic reverence," according to author Kristin Boudreau. "Arthur Dimmesdale seems to stand for empty but seductive rhetoric—which by Hawthorne's day had come to be associated with popular evangelical religions like Methodism."

These men needed to be drawn out, both Catharine Williams and Nathaniel Hawthorne agreed. They needed to be displayed for the boors they were, and then banished into the woods where their tent revivals had ruined so many young women. Rhode Island's attorney general Albert Greene seemed keenly aware of the gravity of the murder trial as he prepared his argument for the grand jury of the Rhode Island Supreme Court.

Greene had been a U.S. senator as well as an accomplished attorney and military man in Rhode Island. Sarah Cornell's death had transcended a conventional murder investigation; the outcome of this trial, Greene knew, could shift the economy, making factories more undesirable places to work, repelling valuable female operatives. There was pressure from the Congregationalist communities to discredit the shifty minister and imprison him, if not expel him from their society.

The forty-one-year-old attorney general sat at his desk, picked up a pen, and began scribbling notes, occasionally blotting out mistakes with a dab of ink. "Newport for Supreme Judicial Court, March Term, 1833" was his title. The grand jury panel convened and listened to evidence: the clove hitch knot, the letters, and the witnesses who began to come forward. The committee of investigation argued that it could piece together what happened that night, that Avery could provide no real alibi. **He is a murderer**, they insisted. After two days of testimony, the grand jury agreed and delivered an indictment on March 6, 1833. It read:

"Ephraim K. Avery, Clerk, not having the fear of God before his eyes, but being moved and instigated by the Devil, upon the body of one Sarah M. Cornell, did make an assault, and a certain cord . . . about the neck of the said Sarah, did put and fasten . . . did kill and murder."

Catharine Williams skimmed the indictment and seemed pleased. "Not guilty," Avery had replied to the standard question of pleading at the arraignment. The judge nodded and the defense attorney requested a short interim before the trial—Avery had been in jail for two months. The justice agreed and set the trial date for Monday, May 6, 1833.

As the wheels of justice began to grind, Avery's church-funded defense team sent investigators across New England to gather gossip about Sarah Maria

Cornell. The group of six included a former U.S. senator who was a celebrated New England attorney named Jeremiah Mason; the team was hired by the New England Conference of the Methodist Episcopal Church. That organization was now naturally pitted against the Fall River Committee, which fronted the interests of the factory owners. Sarah had just moved to Fall River that October, but she represented every young woman that they had employed. Albert Greene's cocounsel, Congressman Dutee J. Pearce, said as much during his opening statement.

"She was, gentlemen, in the parlance of the day, a 'Factory girl,' but she was one of that class of women and children of which we have 7000 usefully and honorably employed in the 150 Cotton Mills in this State," declared Pearce, "a class indispensable to the industry of the country, and whose rights, therefore, the interests of the community require should be protected, and their wrongs avenged."

The Congregationalists engaged their own agents to forage New England for witnesses. Sarah Cornell and Ephraim Avery no longer represented only themselves, nor just class-consciousness, but a deeper benchmark in U.S. history: the burgeoning independence of women and the sexism of a patriarchy that still dominated American culture. Women in the mills were not simply a commodity on the production line, but they fed a growing need for an industry that craved growth within a country that desperately needed a more robust middle class.

"Virtually everyone in New England, from the millowners to the mothers of factory girls and children, had a stake in the success of the textile industry," wrote William McLoughlin in "Untangling the Tiverton Tragedy." "New England's prosperity and the nation's future depended upon this new industrial venture."

Mill owners hoped that Sarah's vindication and Avery's conviction would assure families that their daughters would be safe from predatory rapists cloaked as Methodist ministers. The Methodists prayed for Avery's acquittal and leveraged Sarah's dubious decisions to protect their burgeoning congregations. Catharine hoped to extricate religion from the fallen minister by exposing him as the fallible being he was, not as a man crafted in the image of God.

"Since writing this book we observe there has been a great hue and cry among a certain class that religion was in danger from dwelling upon this subject—that it was better to have it smothered," she wrote. "We firmly believe that religion is not so inseparably connected with E. K. Avery, so identified with him, that it must rise or fall with him, or indeed with any other preacher." Christianity, Catharine argued, would not be besmirched by Reverend Avery, no matter the outcome of his upcoming murder trial.

It's important to return to our original queries: Was Sarah murdered, and if so, was Ephraim Avery the offender? These questions are central to this investigation, and yet they vanish within the pages of Catharine's book. Just because we **think** someone is morally guilty doesn't mean they should be convicted in a court of law. That's both the brilliant substance of American law and the maddening conclusion that crime victims often face.

Between March and May of 1833, Catharine Williams marveled at the shower of attention that flooded New England, particularly Rhode Island, because of the upcoming trial.

"Scouts were out in all directions," Catharine reported, "and oh the racing and chasing there was to look up witnesses."

Catharine noted that investigators, reporters, and gawkers traveled along the toll roads, known as private turnpikes, across New England, all hoping for exclusive information.

"Turnpike corporations and tavern keepers reaped a golden harvest during those two months," she said. "There was scarcely a factory village within a hundred and fifty miles but what underwent a thorough examination."

Sarah Cornell's nomadic lifestyle created a problem for the prosecution and the defense because of her exposure to **so many** people, yet it also lent itself to anonymity. Sarah had changed her name a few times, sometimes referring to herself as "Maria Snow," sometimes simply "Maria." Her social circle was quite large, as was Ephraim Avery's, as both the district attorney and the defense discovered. They interviewed supervisors for numerous factories where she'd worked; they spoke with Avery's parishioners, the ones who were fond of him and those who distrusted him. They interviewed family members as well as friends and coworkers. Both sides needed to prove whether Sarah and Avery could be placed together at the infamous Thompson camp meeting in late August.

There were rumors that Avery had researched methods for pregnancy termination, but the attorney general couldn't prove this. Investigators working for the defense traced women and men who could use personal experience to besmirch Sarah's character. Albert Greene secured the testimonies of Sarah's sister and her husband. Much of this was gossip or hearsay, from both sides. It showed that lies and half-truths, like in **The Scarlet Letter**, could both tarnish reputations, like Hester Prynne's, or rescue them, also like Hester Prynne's. Both damnation and redemption were held in the hands of common townspeople in 1600s Boston and 1800s Fall River. While he sat in the Newport jail, Ephraim Avery appeared subdued.

Catharine regretted Sarah's misfortune—she had

been a wayward ship with no star guiding her home. She had no way of knowing how her reputation, born from a simple mistake at a shop filled with beautiful clothing, could betray her for more than a decade. There was no escaping her past, Sarah had learned—but by then it was too late.

"She did not realize the danger of changing neighborhoods so often," Catharine lamented, "nor know that it was safest for people to stay where they are best known, and where slanderers make out to live upon one old story for a thousand years, but transport it into a new neighborhood and ten thousand will immediately be added to it."

The rumors compounded as Sarah's character—her public reputation—deteriorated. And any gossip that traveled along the roads between New England's villages would strengthen tenfold before Avery's trial began. This case would be the first nationwide known instance of victim-shaming in a criminal trial.

"Possibly the first time that a murdered woman was, in effect, put on trial in order to exonerate her murderer," wrote Shirley Samuels in **Reading the American Novel, 1780–1865**. "The legal precedent was to serve for many rape and murder trials in the years that followed."

The notion that someone's appearance didn't match their character was deeply troubling to many in 1800s America. A man's handshake was often enough to gain a neighbor's trust. A woman's easy smile and kempt appearance should exemplify her own good nature.

"In such a society, the notion that a religious leader could be a secret sinner would necessarily be terrifying," wrote Ian C. Pilarczyk in "The Terrible Haystack Murder."

Soon, Sarah Cornell and Ephraim Avery would go on trial and face a jury. The public yearned for more information on what was rapidly becoming a scandal that reached as far west as Missouri. While that might not seem widespread, newspapers in the 1830s were regional, so a murder in Rhode Island would have to be singular, remarkable to be printed in the **Niles' National Register** in St. Louis. "The trial of rev. Mr. Avery for the murder of a young girl, who is supposed to have been seduced by him, is going on at Newport, R.I. and excites a high degree of interest," the notice read.

The local New England papers were more partisan.

"In the meantime, public indignation could not wait with patience for the issue of the trial, and from time to time it would speak out through the medium of the papers," Catharine wrote. "This the Methodists termed 'persecution.'"

The leaders of the Methodist Church, sensing a shift in New England toward defending Sarah, continued to pronounce Avery's innocence. They complained that the minister was being mistreated in jail—his cell wasn't comfortable enough; a man of the cloth deserved better. They expressed concern over his safety. They feared that a vigilante mob would swarm the jail, drag him from his cell, and beat him to death. There was a conspiracy against Avery, they declared, a conspiracy against **all** Methodists. Yes, he had run away when the charges against him became clear. But, they insisted, it wasn't his choice; his advisors had told him to flee, despite knowing that it would point to guilt. His life was in danger, they argued. Catharine blamed the church leaders.

"It is certain that much of it was provoked by their own imprudence in continually and loudly asserting his innocence," argued Catharine, "and the violence with which they endeavored to bear down public opinion, as well as their ridiculous fidgeting about the safety of his person, and his personal accommodation, through all the stages of his travels."

The Methodist parishioners across New England began to coalesce around Avery's defense, regardless of the evidence against him. Meanwhile, most of the Congregationalist factory owners declared that he was certainly guilty.

Catharine Williams declared that Ephraim Avery lacked character and she was certain that God would never forgive him—he was destined to spend the latter half of his life in prison. Sarah Cornell would receive justice, she believed, and the Methodists would be rightfully humbled.

CHAPTER NINE

~~⁓~~

THE WITNESSES

CATHARINE WILLIAMS'S HOME STOOD
at 20 Olney Street in Providence, Rhode Island,
once the site of the Liberty Tree elm and Joseph
Olney's tavern, both featured as landmarks during
the Revolutionary War. Her house has now been
replaced by a stoplight at the intersection of Main
Street and Olney. The home she shared with her
young daughter, Amey, was within walking distance
of her family's tomb in the North Burial Ground.
By 1833, Catharine was entrenched in Providence's
community, spending many days at the nearby
Episcopal church.

She and Amey were thriving on the income of
her three latest books, each centered on the theme
of patriotism. The latest, titled **Aristocracy**, was so
successful that it was the first work she bothered
to copyright through the U.S. Congress; in 1831,

America revised its copyright law, which extended the original copyright term from fourteen years to twenty-eight years, making copyrighting more attractive to authors (the process to apply could be laborious). As Catharine grew older and faced more trials and frustrations, her self-confidence seemed to grow amid the hardships of a divorce and her troubles rearing an ornery child. It's easy to see her progress in her writing, along with her indignation. With each page of **Fall River**, her anger at Ephraim Avery, at the Methodists, swelled. Really, Catharine blamed the distorted morality of the evangelical Methodists for all of Sarah's troubles. She was trapped, Catharine contended. At a Methodist meeting, with the moaning and jerking, earnest prayer enveloped in suggestive motions, Sarah and other young women like her were closely watched and quietly criticized by hypocrites.

"If they go and return protected as they ought to be by one of the other sex, barbarous insinuations will sometimes be made," Catharine argued. "If on the contrary they wander about from meeting to meeting alone, they are immediately censured."

A woman like Sarah was cornered—how was she permitted to be fanatical at meetings but simply demure at work and home? How could they expect her to exude her love of God, then quickly conform to the stern standards of the Puritans in her everyday life? Sarah was unable to.

Catharine Williams stood near the Old Colony

House, the redbrick, Georgian-style courthouse in Newport, on the morning of Monday, May 6, 1833. The murder trial would take place on the lower floor of the two stories; horse and buggies ringed the large brick building. Had she lived, Sarah would have turned thirty-one just three days earlier. Catharine watched in amazement as a procession of supporters for Ephraim Avery arrived. She described them as "an army of preachers, stout muscular men . . . followed by a company of women as a 'corps de reserve'—and flanked by a hundred and sixty witnesses." She noted how the city swarmed with people from every religious denomination, all curious to see the Methodist minister who was accused of murder. Catharine began referring to Avery as "the prisoner." Both sides felt immense mistrust for the other.

"There was a deep anxiety that truth should be brought to light by the friends of justice and humanity," she said, "and a restless and watchful one with others, to prevent, if possible, its development."

At 10:00 a.m., the two supreme court justices sat on the bench, peering down at the defendant's table and then over to the spectator gallery. The case of the **State of Rhode Island v. Ephraim K. Avery** was set to begin nearly five months after Sarah Cornell died. The prosecution and the defense reviewed their notes and attempted to anticipate juror questions: Was Ephraim Avery spotted near John Durfee's farm in Tiverton the night of Sarah's

death? What was her mood the night she left the
Fall River boardinghouse, determined to complete
a secret errand? Who was the author of the mysterious anonymous letters found in her trunk, the notes
that very likely drew her to her death? I hired a document examiner who will later tell us conclusively
who the author was.

Did Sarah suspect that she was in peril, thus penning that foreboding message that named Avery? Or
was it innocuous? What was the timeline of Sarah's
death? Was there an attempted abortion? And, most
crucially, did Sarah Cornell take her own life or was
she murdered by Reverend Ephraim Avery?

Catharine Williams declared that she knew the
answers to each of those queries, and every piece
completed the puzzle of Sarah's final hours. As the
author sat in the court's gallery, hands on a notepad,
she glared at Ephraim Avery and issued an unflat-
tering description.

"The trial came on, and the prisoner was produced," she wrote. "He was a middle-aged man,
tall, and of very stout frame, and a face that might
have passed for good looking, had not a certain iron
look."

Like most ministers in the 1800s, Avery was
dressed in black with a broad-brimmed black hat.
He had a cool air about him, according to most people there, though he seemed to have suffered from
poor health after five months in a frigid jail cell.

"His face is great attenuated," said one observer,

"and its complexion might almost be described as cadaverous."

Avery nodded at the pair of judges and each attorney before they all took their seats. Now the chore of selecting a jury commenced, and it was an epic struggle for both sides. Defense attorney Richard K. Randolph glanced at the pool of fifteen men and shook his head. These men should come from elsewhere, not locally, he declared. He requested a larger selection of potential jurors, from an array of neighboring counties. The chief justice declined the request to cherry-pick from different districts but agreed to offer both sides a larger selection. An additional forty-five men were added to the pool, and selection began the following day. On Tuesday morning, the courtroom was filled with sixty potential jurors, all eyeing the prisoner. Avery seemed stoic but even more worn than the previous day.

"He appeared feverish and somewhat less composed than yesterday," reported one observer. "He was dressed in a dark frock coat, black vest and pantaloons, and an overcoat of nearly the same color as the under one; he wore spectacles of a purple hue."

Catharine refused to believe that Avery felt a bit of fret as he hovered over the defense table. He seemed to even appear mildly haughty.

"[He] 'looked like no fool'; or to use the language of the spectators, 'looked as though he knew more than he told for,'" she wrote.

Avery was placed at the bar and asked once again

how he pleaded, to which he replied, "Not guilty." The clerk asked, "How will you be tried?" Avery replied, "By God and my country." The clerk said, "God send you a good deliverance."

As Avery sat with his attorneys, Catharine marveled at the great suffering the attorney general had endured before testimony even began. Sixty men each needed to be thoroughly interviewed for latent biases against Sarah Cornell. Jury selection is, in many ways, the most important exercise during a criminal trial. But the defense found it difficult to find impartial jurors, thanks to the fervor churned up by the local press. The attorney general asked each of the jurors these three questions: "Are you related to the prisoner or to the deceased? Have you any conscientious scruples against finding a man guilty of a crime punishable with death? Have you formed any opinion of the guilt or innocence of [the] prisoner?" It was the final question that seemed to stall jury selection—**do you have an opinion about this case?**

"So strong was the presumption of the prisoner's guilt that it seemed almost impossible to find a man who had not made up his mind," wrote Catharine, "and this mind was pretty rudely and unequivocally expressed by all on the spot."

Catharine observed that few people claimed to be neutral and only one felt empathy for Avery.

"It was not until after one hundred and eight were challenged that a jury could be found," she wrote. "The difficulty was materially increased by the prisoner's counsel . . . who fought the ground inch by inch with so little apparent reverence to the authorities of the law that many a native of Rhode-Island blushed to hear the highest court in his state dictated to thus by a Boston lawyer."

Catharine held biases not only against churches other than hers but also against self-righteous lawyers from such uncivilized cities as Boston. Her quip likely produced a snicker from her likeminded contemporary admirers, but it reads like pretension to me.

The attorney general gazed at the man sitting before him. Both sides had already dismissed numerous candidates who simply couldn't remain open-minded. Albert Greene asked the man, "Have you so far made up your mind as not to be able to give the cause an impartial trial?" The juror thought for a moment and replied, "I do not think I have." The defense attorney walked over and asked, "You think then, notwithstanding your bias, you could give this cause an impartial hearing?" The juror nodded and replied, "I think I could." Both men agreed that this juror was acceptable.

The clerk turned to Ephraim Avery and said, "Juror, look upon the prisoner, prisoner, look upon the juror. What say you prisoner, will you be tried by this juror? If not, make your objection, and you will be heard."

Avery eyed the man and responded, "I have no

objection." The juror then placed his hand on the Bible, swore to God, and took his seat in the jury box. By the end of the day, Ephraim Avery's jury was still in need of six jurors. The court ordered sixty more potential jurors to appear the next day to the chagrin of everyone, including Avery. By the conclusion of Wednesday, the jury was complete. The following morning, Ephraim Avery faced his adversaries, Attorney General Albert Greene and Congressman Dutee Pearce. The latter opened for the prosecution and laid out the case.

"We shall show to you that on the 21st of December, 1832, Sarah Maria Cornell was found dead, suspended at a stake near a stack of hay, on the estate of John Durfee, in the town of Tiverton, one half, or three fourths of a mile from the village of Fall River," declared Pearce. "That she left her boarding house in Fall River, the preceding evening, at six o'clock, in health, and in usual spirits."

Pearce contended that the physical evidence, including the position of her body, showed conclusively that Sarah could **not** have taken her own life. Sarah had been strangled, he asserted, her neck was not broken, as he believed it would have been in a suicide. The clove hitch knot was impossible to draw with one hand, he declared. Pearce believed that "the body [had been] subsequently carried to the stake and fastened there, to give an impression that she had committed suicide." There were marks and bruises on her corpse that were unexplained—large hands had caused at least some of them. There were signs of a struggle—her expensive, precious comb had been broken in two. **This was murder**, Pearce bellowed to the jury.

"This is the starting point for your inquiries in this case," said Pearce. "The next consideration will be, from whose hands did that violence proceed."

Avery shifted in his seat. Pearce detailed the supposed relationship between the minister and the mill girl: he promised to prove, through letters and witnesses, that the two had a contentious, intimate relationship that eclipsed that of preacher and parishioner. He was an abuser, a rapist, and she had been his victim. If the jury indeed believed that Sarah Cornell had been murdered, then her killer could be no one other than Ephraim Avery.

"If we show her situation, previous to her death to have been such as to render her removal, out of the way, desirable to the prisoner," insisted Pearce, "and that the circumstances attending her death were such as to induce a strong presumption that he was the author of the violence, we shall have presented to you a probability of the guilt of the prisoner."

A litany of information I had never heard before spilled out at the start of the trial. Pearce promised to challenge Avery's dubious alibi for December 20, 1833. **Where was he?** Avery claimed he had been alone on a walk near the village of Fall River. But the State claimed it could trace him from his home in Bristol to Tiverton to John Durfee's farm and then back to Bristol again. There was a roster of witnesses gathered, waiting to take the stand.

"If, Gentlemen, these circumstances are proved to you, in a chain of connexion beyond a reasonable doubt, we have made out a case of strong, irresistible, presumptive evidence, from which it is impossible to escape without a conviction of his guilt," argued Pearce.

The State was certain of its evidence: Ephraim Avery was a sexual predator, preying on naive factory girls; he attacked Sarah Cornell, got her pregnant, and when she demanded child support, he snapped. He premeditated her murder, drawing her to John Durfee's farm late one December night with unsigned letters, promising to listen to her pleas. He might even offer child support. Instead, he tried to abort the baby through physical violence, and when she fought back, Avery strangled Sarah and then staged it as a suicide. His facade of a pious, evangelical reverend ministering to grateful parishioners and preaching the word of God was crumbling. Greene and Pearce acknowledged that their case was largely circumstantial. But frankly, most cases in the 1800s were circumstantial because of a lack of reliable forensic tools.

"I am aware it will be said that there is no **positive** proof," said Pearce. "But there are some of the strongest cases of conviction, where there is no positive proof. Positive proof can be rarely found, in the commission of such crimes."

Even today, oftentimes the strongest cases **are** circumstantial. Most prosecutors would prefer a bevy of circumstantial evidence rather than one positive DNA sample that can be disputed. But forensic investigator Paul Holes, who helped solve the notorious Golden State Killer case, told me that circumstantial evidence can be subjective, based solely on the investigator's own experience. And his gut instinct has led him in the wrong direction before.

"Based on my own personal experiences," he said, he has often been faced with circumstantial evidence "that makes it seem like this person is responsible," until additional evidence takes the case in a new direction. "That's what I have seen, particularly with the Golden State killer, where I made what I felt were very strong circumstantial cases against multiple suspects—only to have them eliminated by DNA." This, he laments, "shows the weakness of utilizing our intuition"—or at least, **only** our intuition.

Juries in the 1800s demanded definitive proof of guilt, as do juries in the twenty-first century.

"We've seen too many people that were convicted on circumstantial cases that today are being exonerated by DNA," Holes warned.

The jurors staring back at Pearce silently hoped for a witness to the murder, someone who would definitively tie Avery to Sarah Cornell's death. Pearce assured them that an eyewitness wasn't necessary in this case.

"Suppose two witnesses swear positively that they saw the act committed, and know the perpetrator," said Pearce. "A jury would not hesitate to convict. And yet where is the certainty in this case? The verdict may be wrong; the witnesses may have been deceived, or they may have perjured themselves."

But a trail of circumstances can seem unbreakable. A retired district attorney once compared a circumstantial case to a stack of pencils. Take each clue on its own and it could be easily snapped, but together the stack of clues is solid. Albert Greene and Dutee Pearce assured the panel that they had an unbreakable case.

"Any man can swear that he saw a murder committed by a certain man," said Pearce. "But a chain of circumstantial evidence must be made out, and put together, link by link, by persons so situated as to preclude the possibility of design, concert, or perjury."

The twelve men fidgeted in the jury box. This was a capital case—if convicted, Ephraim Avery would swing from the public gallows, and despite their punitive leanings, jurors in New England felt queasy at the thought of executing an innocent man. Dutee Pearce assured them that Ephraim Avery was **not** virtuous. He was a depraved wolf, searching for a flock of sheep to follow his word until they were no longer useful. Sarah Cornell, a factory girl, was ambushed by him almost from the start. After lecturing the courtroom for forty-five minutes, Pearce stood before the jury, paused, and issued a warning.

"If you have taken your seats in that box, with the oath of God upon you that you stand equally impartial between the prisoner and the state," he said, "and are actuated by other feelings and wishes than those I have described, let me tell you, you are in a worse situation than the man whom you are to try. You have already committed perjury."

With that admonition, the attorney general and his cocounsel turned to the gallery and called their first and, in some ways, their most important witness: Tiverton farmer John Durfee. As he sat in the witness chair, Durfee recounted the morning he discovered Sarah Cornell hanging from a haystack pole, just as he had done for Catharine.

"Her hair was over her face in such a manner I parted it a way, to ascertain if she was dead or alive," he testified. "Her shoes were off, and feet standing as close together as if they had been tied together. Her toes on the ground. Knees bent nearly to the ground."

The farmer stood up and then stooped down to demonstrate.

"Her heels nearly perpendicular, and her knees nearly to the ground, at a right angle," Durfee said.

Durfee explained how he and his father, Richard, had cut her down from the pole. He loaded her body onto a horse-drawn cart to prepare for her burial before leaving for Mrs. Hathaway's boardinghouse to retrieve burial clothes. He and the matrons discovered the four letters in her trunk, as well as the slip of paper naming Avery in her bandbox. The court clerk handed a file of papers to Durfee, and he selected four from the stack, each letter confirmed to be one found in the trunk. Three were anonymous and addressed to Sarah; one was sealed and penned in her own hand, the one addressed to Reverend Ira Bidwell. Durfee described the knot on the marline rope around her neck, the clove hitch knot; he explained how he had exhumed Sarah's body twice. Durfee also described a man near his house on the night of December 20, a stranger. The farmer said the man was a quarter mile away and had his back to him, but he did notice some features.

"The person I saw was a tall man. He had on a surtout and black hat. The size of the hat appeared rather a larger brim than usual," he testified. "The crown I thought was higher than common. I did not see his face, and did not see him move."

Durfee was able to corroborate physical details of the scene at his farm. Next on the witness list was Williams Durfee, John's brother, who also reported to the homestead that morning; he had been the first to examine Sarah's neck and quickly identified the type of knot as a clove hitch.

"I tried to pick the string out with my fingers, and could not, my nails being short and I called for Joseph Cook to help me," said the retired mariner. "He called for a knife and I told him not to cut because it would wound the flesh. I discovered that the string of her calash was under the cords round her neck."

Sarah had been wearing her headdress when she was hanged from the pole, Williams Durfee was certain. Durfee's most important note was his certainty that the knot was a clove hitch: much of the State's case rested on its contention that Sarah could not have tied a clove hitch to take her own life.

Another witness, Seth Darling, took the stand. The elderly man had rushed over and examined the rope on the haystack pole as others tended to Sarah's body.

"I then examined the string on the stake," said Darling. "The stake, I judge, was five feet high, or five and a half-high. The string appeared to be four strands, hanging from the stake, the ends about four inches from it."

Sarah was slightly taller than five feet, so she certainly could have tied the rope to the stake herself, and no one seemed to dispute that. Darling also confirmed that the rope around her neck was tied with a clove hitch. That seems unusual to me; according to the witnesses, the end of the rope around the top of the stake was a slip knot, but the knot around her throat was a clove hitch. Seth Darling was curious too.

"I was surprised, when I saw the cord taken off that it went round twice," he told the jury. "Up to that time I supposed she had committed suicide."

"Why were you surprised?" asked the attorney general.

"I had been impressed it was suicide," said Darling, "and finding a knot so different from any I supposed, I could not account for it."

Darling subscribed to the same theory: if a simpler, more foolproof knot could be used in a suicide, why not use it? It seemed so haphazard. But that was also the case for murder—why would a killer use two different knots?

Seth Darling was helpful because he served as the prosecutor's entrée into the controversy over the three anonymous letters found in Sarah Cornell's trunk. She had told her family that she had written to Avery, which of course he denied. But Darling was at the post office in Fall River on November 19, one month before Sarah died; he saw two letters from the same customer drop into his box: one to Sarah's brother-in-law and one to Ephraim Avery. The insinuation was that the postal customer was Sarah Cornell.

"I made up the mail on Monday morning, the 19th of November," testified Darling. "My impression is—"

"Don't bring in any impression," snapped one of Avery's defense attorneys.

"My recollection, as far as it goes, is that a letter came to the office that day, directed to the Rev. E. K. Avery, Bristol, and one to Grindall Rawson of South Woodstock."

Richard Randolph, with the defense, eyed the elderly witness. Darling recalled that as soon as the name Ephraim Avery came up regarding Sarah's death, he remembered the letter.

"Are you willing to swear that the letter was directed to Avery?" demanded Randolph.

"That is my impression, powerfully," was the reply.

The attorney general was building his circumstantial case with each witness, and so far, he had effectively made these points: Sarah knew Ephraim Avery and she had responded to his letter, which was certainly one of the anonymous letters. The clove hitch knot was impossible to use during a suicide—and not a logical choice. Why not use a slip knot? And a mysterious man matching Ephraim Avery's physical description was in the area the night of Sarah's death. The case against the Methodist minister was solidifying.

Dr. Foster Hooper braced himself as he sat down in the witness chair. The young physician suspected that the defense would try to undermine his medical expertise, particularly concerning Sarah's injuries and the age of the fetus. Dr. Hooper was just five years out of medical school, but he was dauntless as he replied confidently to Albert Greene. Dr. Hooper described the extensive injuries on Sarah's knees, her thighs, her hips, and her abdomen. Her neck had not been broken; the twine had strangled her, but it could have been murder or suicide.

"The uterus was examined, in which was found a female fetus, supposed about half grown, gone about half her time," testified Dr. Hooper. "It required rather minute examination to ascertain the sex."

He described her throat, her lungs, and her heart before decomposition had advanced. When Greene asked if she had appeared to be manually strangled, Hooper said her face seemed paler than he would have expected of someone who had hanged herself.

Richard Randolph, the defense attorney, jumped up from his seat for cross-examination.

"Did you not commence the examination with a strong impression that the deceased had been murdered?"

This seemed accusatory, but Dr. Hooper remained calm.

"I had the impression from the first examination that the death was by violence," he replied.

Randolph glared at the young physician, and his questioning took a sudden turn.

"Did you not deliver an anti-masonic lecture in Swanzey?"

Dr. Hooper paused and replied, "I did."

Confused, the chief justice interrupted: "Mr. Randolph, I do not perceive what that has to do with this trial."

Randolph replied that after this lecture, in which Dr. Hooper criticized the Freemasons, privately the physician told people that he believed Ephraim Avery and the two examining judges from Avery's initial hearing in Bristol were all members of the secret fraternity—he seemed to be the source of that rumor. The State objected, but the defense replied: "We wish to show the state of mind under which the witness testifies." The chief justice considered the argument.

"Anything which shows the feelings of the witness toward the prisoner is undoubtedly proper."

Dr. Hooper sat up, relieved to be allowed to explain. He looked at the judge and the jury and said that someone credible had offered him the information about the Freemasons. But his medical opinion in this case was sound.

"Have you any prejudices, or have you ever had any, against Mr. Avery?" asked Dutee Pearce for the State.

"None at all" was the reply.

Randolph then stood up.

"Can you tell the precise age of a fetus from its length?"

"I do not know that I can," replied Dr. Hooper.

"You were brought here as a scientific witness," Randolph retorted, "and I should think ought to know."

Dr. Hooper replied that, according to his medical

books, the fetus was roughly four months old. Sarah likely became pregnant at the end of August, as she had claimed.

So far, the witnesses had all bolstered the State's claim that Sarah was truthful. The next day, Dr. Thomas Wilbur took the stand for a contentious battle with the defense. He described his tearful meetings with Sarah months before her death. Wilbur still seemed shaken as he detailed his examination of her body. He had been bothered by her cloak—it was heavy and hooked; the opening where she could have stretched her arms through was just about a foot. Randolph asked, "What did you see that day that led to suspicion of violence?"

"The tightness of the string around the neck, the situation of the cloak and the gloves, led me to suspect," said Wilbur. "I said to my family after getting home, I thought it possible, but for the cord, that she might have got her hands out of the cloak, and hung herself."

Randolph replied sharply.

"Might she not, with sufficient resolution have drawn a common slip noose as tight as this was?"

Dr. Wilbur scoffed. He estimated that Sarah weighed no more than 115 pounds.

"That young woman's weight sagging down on the string could not have drawn it so tight, I think."

Remember what Paul Holes told us earlier: the weight of a petite person would have tightened a clove hitch knot sufficiently. But Dr. Wilbur was sure that his patient was dead by someone else's hand—he believed that she must have been horizonal when she received those injuries.

"The ground from the place where her comb was found is rough, some briars and pudding stones," he said. They might have caused some of her injuries. But investigators found no blood evidence on the ground below her or nearby.

When Dr. Wilbur stepped off the stand, Catharine admired him. The testimony of men like John Durfee and Thomas Wilbur strengthened the State's case against Avery. But the author was saddened as each witness concluded his testimony, adding pieces to the puzzle of Sarah Cornell's final moments.

"Every succeeding one brought to light new barbarities, and imagination sickens at the idea of the cruel butchery which this most unfortunate girl must have undergone, previous to her being strangled," wrote Catharine in **Fall River**. "No person could hear them unmoved."

Benjamin Manchester, one of the laborers who discovered the cord missing, took the stand next. He had reported to the stackyard when John Durfee called for him that morning.

"I noticed the cord, because someone said they guessed she was a weaver; she had got a weaver's knot round the stake," said Manchester. "I took hold the line and replied, I guess she was more of a sailor than a weaver, for she has taken two hair hitches round the standing part."

Now a handful of witnesses had confirmed that the knot situated by Sarah Cornell's neck was a clove hitch. Manchester also believed that Avery was the man he had seen near the Durfee farm on the night of December 20, though he wasn't close enough to see his face. The matrons who dressed Sarah's body all testified to evidence of "rash violence" found on her body—but they weren't certain of what **type** of violence.

"I have said she looked as if she had very harsh means used upon her, and I think so now," said Meribah Borden, John Durfee's sister. "I can't tell if she had violence."

Randolph turned to Borden and accused her of backpedaling from her opinion during the previous hearing in Bristol, where Avery was released from charges.

"Did you not say she had been forced?" he barked.

"The question was not asked me at Bristol," Borden calmly replied. "I am not obliged to tell all my thoughts. I will tell all I know. Whether he had done it, or any other man, it is not for me to say. She looked as if she had been shamefully abused, but what means were taken, it is not for me to say."

The other women had described the extensive injuries, including the image of fingerprints that seemed to belong to a man, imprinted on her body.

Dorcas Ford said she believed that Sarah had been sexually assaulted. Randolph attacked her credibility too.

"What did you say at Bristol? Did you not say you thought she had been forced?"

"I was asked if there had been an attempt to produce abortion, and I said no," said Ford. "My opinion is she had been dreadfully abused."

Then Dorcas Ford gave a fascinating answer to a simple question by the State: Did you believe that a man killed her?

"I suppose her life was forced from her," replied Ford. "And you must judge in what way yourselves."

Her vague reply was maddening for the men at the defense table, but I think it's quite smart. Ford seemed to be saying that whether Sarah Cornell had died by her own hand or by someone else's hand . . . that a man was responsible. The chief justice asked her the question again and her response was the same.

"I shall give no other answer than I have."

Randolph for the defense rose and angrily declared in Ford's direction: "The witness says she shall give no other answer, and as I have only two courses to pursue, to move to commit her, or let her go, as she is a woman, I prefer the latter."

And all this, in just the first week of testimony.

CHAPTER TEN

~⸙~

THE LETTERS

SARAH MARIA CORNELL HELD THE yellow paper in her hand about one month before her death. She reflected on her visit with her personal physician several weeks earlier. Dr. Thomas Wilbur had been so helpful to her, the way a father might guide his child. Sarah had disclosed that Reverend Ephraim Avery had tried to convince her to take the potentially deadly oil of tansy to induce an abortion. The physician seemed appalled, and then strongly encouraged her to demand financial support from the minister. Sarah wept but agreed. Now, in November, she told her family that she had received a response from Avery on November 13, after requesting funds.

"I wrote to him last week informing him my fears," Sarah wrote on November 18, 1832. "I told him he must not deny it, if he did I should expose him immediately. I have received the following answer without any name."

Catharine Williams now examined the anonymous reply on yellow paper. She examined the neat, slanted writing, penned in what seemed like a rush, with a nervous flair at the end. She later transcribed it for her readers. If the author of the yellow letter was indeed Avery, then the Methodist minister responded to Sarah the next day from a post office in Warren, Rhode Island. Sarah told her family that she disclosed to him that she was pregnant, but without Sarah's letters, it's hard to know precisely what she said. The letter writer's response felt urgent, even desperate.

"Miss Cornell, I have just received your letter with no small surprise, and will say, I will do all you ask, only keep your secrets," it read. "I wish you to write me as soon as you get this, naming some time and place where I shall see you, and then look for answer before I come; and will say whether convenient or not, and will say the time. I will keep your letters till I see you, and wish you to keep mine, and have them with you there at the time. Write soon—say nothing to no one. Yours in haste."

If this was written by Ephraim Avery, as Catharine suspected, then he was arranging for their meeting the following month on John Durfee's farm— and he also seemed to be issuing a warning about keeping secrets. Five days later, Sarah wrote that letter to her sister, Lucretia, and Lucretia's husband, Reverend Grindall Rawson. Sarah's letter was not admitted into evidence, likely because it was hearsay. Catharine didn't mention Sarah's letter about the anonymous note in her book. Either she wasn't aware of it or she purposely omitted it. The latter seems unlikely, because it was very damning. Catharine didn't believe that Sarah had ever mentioned Avery by name in any of her letters. And she felt confused by it.

"As to the opinion of attachments on the part of S. M. Cornell towards her minister," wrote Catharine Williams in 1833, "we ground it on these facts. First, by her letters themselves, not merely because they show a decline in religious zeal . . . but from this circumstance—that the name of Avery is never mentioned by her in any of them."

Catharine wondered why Sarah never mentioned Avery, yet the names of other ministers peppered her letters. Was she protecting Avery out of reverence, embracing the religious milieu in New England?

"His name she studiously avoids," wrote Catharine. "Whether it was by her contrivance or his however, it is impossible for us to say, since she cannot tell, and he won't tell."

But now I know that Sarah **did** name Ephraim Avery, openly criticizing him to her family. Sarah Cornell had clearly lost her patience with the minister; she was preparing to stand up for herself. She described her angst at seeing Avery at a prayer meeting in Fall River two days earlier. The contents of Sarah's writings are heart-wrenching. She first tried to talk with him, but he declined because there were too many people around after the meeting. She threatened to visit him in Bristol, where he lived. He paused and promised to see her in Fall River soon. **Don't come to Bristol**, he urged her. When Sarah and Avery met, they spoke about her pregnancy for about an hour.

"He said . . . that if that was my case it was not his, and said I must go to a doctor immediately," she wrote to her sister and brother-in-law, "said he had burned my letters—if he had known what would have happened he would have kept them."

It sounded to me as if Avery was threatening to blackmail her, and he wished he had not disposed of her letters. Sarah said Avery told her he would help, but she needed to stay quiet.

"[He] said I must never swear to it, for if that was my case he would take care of me," she wrote.

I didn't read that last section as a threat, but as a promise to take care of her if she stayed quiet. He seemed effusive about his wife and family, almost begging her to stay silent, for his sake. Sarah wrote:

"[He said] I must say it belonged to a man that was dead, for, said he, I am dead to you—that is I cannot marry you. He owned and denied it two or three times."

Avery said that if she didn't reveal that he was the father, he would support her. She begged her brother-in-law to avoid exposing Avery, but only if he made the financial concessions.

"I pledged him my word and honor I would not expose him if he would settle it," Sarah wrote to her family. "Therefore, you must not mention his name to anyone. If it should come out, you can say it belonged to a Methodist minister, but that we settled it, and that I do not choose to tell whose it is."

Sarah then transcribed Avery's response to her, his shock at her threat to unmask him if he didn't comply with her request.

"I suppose he wishes me to return his letter, therefore I have copied it," Sarah told the Rawsons. "I have written to him again, and am expecting any answer every day. What the result will be, I know not. I still have hopes and fears."

She told her family that there was a woman in her mill who had a child and began working six weeks after the birth.

"She gets her child boarded for fifty cents a week," Sarah wrote. "Shall try to save six dollars a month this winter."

Sarah seemed determined to raise the baby, with or without Ephraim Avery's help. She felt frightened but invigorated. A child might offer her a deeper purpose than simply embracing her independence— unconditional love. Her closing at the end of the final letter they received from her felt sorrowful.

"My love to my mother. You must burn this letter. Farewell. Your sister, Sarah M. Cornell."

Sarah apparently responded to Avery, pressing her demand for money and a meeting. This is where the trial of Ephraim Avery continues. The prosecutor detailed how, weeks after she sent that letter, Avery decided to meet with her.

———

John Orswell bundled up as he stood on the steamboat **King Philip** when it was moored in Providence, Rhode Island, on November 22. Orswell was the engineer that day, the person who would guide the boat from Providence to Fall River. Between eight and nine o'clock that morning, a man strolled down the steamboat's gangplank, pink letter in hand. He asked the engineer to hand deliver it to the Cole family in Fall River, the owners of the house where Sarah was boarding. Orswell pointed to the letterbox, but the man shook his head.

"He said he did not want it to go in the letter box, but wanted it delivered, as soon as it got there," he testified. "He insisted upon me carrying it; said it would do him a great favor, and took the letter from under his cloak, and handed it to me with a ninepence."

Orswell agreed and took stock of the man—tall and thin with a dark jacket. He believed the man to be Ephraim Avery, but like many of the other witnesses, he refused to swear to it because he had never met the minister.

"Are you positive that Mr. Avery is the man?" asked Richard Randolph, the defense attorney.

"According to the best of my recollection and judgment he is the man," Orswell replied. The engineer's testimony would be important because of the contents of the envelope, sometimes called in court "the pink letter." The anonymous author wrote, in part:

"Dear Sister—I received your letter in due season and should have answered it before now but I thought I would wait till this opportunity—as I told you I am willing to help you."

"Sister" would have been a common term for a woman in the Methodist Church, just as "brother" was. The writer of the pink letter suggested that they meet on December 18 or alternatively, if the weather was bad, on December 20. He left detailed instructions on where to meet and begged for a reply if the proposed plan wouldn't work for her.

"Write me soon and tell me which," he wrote. "When you write direct your letters to Betsey Hills and not as you have done to me. Remember this your last letter I am afraid was broken open. Ware [sic] your calash not your plain bonnet. You can send your letter by mail. . . . Let me still injoin the secret—keep the letters in your bosom or burn them up."

That letter was posted on November 22. The next anonymous letter was sent December 8 from Fall River. The prosecutor wanted to show that Avery was in the town on that day, buying stationery and then posting the letter. A witness who recognized Avery sat now on the stand. He recalled that the minister was in his stationery shop in Fall River on December 8, 1832, twelve days before Sarah's death. This witness was interesting, because Iram Smith knew Ephraim Avery, as well as Reverend Bidwell; both men were in his store that morning. Neither man denied it, as Avery had spent the night at Bidwell's home. But the minister denied writing any letter addressed to Sarah Cornell. And the witness couldn't verify that either.

"As to what Mr. Avery did, I cannot say," Smith testified. "I have some recollection of his asking for paper. If he got it; he got it himself. . . . My impression is that I saw Mr. Avery at the desk."

A clerk in Smith's store remembered a man who was purchasing paper, a sheet of white paper that seemed to match the paper of one of the anonymous letters received by Sarah; the man, according to the clerk, mentioned writing a curt letter to the local newspaper, the **Fall River Weekly Recorder**. He **might** have torn the paper in half and penned something on the paper at the store's desk, but the clerk wasn't sure—he had tended to many customers since. Here's what that letter, dated December 8, allegedly said: "I will be here on the 20 if pleasant at the place named at 6 o'clock. If not pleasant the next Monday evening. Say Nothing."

The man opened the door of the store and turned

in the direction of the post office. The deputy postmaster believed he saw Avery drop a letter into the
mailbox, and that the deputy postmaster retrieved
the letter, which was apparently addressed to Sarah
M. Cornell. Days later, when Harvey Harnden,
the deputy sheriff, reported to Smith's store for evidence, Smith located the remaining half sheet of
paper and attempted to match its fibers to that of
the letter addressed to Sarah.

"It compared very well with the written half sheet
[the letter of December 8]," Smith testified. "I compared them; I did not see any difference. I handed
the half sheet to Col. Harnden."

This was certain proof, according to Catharine,
of Avery's lies when he denied writing and mailing
the anonymous letter on white paper on December
8 from Fall River.

"The circumstances of the letters were sworn to,"
wrote Catharine, "and half a sheet of paper found
in the store where the letter of the 8th of December
was supposed to be written, which exactly matched
one of the letters, both the water mark and even the
very fibres of the paper."

Again, this was a common paper, and the testimony was of no real value, just more vague circumstantial evidence, though it did place Avery
at a stationery store and near the post office. And
Iram Smith was unsure of many things, despite
Catharine's insistence that he could trace Avery's
movements. Attorney General Albert Greene asked

Smith to be more precise about his observations of Bidwell and Avery.

"State distinctly what you recollect about his using a piece of paper, or writing in your shop," Greene insisted.

"I don't know as I can state any more particular. I should not be willing to swear to any thing positively," replied Smith.

The chief justice asked, "Can't you tell what was done?"

Smith looked at the judges and shook his head.

"I can tell what I think I recollect."

Greene seemed frustrated.

"What does your doubt arise from? Have you any doubts now?"

"Sometimes," replied a defeated Smith, "and sometimes I have not."

He was not an especially helpful witness for the State, but Albert Greene carried on. There seemed to be no lack of people who had spotted Avery in Smith's store on December 8. Jeremiah Howland was browsing the products when he greeted the pair of ministers. Avery had a section of white paper in his hand, and he mentioned writing a letter to the newspaper, but Howland believed he heard Avery indicate that he would wait and write the letter at home.

There had been a lot of debate over witnesses and their unreliable memories—the defense constantly countered their testimony with phrases such as "Are you willing to swear he is the man?" Avery **might have** received a letter purportedly from Sarah on pink paper, but it was never located. None of it resulted in definitive evidence of even an intimate relationship, let alone murder. Avery could not be convincingly connected to the anonymous letters.

In modern times, the letters could be tested for DNA—though a sealant called a wafer was used in the early 1800s to seal envelopes, so saliva was not likely present. Today, the paper or the envelope could be examined for fingerprints; there would likely be CCTV footage, perhaps even inside Smith's store. The letter could be traced through the U.S. Postal Service. But, as I've discovered through decades of historical research, investigators in the nineteenth century had few forensic tools. Today we also have document examiners, and I hired a nationally renowned examiner to inspect the anonymous letters. I was hoping she'd tell me whether Ephraim Avery was the author, or perhaps it was Sarah. Or someone else entirely. What the expert would reveal, Paul Holes told me, could help make the case for murder.

"If everything seems to add up on that front, then there's a level of physical evidence there," he said.

The attorney general hoped that this series of letters created a picture for the men of the jury: Sarah Cornell had threatened to expose Ephraim Avery. Numerous witnesses could connect him to each letter, despite his denials of being the author. He had arranged a meeting with her for the night of her death. The letters, in addition to her note to her family, seemed to make the State's case: Ephraim Avery felt trapped by Sarah's threats, and he felt compelled to murder her. But could it be proven that Avery was the author of the letters? The attorney general said yes. But the defense claimed that Sarah herself had written them, to frame the Methodist minister. Who was right?

———

Richard Durfee understood death. The seventy-four-year-old was a church deacon and a retired military captain. He had ministered to the living and prayed for the dead. The father of ten had only five surviving children by December 1832, when he squinted down the hill from his front porch toward the haystack. His son John was yelling to him that morning, waving him down. Richard slid into a heavy coat and traversed the slick, muddy grass down the slope to join his son and two other men.

"[I] went to the stack, and looked over the fence," he told the court on Friday, May 10, 1833. "Saw her hair hanging in the most frightful manner I ever saw. Saw no sign of any thing on the ground, no appearance of any person having moved about in the stack yard. Her cloak and bonnet were in proper order, as though she had been living."

Few things shocked the seasoned soldier, but that

morning Richard Durfee was aghast. Catharine watched the faces of the two judges as they listened to Durfee's testimony. He described the vision of Sarah's frozen body swaying from the haystack pole.

"No person could hear them unmoved," she wrote; "the very judges, though used to the delineation of crime and pictures of violence, wept upon the bench; they wept like children at the description of her mangled person."

Richard Durfee detailed Sarah's burial as Catharine Williams watched the elderly man handle questions deftly on the stand. She felt anguish for Sarah Cornell, who had come to represent the struggle of a generation of young women, yearning for independence but in fear of the inevitable vulnerability bound to it. Sarah's somber burial in a barren, icy ground illustrated society's failure to protect its women.

"It was in the coldest part of the year," Catharine mused. "She had been laid in a dry and marly soil, was frozen when she was buried, and the earth frozen that was thrown upon her."

But Sarah Cornell had acquired advocates after death who never appeared in her short life. And now five months after her supposed murder, a small cadre of distinguished attorneys, who would have likely shunned her in life, were defending her honor in court.

The attorney general, Albert Greene, needed to establish a timeline. Sarah left Mrs. Hathaway's boardinghouse in Fall River sometime before dark on the night of her death, December 20, 1832. According to those anonymous letters, she was scheduled to meet someone at Durfee's farm in Tiverton around 7:00 p.m.

Near the Durfee property, a Welsh woman was cleaning dishes when she heard a meeting bell ringing: it was 7:30 p.m. Eleanor Owen's house was about a quarter mile from the stackyard—she could see it from her parlor window. As the bell tolled, she heard a screeching. She yelled to her son to go to their front door and listen.

"I sent the boy to the door; one boy was a coward," Owen recalled, "and said to another you may go. I told him you must go, and he did go, and when the door was open, then I heard the meeting bell." Her scared son carefully cracked open the door and reported that he heard nothing but the bell. But the time stamp was significant: Owen heard a scream thirty minutes after Sarah was scheduled to arrive at the farm.

Next, the attorney general called William Hamilton, who had been a crucial witness from the neighborhood that night. Hamilton was walking past the Durfee property at about 8:45 p.m., which is a little more than an hour past the time that Eleanor Owen heard the screams.

"In a hollow, past Durfee's house, the back part, I heard screeches, what I called squalls. Thought it was a human voice," Hamilton testified, "some female in distress, as though some person was beating her. Stifled groans continued until I started. When I got on the hill in front of the house, I stopped again, and heard nothing."

There's a troubling inconsistency because both witnesses seemed certain of the time: one used the predictable meeting bell; the other had a watch. Perhaps the first scream came from the attempted abortion, and, after being calmed, Sarah died— either by her own hand or by her killer's. The prosecutor didn't debate the difference—Albert Greene just wanted the jury to feel certain that there were screams coming from Durfee's farm that night. With that, the court recessed.

———

At nine o'clock the next morning, a Saturday, Catharine examined the jurors as they filed in. She knew that today the State would try to discredit Ephraim Avery's alibi. The minister had categorically denied ever seeing Sarah Cornell in Tiverton, or even visiting that area—he had left the morning of Sarah's death for a walking trip on a nearby island; he claimed that he wanted to visit an area where his father had fought during the Revolutionary War.

"I most solemnly declare that I was not at Fall River on the afternoon or evening of the 20th of December, 1832," Avery said, "that I had no interview with, nor saw Sarah M. Cornell on that evening."

The minister stated that he had left his home around two o'clock, walked to the ferry station, and took the boat from Bristol to Aquidneck. He had then proceeded on a solo adventure in the wilderness. The attorney general set out to prove that, instead of staying on the island, Avery took the old stone footbridge over to Tiverton to meet with Sarah. Catharine thought Avery's claims were preposterous.

"It was proved that the prisoner left his home on the 20th Dec. without any good reason without informing his family where he was going or assigning any excuse for absenting himself," she reported. "He observed he had been on a walk of pleasure and observation, walking about the island towards the coal mines, near the Union meetinghouse," wrote Catharine.

In fact, Avery claimed that he had come across several people on his travels: "When near the mines, I met a man carrying a gun, dressed in coarse old looking clothes, and an old hat, somewhat dented in on the front part of the crown," said Avery. "I soon came to a gate, one side of which was either painted white or white-washed; and after going through the gate, I passed between two houses, continuing nearly in the same direction. I came into a lot where were sheep and young cattle. Here I saw a lad 10 or 12 years old."

Avery's story was **very** detailed with notes about the terrain— "I passed over low, moist ground;

the travelling was across pastures, over walls, and through fields very rough and uneven."

He recalled which direction he traveled: "I crossed the west road, (which at that time I supposed to be a bridle way) bearing to the east." Avery explained his various ponderings for much of the trip as he searched for a parishioner at her home, whom he hoped to visit: "It being dark, I thought I might be troubled to find it, and so took the direction for the ferry," said Avery, "calculating I might, if too much fatigued, stop at Mr. Cook's, three or four miles up the Island."

When Avery arrived at the ferry house, he knocked. When the captain answered, Avery asked to be taken across to Bristol. The old man peeked outside and shook his head.

"I told him it was late, I told him it was inconvenient to cross as it was blowing hard, and very cold," testified Jeremiah Gifford. "He wanted to cross that night. He said Brother Warren had told him he could cross at any hour. I told him the weather was so tedious I could not cross."

Captain Gifford shivered inside his house as he eyed the stranger. He seemed fine.

"He had on a brownish colored surtout, rather longer than a box coat," said Gifford, "about the color of my coat. He had on a black hat. Brim rather wide. No spectacles at any time, to my recollection."

Incidentally, this description tallies with the

appearance of the stranger that witnesses spotted near the Durfee farm earlier that night.

"The man had on a dark colored surtout," Benjamin Manchester recalled, "and dark hat with a wide brim."

Still, as suspicious as it seems, those details are still circumstantial. Captain Gifford invited Avery inside to stay the night, and the next morning, the captain's daughter Jane Gifford made small talk.

"I shook hands with him, and asked how he did, and he asked me," she testified.

The young woman watched Avery holding a cane as he moved about the room.

"I did not know you preached on the island last night," Jane Gifford told him. "He said, 'I did not— I was over on business.'"

It's curious that Avery didn't tell Jane that he was simply taking a constitutional, but her testimony seemed to make the defense uncomfortable. The following week, they would try to discredit Jane's testimony. Avery arrived home in Bristol via rowboat helmed by the captain's son—he said he was desperate to return because his wife, Sophia, was ill. Sarah Cornell was discovered around the same time that morning.

Avery's description of his travels seemed too detailed to me, and I asked forensic investigator Paul Holes about it. Holes replied, "Tell me in great detail what you did two days ago." Of course, I couldn't.

"When you start to see an overabundance of detail, it's almost as if it's rehearsed," said Holes. "You know, they're trying to account for too much, because the average person doesn't remember their day-to-day activities."

I asked Holes about the circumstances—wouldn't you remember what you did on the day that changed your life, like the murder of someone you knew?

"If he's truly innocent, he doesn't know your victim is being killed or is committing suicide, so he's just going through his normal life," Holes replied. "And we may have snippets from a few days ago of what we did that day. But there's nothing substantive related to the victim that is going to be something that we will cement to our memories. It's almost like he's trying too hard to establish an alibi."

Catharine Williams didn't believe all those details from Ephraim Avery's day either.

"Crossed a brook, went through a white gate, saw a 'man with a gun, and a boy with some sheep,' and finally wandered back to the ferry somewhere about ten o'clock, on a cold December night, without any supper or appearing to think of any," wrote Catharine. "No man with a gun, or boy with sheep, could be heard of in that part of the country from anybody but himself, and no one saw him, through all that route."

The defense couldn't locate any of these witnesses; Avery was last positively identified stepping off the ferry that came from Bristol in the midafternoon and then when he knocked on Captain Gifford's door. There were as many as seven hours that were unaccounted for. Avery said that the witnesses who declared that they saw a tall man in black who seemed to resemble him near the Durfee farm were all mistaken—it wasn't him. But Catharine said there were more witnesses who could identify him in Tiverton than on a ramble on a remote island.

"No person had been seen on the route he pretended to have taken on that afternoon, but that a man answering his description exactly was traced step by step all the way to Fall River, even to the very stack yard," wrote Catharine.

Catharine followed the trial closely, summarizing the State's account of Avery's travels on December 20 and 21. But her details in this narrative were evasive—no one could **definitively** challenge Avery's alibi because no witnesses could positively identify him. Still, Catharine used phrases that were misleading to her readers and me.

"One man, Mr. Cranston, at Howland's ferry bridge, swore to his identity," she wrote. "Mr. Lawton, the man on the Tiverton side, remembered a person of his exact description passing at the same hour, three o'clock."

But that's not how the trial transcript reads. Peleg Cranston was the toll keeper that cold night; he remembered a stranger crossing as he stood bundled up inside the small tollbooth.

"He looked like a doctor, lawyer, or minister," Cranston testified. "He came up and said it was a cold, blustering day. He had his money in his hand. I asked him to walk in and warm. He said no, he was obliged to me, or thanked me; he was going to Fall River, or toward Fall River, and walked on."

Cranston indicated that the man was not known to him, which is quite different from Catharine's claim that he could swear to his identity. Cranston believed that Avery was the same man, but by that time, this story had circulated across New England.

If the attorney general could trap Avery in a lie, then he could discredit the minister's defense, but by the second week of testimony, there simply wasn't enough information to prove that Avery had gone to Tiverton. This was a common theme of all the witnesses who saw the mysterious man with the broad-brimmed hat: he **could** have been Avery. But again, what if it **had been** Avery? What if Sarah and Avery did meet, he tried to force an abortion on her but then left, and she took her own life? That's what we were trying to uncover.

Next, Catharine focused on the cord, the marline twine made of hemp, that was wrapped around Sarah Cornell's throat.

"The cord was identified as belonging to some bags that lay in a cart of Mr. Durfee's within a few rods," she wrote.

That's not exactly true. Abner Davis testified that there was cord missing from several bags nearby, but there was no way to prove where it came from. Besides, Sarah herself could have taken the cord in preparation for her suicide attempt. But if Avery **did** kill Sarah, the cord meant that, perhaps, her murder wasn't premeditated. He might have hoped to talk her into having an abortion, and when she refused, their confrontation escalated.

On the night of Sarah's death, Gardner Coit stood behind the bar of Lawton's Hotel in Fall River, tending to customers. The clock read 5:45 p.m. when a tall man in a fur cap requested supper and a glass of brandy. Coit nodded and served him food, after the server handed him the snifter. They both watched as the stranger left the hotel's sitting room.

"I do not think I could recognize his features. Do not know that I have seen him since," Coit testified. "He went out after paying for his supper. He came alone and went alone. He was dressed in dark clothes."

Neither the barkeep nor the waitress could say positively that Avery was the man they had served. But Catharine's version of their testimonies veered from that in the trial transcripts.

"A man answering his description went into the back room of Lawton's hotel, early in the evening on that day, and had a glass of brandy carried in," wrote Catharine. "They did not know Avery, but upon seeing him, believed him to be the same person."

In fact, each of the handful of transcripts have slightly different tilts, depending on the reporter.

Some favored the defense, while others favored the prosecutor. Now I must consult not only the main trial transcript but multiple versions of it from different reporters to create an accurate picture.

As the reader moves through Catharine's book **Fall River**, it's difficult not to be swayed by her argument: Catharine offered seemingly irrefutable proof of Avery's guilt. But as Rhode Island's attorney general called witnesses to the stand during the second week, it became clear that the State's circumstantial evidence lacked the potency that Catharine so deftly presented on her own pages. A litany of witnesses all walked past Ephraim Avery, each swearing to tell the truth. Some declared that a man who looked just like the Methodist minister was in Fall River on December 20, but none could say with absolute certainty. The color of the man's jacket, even its style, varied. The estimation of the man's height was inconsistent; even the size of his hat seemed off. Ephraim Avery's features appeared to be nondescript, unfortunately for the attorney general: he was tall and prone to wearing dark clothing and large hats. Sometimes he had facial hair and sometimes he wore spectacles, which complicated the identification. Sometimes he carried a cane. Avery denied crossing the bridge between Tiverton and Rhode Island, but some witnesses suspected it was him. But as each took the stand, Avery's defense attorney dismantled their testimony—either they were too far away or too distracted, or it was too dark outside to see well. They testified to the man's gait, but even that changed depending on the time of day. George Lawton owned the hotel where Avery allegedly had supper that night. He believed that he saw him crossing the bridge toward Tiverton on foot around three o'clock on the day of Sarah's death.

"It looked so much like the man, I had seen on the bridge, I had quite a serious feeling," Lawton testified. "I can't describe what the feeling was."

Avery's attorney jumped up from his table on cross-examination and addressed Lawton.

"Can you swear to the jury that Avery is the same man, you saw on the 20th on the bridge?"

Lawton took a moment and replied, "I do not swear it was the same man, I say it resembles the man."

Richard Randolph pressed Lawton: "What do you understand by identifying a man?"

Lawton tried to clarify by answering that identifying a man meant swearing under oath that he could recognize him.

Well? Randolph said.

"I do not swear positively that is the man, I saw on the bridge," Lawton admitted. "He resembles him."

A parade of witnesses claimed to have spotted him around Fall River and Tiverton that day—but none was certain, which is dangerous, even today. According to the Innocence Project, "Eyewitness misidentification contributes to an overwhelming majority of wrongful convictions that have been overturned by post-conviction DNA testing."

Witnesses are often unreliable, especially if they're witnessing or surviving a traumatic crime. For his part, Avery could not provide a witness who saw him strolling along the paths of the rural island where he claimed to have been that day. The timing of the screams from John Durfee's farm were conflicting, with one estimation at 7:30 p.m. and the other around 8:45 p.m. Who was right? Were they both?

Harriet Hathaway had welcomed many young women to her parlor over the years. Her boardinghouse in Fall River catered to the ladies who toiled for much of their adult lives in the city's factories. Three weeks before Sarah Maria Cornell died, the middle-aged landlord shook the thirty-year-old's hand and offered her a room; she was her only boarder at the time. On Saturday afternoon, May 11, Hathaway recounted the final hours of Sarah's life for the jury, and it saddened her. The night was approaching as the wind blew against Hathaway's front door on December 20. Sarah descended the staircase and reminded the woman that she had hoped to eat supper before her appointment. Sarah told Hathaway that she was meeting someone at John Durfee's house, not the farm, which was curious. Sarah had left her factory job early that night, around 5:30 p.m., with the permission of her overseer—she normally clocked out around 7:30 p.m. Sarah told everyone that she was expected in Tiverton before dark.

Hathaway served Sarah her meal as she watched the young woman eat alone. Sarah had never entertained men at the boardinghouse—she was never immoral, or even impolite. And this evening, Sarah smiled at Hathaway as she adjusted her dark cloak. Mrs. Hathaway knew that the small key to Sarah's trunk stayed safely in her pocket. The matron had noticed a slight shift in her boarder's countenance.

"She appeared more cheerful than usual," Hathaway noticed. "Had been more cheerful throughout the day than she usually was. She was sometimes cheerful, sometimes dull."

Mrs. Hathaway described to the jury how, upstairs in her room, Sarah had stripped off the tattered cloak she typically wore to the mill and put on a nicer one, as well as her calash. It covered her short hair when she drew the strings tightly. Sarah bid Mrs. Hathaway good night and assured her that she would be home before 9:00 p.m., several hours after dark. Sarah hoped that she might return immediately—she was praying for a brief resolution to something she held privately. Mrs. Hathaway nodded as Sarah shut the door behind her.

About ten o'clock that evening, the landlady didn't seem concerned, though she had waited up for Sarah; Mrs. Hathaway decided it was time to retire, despite the tardiness of the young woman in her charge, so she left the front door unlatched and went upstairs to bed.

After hearing about Sarah's horrible death, Harriet

Hathaway remembered seeing those letters, the ones that the matrons found in Sarah's trunk. Sarah had had them in her lap about three days before she died—she was discussing them with Mrs. Hathaway's daughter, Lucy. The two young women both worked in the same weaving room in the factory; about a week before her trip to John Durfee's property, Sarah had told Lucy about her meeting.

"She was usually silent and depressed, and was especially so on the Tuesday before," testified Lucy Hathaway. "She appeared afraid the overseer would not let her go out on the 20th and was fearful of losing her place, because she said she should go whether he would let her or not, if she lost her place."

But the overseer did let her go. Sarah asked Lucy to please tend to her weaving loom—she wanted to be ready for work by Monday. She wanted some extra yarn from the waste pile so she could do some pleasure knitting. The defense attorney cross-examined Lucy and asked specifically about the twine used at the mill. Lucy admitted that she had seen a similar twine to that found around Sarah's neck.

"There is one kind of string similar to it, used in the factory, in an upper room for hanging the harness," Lucy Hathaway testified. "It is of the same material but smaller. There were no such strings in the weaving room. I never saw any string as large as that used in hanging harness in the factory."

No luck for the defense attorney, who was

searching for inroads to prove that Sarah had carried the twine herself to Durfee's farm to take her own life and frame Ephraim Avery.

Sarah didn't tell the Hathaways that she was pregnant, only that she wanted an easier life, a more restful time. She was quiet when Lucy asked about her health—she seemed ill quite a lot.

"I knew she was out of health, from what she said to me, and from my own observation," Lucy said. "She said she had been out of health ever since she came from the camp meeting at Thompson."

Sarah was referring to the event where Ephraim Avery allegedly sexually assaulted her, but she didn't disclose that to the Hathaways; she only alluded to health problems originating from that meeting.

"What did she say?" asked the attorney general.

Lucy Hathaway paused, composed herself, and very delicately recalled Sarah's angst over her life, starting with that camp meeting.

"She said I never will go there again, and then spoke of her health, that she had seen something which occurred there so disgusting, things which took place between a minister and a church member, and then says, a married man too."

Catharine thought about that statement, how full of sorrow Sarah must have felt. She told few people the minister's name—and very few knew the story of what happened at the campground. But it was clear that Sarah had soured on those meetings, and Catharine felt shame for the victim. The court reporter Benjamin F. Hallett also watched Lucy Hathaway closely as she described Sarah's pitiful story. Hathaway, a young woman, had stayed poised, despite describing a dreadful, lascivious event that might have wilted most female witnesses.

"The reporter cannot here refrain from expressing the respect which was universally felt, by all who witnessed the delicate, unaffected and lady-like manner in which this young female acquitted herself," wrote Hallett. "Polished society might find it not a little difficult to furnish a representative to discharge so painful a duty, with as much of the true dignity of modesty as was here evinced by a 'Factory Girl.'"

As I said earlier, almost all the heroes in this story are women. The female witnesses struggled with modesty as each took the stand, but they did their best: The matrons who found Sarah were nervous about using offensive language when describing Sarah's physical injuries, particularly those associated with a potential abortion attempt. The women who once worked with Sarah were timid when asked about Sarah's torrid reputation. Catharine reminded readers that proper women should remain vigilant about the sensibilities of the jury, as she was with her readers.

"We shall endeavor to give a summary of the evidence, though in a very brief and perhaps superficial, manner," she wrote, "without going into the whole revolting particulars."

Lucy Hathaway's testimony, details laden with sadness from a former friend, had ended the day of Saturday, May 11. At seven o'clock, the chief justice signaled to the court crier that the court would adjourn, and he made the announcement. Sunday was reserved by all for worship, and they would return to the courthouse at nine o'clock on Monday morning. Four court officers approached the men on the jury and directed them to stand up and follow them through the large doors. The panel would be sequestered, sort of. The jurors would be allowed to explore Rhode Island together and talk among themselves. They could visit with their families, but only if they were in the presence of one of the officers. Not one word could be uttered about the case. Attorneys on both sides prepared for a long day of testimony, including that of Harvey Harnden, the deputy sheriff who had pursued Ephraim Avery months earlier, tracking him from Rhode Island to rural New Hampshire. Harnden eventually arrested Avery and returned him to Bristol for the preliminary hearing that led to his release—the deputy testified that the minister had presented no problems as they traveled back to Rhode Island. But Avery **had** fled, which seemed suspicious.

Witnesses for Attorney General Albert Greene had testified to Sarah's good character. An elderly man named Elijah Cole had roomed in the same house as Sarah, before she moved over to the Hathaway boardinghouse. Cole remarked that no men had ever visited Sarah at the house, though the defense could have argued that she was pregnant and generally not feeling well enough to entertain the cadre of male visitors she used to. Cole agreed that Sarah was respectful of herself and others— and she was God-fearing, attending many nightly Methodist meetings.

"[I] did not mistrust her situation. Sometimes, she was more cheerful than occasion seemed to require, than was common in my family," said Cole on the stand. "At other times lost in thought, I did not think melancholy. She went out evenings, to meetings. At other times with my family, generally."

Cole's observation of Sarah's personality seemed consistent with both supporters and critics: she experienced mood swings, likely from pregnancy hormones, as well as trauma from the sexual assault and angst over being a single mother. She might have also suffered from a mental illness—we don't know. Witnesses who would later castigate her on the stand would label her as "erratic" and "unstable." But it seems clear to me that Sarah was simply struggling through life, isolated from family but surrounded by well-meaning strangers. She had lived in fear of Avery until she gained some measure of control over him; she demanded child support and threatened him. The lack of financial support from the father is another parallel between **The Scarlet Letter** and **Fall River**.

"What Sarah Maria Cornell apparently sought in her final fatal meeting with the Reverend Avery was support for her unborn child," wrote Shirley Samuels. "Pearl is the lost child of **The Scarlet Letter**." Both Reverends Dimmesdale and Avery are failures to the women, to their children, and to their communities.

In Hawthorne's novel, Hester Prynne mused, "My child must seek a heavenly father; she shall never know an earthly one."

———

In 1832, Sarah Cornell wrote a letter that she intended to mail to Reverend Bidwell, declaring her intent to leave the Methodist Church. Yet it wasn't until the end that Sarah expressed bitterness toward Avery.

During her five visits with Dr. Wilbur, he noticed that Sarah never disparaged Avery. Albert Greene had asked Wilbur as he sat on the stand, "In any conversation with you did she speak of Mr. Avery, and did she express feelings of kindness or unkindness, towards him?"

"Sarah Maria Cornell called on me five times, at each of which times she spoke of Mr. Avery," he replied. "She never did in my bearing express any but feelings of kindness and sympathy for him, and his family."

But in letters to her family right before her death, Sarah was clearly angry; in comments to friends, she revealed her disgust over his behavior at the Thompson camp meeting in August.

Many people, including Elijah Cole, had seen Sarah with the three anonymous letters of differing colors, but none had read them.

The camp meeting in Thompson, Connecticut, in August was featured prominently on the prosecution's witness list. A man who drove Sarah from her sister's home to the campground, about five or six miles away, could confirm only that he dropped her off and saw her twice at the meetings over the four days he was there. He didn't know Ephraim Avery, so he couldn't confirm that Avery was there. The attorney general pressed him about his perception of her character and, once again, a witness confirmed that she was a proper young woman.

"As far as I ever knew, her conduct was modest and correct," testified J. J. Paine.

Defense attorney Richard Randolph requested cross-examination, and the attorney general became alarmed. Randolph seemed to slyly suggest that perhaps Paine and Sarah had a liaison because they traveled to the campground alone and . . . Sarah's dubious character suggested that she would be willing to sleep with any good-looking young man. **That's how she was pregnant in late August,**

declared the defense. **The cart driver was the father.**
Paine shook his head.

"Nothing improper in her asking me to carry her
to the camp meeting in the manner in which it was
done," replied Paine.

Albert Greene was livid at the defense attorney for
his line of questioning. He turned to J. J. Paine and
asked a startling question.

"I will put a question to you which you are not
bound to answer," he said. "Is there any fact within
your knowledge, from which you have any reason
to know who was the father of the child?"

"There is not," replied Paine.

Greene pressed on, staring at the defense attorney.

"Do you know of any illicit intercourse between
Sarah M. Cornell, and yourself or any other man?"

"I do not," Paine affirmed.

Richard Randolph stood up and looked at the
witness, denying he made an unseemly accusation.

"We do not say there was."

Greene glared at Randolph and replied defiantly,
"I know it, but you seem to infer it, and I choose to
settle that question, as we go along."

The attorney general suspected early on that
Avery's well-appointed defense team would continue to subtly disparage Sarah Cornell's character
for the duration of the trial, to insert reasonable
doubt in the minds of the twelve men before them.
**Why would a minister even tolerate the presence
of a wanton woman, let alone sleep with her? She**

had bedded many men, so the father could have been any of them.

Next, a young woman took the stand to begin her testimony, perhaps the State's most crucial witness; Lucretia Rawson, who also went by Nancy, was Sarah Cornell's beloved older sister by about two years. Lucretia had met Sarah at the Thompson camp after J. J. Paine dropped her off. But about a week or so before, Sarah was at her sister's home in Woodstock, Connecticut—she had been staying with the Rawson family for almost two months. The sisters hadn't seen each other for about four or five years before their visit.

The attorney general walked a fine line with his questioning: he wanted to know from the thirty-three-year-old if Sarah might have been already pregnant at the camp meeting, when she was allegedly sexually assaulted by the minister. **No**, replied Lucretia. She had not been pregnant, and she knew this for sure. Sarah had been on her menstrual cycle.

"Do you know any fact," asked Greene, "respecting her being unwell as females are?"

"A week and one day, before the camp meeting, she was unwell in that manner," Sarah's sister replied. "I had the means of knowing, because I did the washing. That is sufficient."

The defense had insinuated that perhaps Sarah was pregnant before the camp meeting, and if that were the case, then she had lied to Dr. Wilbur about the sexual assault. But if the jury believed Lucretia

Rawson, then Sarah was certainly not with child fewer than two weeks earlier. On average, a woman's luteal cycle, the time between a woman's period and her ovulation, can be around ten days. Some women have shorter cycles. The timing of the multiday camp meeting allowed for Sarah to become pregnant two weeks later at the end of August. Lucretia testified that Sarah stayed with her and her husband for an additional month, until October 2, 1832. Lucretia reported that after the camp meeting, Sarah's period did not return when she would have expected it, four weeks later. Lucretia, who did the family's laundry, had tracked Sarah's menstrual cycle. Her period stopped after the camp meeting.

"Previous to that time she was regular in this matter," she said. "Before she left Woodstock, she told me what she feared might be her situation."

Richard Randolph, the defense attorney, hopped up for cross-examination, but it was brief. He asked Lucretia if her sister had ever seemed suicidal.

"I never knew any attempt on her part to commit suicide, or any alarm to the family on that account," she replied. Sarah might have been unstable at times, Lucretia admitted, but she would never take her own life, particularly once she became pregnant. And besides, Sarah was a good Christian woman.

Another member of the large Durfee clan testified the next morning. Amy Durfee worked with Sarah in the weaving room of the mill in Fall River. The two worked together closely, and Durfee had noticed Sarah finishing her work on her loom early on the night of the twentieth. Like other witnesses had reported, Sarah told Durfee that she was leaving two hours early for a meeting at the Durfee farm.

A friend of the Averys', Nancy Gladding, testified that earlier in the week she had invited the minister and his family to visit her home on Thursday, in fact on the night that Sarah died. Ephraim Avery declined, giving no real reason. He insisted that they visit the Gladdings the next day, Friday. Gladding assumed that someone in the family was ill, like one of the children. Avery turned to his wife, Sophia, as Gladding stood nearby.

"He said to his wife 'you must take this visit,'" she testified. "He said it would be necessary for her to go in a carriage. She came on Friday, not in a carriage. . . . They came to my house on Friday at 4, and remained till 6. I had not heard of the death of the girl. Nothing was said about it, and nothing about his having been absent the night before."

But Avery had heard about Sarah's death because Reverend Ira Bidwell had rushed to deliver the news to him earlier that day, after she was discovered.

"He then stated that the girl we were conversing about (S. M. Cornell) was dead," said Ephraim Avery. "I inquired what was the matter? He replied, that she had hung herself; adding that on that morning he had visited the place where she was hung, had ascertained who she was, and had received information from Dr. Wilbur, which implicated me as having had illicit intercourse with her."

Avery had denied an affair with Sarah. Later that day, his family visited the Gladdings and he refrained from gossiping. Of course, the minister realized that talking about Sarah, as one of his former parishioners, would be uncomfortable for everyone, including his wife, who had supposedly ejected her from their home for flirting with her husband.

A young woman described one of the only encounters reported of seeing **two people** who fit the descriptions of both Ephraim Avery and Sarah Maria Cornell in Tiverton on the night of her death. Zeruiah Hambly lived close to John Durfee's farm.

"The evening of the 20th Dec. I went out, and overtook a tall man, a very tall man, with a lady much shorter, passing down the corner, not far from 7 o'clock," said Hambly. "The bells had not rung for half past 7. The lady had on a cloak. They turned down the lane that goes by Mrs. Owen's house. It is next but one to ours, and is in sight. Did not notice his hat."

This pair vaguely fit the description of the minister and the dead woman. The court reporter Benjamin Hallett noted that this was perhaps thirty minutes before Mrs. Owen had reported hearing screams coming from Durfee's stackyard, right around when they were supposed to meet. But like many witnesses, Hambly had only a fleeting encounter with them, so her details were vague.

"It was dark; should not be willing to say what kind of coat he had on," Hambly testified. "I was close to them, as near as to you, (within 10 feet) walking the same way, but did not pass them. Did not notice the lady's bonnet."

A witness detailed how he spotted Avery the morning of December 21 in Bristol as the minister apparently exited the ferry. William Lawless said that Avery seemed to try to avoid him as Lawless stood outside his home.

"I spoke to him, and knew him. I first saw him early in the morning, as I was standing at my gate," Lawless testified. "I undertook to overtake Mr. Avery. When I came up he appeared to wish to let me pass."

Lawless caught up with him and asked if he had returned from preaching on the island the night before. Avery offered the same vague explanation as he did to Jane Gifford: he was simply there on business. Preaching would have offered investigators witnesses, but business was nebulous.

The stagecoach driver, Stephen Bartlett, testified that he had carried Ephraim Avery from Bristol to Fall River as many as six times before Sarah's death, often to have a meal and a drink at Lawton's Hotel. This is the same place where a tall man fitting Avery's description was spotted on December 20. Despite Catharine's contention that Avery had once abused his horse, Bartlett insisted that the minister seemed fond of his carriage's horses.

The jury listened as Bartlett described Avery's conversation with him about Sarah Cornell, after Reverend Bidwell had warned him that Sarah had died, that she was pregnant, and that the minister might need to be prepared to answer questions, thanks to Dr. Wilbur's incriminating recollection of Sarah's accusations against Avery. Bartlett recounted the minister's tense conversation with Bidwell and insistence on visiting Lowell to gather evidence against her character. Avery had ordered Bartlett to drive to Bidwell's home and request permission to visit the town immediately. There was not time to waste because the rumor mill churned quickly in Fall River.

"He said something about her being a bad girl, and thought if it was known in Fall River it would destroy her testimony," Bartlett testified, "and I understood him to say she was a loose girl, and had threatened to revenge herself of him for having excommunicated her."

Bartlett listened as Avery grew more anxious in his stable, and angry. The minister was determined to locate people in Lowell to testify to Sarah's bad character, to her vengeful nature. He repeated his recollection that Avery wanted Sarah framed as a "common prostitute," which would absolve him of sleeping with her. Avery confirmed this in his own story and recounted the devastation he felt when relaying the accusations to his wife.

"This intelligence, so unexpected, so gloomy in its

character, and so well calculated in its nature to be a source of affliction and distress," said Avery. "I felt immediately to commit my case to God . . . after having in as suitable a manner as I could, communicated the heart-rendering and soul-chilling intelligence to my wife."

This began the story of Bartlett's visit to Dr. Wilbur to discover the physician's story on behalf of Avery and Bidwell; Wilbur told him nothing and instead privately warned John Durfee and Harvey Harnden to locate the minister quickly. Bartlett also confirmed that he carried Ephraim Avery on his coach from Fall River to Bristol on December 8, the day the mysterious letter was written. There was a litany of other witnesses for the attorney general who tried to establish that Avery was the author of the letters or was spotted in Fall River at crucial times, which tied him to Sarah's death.

But then a handsome young minister took the stand. As the jury collectively leaned in for his testimony, the defense would begin to reveal its strategy—Sarah Cornell was a wanton woman, not only sleeping with any man she encountered but also trying to lure away her sister Lucretia's husband. Reverend Grindall Rawson took the stand near the end of the prosecution's case, and it would become the most uncomfortable testimony of the trial. Would the jury believe him?

~~

CHAPTER ELEVEN

THE HITCH

"HER MOTHER SAID HER CORRECT name was Sarah or Sally Maria Cornell," replied the handsome witness. "We always called her Maria."

Grindall Rawson shifted in the witness chair; his sister-in-law's reputation could be altered by his testimony. Of the men Sarah Cornell had encountered in her life, the twenty-nine-year-old minister had been the most trustworthy. She briefly lived with Grindall and Lucretia in 1832, and when she left, Sarah wrote him letters. Sarah had made him laugh, and the three shared a love of Methodism. And they all adored going to camp meetings. In 1830, Sarah wrote to her mother about a lively meeting she'd attended that lasted for ten days—she thought her brother-in-law would have appreciated it.

"Had about twelve sermons preached on board, and one on the shore," Sarah told her mother, "dug clams—had plenty of good codfish, crackers and coffee—and on the eleventh day reached Boston wharf in better health and better spirits than when I left—having had about six good hours sleep in ten nights. Just at this moment one of Brother Rawson's Camp Meeting stories has popt into my head and methinks I hear him say, 'Well Maria this is one of your Camp Meeting scrapes.'"

Grindall offered her sage, brotherly advice, even when the subject was awful. He had pressed her to pressure Ephraim Avery for financial support after he raped her and she became pregnant. He was appalled that a minister had attacked a parishioner, especially a woman as kind as Sarah. Grindall Rawson, it appeared to all, was a good man. On the stand, he described how Sarah, whom he called Maria, worked at his tailoring shop in Woodstock, Connecticut, the summer before she died. He had arranged for her to ride with J. J. Paine to the Thompson campgrounds in August. Grindall watched her mingle there with kind Methodist parishioners, sharing their love of God. Nothing seemed amiss. But eventually, Sarah told her sister about the rape.

"When she first stated to me the occurrence at the camp-meeting, she told it to me and my wife with great reluctance," Grindall recalled. "My wife got up one night, after we had been to bed; Maria had come down, and Mrs. Rawson said to me that

Maria was in trouble. She had confessed her situation to Mrs. Rawson, and Maria then told it to me."

Albert Greene, the attorney general, nodded at Grindall. He asked if he knew of Sarah ever sleeping with a man—had she ever had intercourse, aside from the sexual assault?

"I never knew of any illicit intercourse between her and any man, before this," he replied. "It came out directly to me, first from Maria herself, that Mr. Avery was connected with the transaction at the camp-meeting."

This was when Grindall rushed to consult a trusted Presbyterian minister as well as an attorney. They suggested that Sarah pack up her things and move to Rhode Island, where Avery lived, so that she could legally demand financial support from Avery.

"She herself proposed to go to Fall River and work there in a factory while able to work, and until he should make some provision for her," wrote Catharine Williams.

When Grindall paused during his testimony, defense attorney Richard Randolph popped up.

"What did she say concerning Mr. Avery, at the camp meeting?"

Grindall thought for a moment and replied, "Do you wish to know the whole she said?"

"Yes, the whole," affirmed Avery's attorney.

Grindall unfurled a harrowing story told to him

by his sister-in-law, how Avery drew Sarah out into the woods alone. It was perhaps the most compelling testimony of the trial. Sarah Maria Cornell had detailed the sexual assault to her sister and her brother-in-law. Now Grindall wanted to put Sarah's story on the record.

"They went arm and arm into the woods. He asked her to take her glasses off. They sat down; some conversation followed about Avery having burned the letters," Grindall testified.

The letters he was referring to had been the notes of confession that Sarah had written for Avery, as an atonement for her sins and an avenue to return to the Methodist Church. Sarah had hoped he would return her letters so she could start anew in another town. But as they sat near each other in the woods, Avery confessed that he still had them. Sarah felt confused. **You promised**, she told him. He assured her that he would destroy them, but on one condition. Grindall Rawson braced himself for the next part of the story.

"At that time he took hold of her hands, and put one [of his] onto her bosom, or something like it," recalled Grindall. "She said she tried to get away from him, but could not. She said he then had intercourse with her."

Sarah felt betrayed, and victimized, and certainly humiliated. If it were true, then Avery, I imagine, was smug that day in the woods. It sounded like he treated the rape as a transactional meeting; the minister stood up, brushed himself off, and nodded for them to return to the camp. He glanced at her and promised to burn the letters when he returned home to Bristol.

The courtroom grew quiet as Grindall concluded his testimony; the details of the sexual assault of Sarah Cornell echoed across the courthouse walls. Very rarely had words like "bosom" and "intercourse" been used in a New England court of law, especially in a case involving a minister. While many of the witnesses were taciturn on the stand, Grindall Rawson was articulate, determined to protect his sister-in-law in life as well as in death. The defense attorney eyed Grindall.

"What was her character for chastity?" he asked.

Albert Greene barked about the meaning behind the lurid question, and Richard Randolph quickly moved past it. But it was clear what the defense's strategy would be—blaming the victim.

Exploiting the character of the victim deflects and lessens the impact of the crime: "she deserved it" becomes the subtle mantra. In 1947 Theodor W. Adorno defined what would be later called "blaming the victim," as "one of the most sinister features of the Fascist character." Sarah Cornell was being blamed for her own death. Attorney Sharon Vinick said the tactic is deplorable, and it would not likely work today.

"Not only are they victim shaming, but they're also doing things based upon her actual character," said Vinick. "So these witnesses, they wouldn't all come on the stand to say that she stole; she was lascivious; she spit on the floor. Whatever nonsense it is that they're bringing in, that would all be excluded."

But in the 1800s, there were no laws protecting rape survivors—women were often not believed or were blamed for instigating the attack, if the case even made it to court. Grindall Rawson, regrettably, would play an unwilling part in the victim blaming very soon when the defense would focus on his relationship with Sarah.

———

After six days of testimony featuring sixty-eight witnesses, Albert Greene and his prosecution team wound down their part of the trial. The attorney general's finale was to have one very important piece of evidence admitted to the trial so the jury could read it—it was the small note found in Sarah's trunk, written in her hand, the short missive about her whereabouts. Albert Greene implored the court to read it aloud for the panel of men, so they could better understand her state of mind as she left for her meeting in Tiverton on December 20. **She was not considering suicide**, insisted the attorney general. **She was concerned about being murdered.** The defense strongly objected, saying the slip of paper proved nothing against Avery. **We agree**, stated Chief Justice Samuel Eddy.

"The paper in pencil being proved to be her handwriting, is admissible to show the state of mind of the deceased, in connexion with the presumption of suicide," he ruled. "It does not go to the jury as evidence of any act on the part of the prisoner, but merely to prove, as far as it goes that she did not go out with the intention to commit suicide."

Albert Greene sighed. He thought the night was the manifestation of Sarah's fears. Dutee J. Pearce held the paper in his hand and turned to the twelve men. "If I am missing enquire of Rev. Mr. Avery of Bristol; he will know where I am gone. S. M. Cornell. Dec. 20th," he read.

Over the past two centuries, much has been made of that small slip of paper, a key piece of evidence in the murder trial of Ephraim Avery in 1833. Its phrasing might have seemed innocuous, had its author not died hours later with twine around her neck. Within that framework, Sarah Cornell's short message, "If I am missing," became a signature line of mystery books for countless wordsmiths to follow. The phrase has been repeated by a handful of real murder victims, hoping to leave clues about their demise at the hands of their spouses. Often Sarah's note is interpreted as ominous, as if Sarah had heard a murmur from a spirit warning her that Ephraim Avery was dangerous. Even Avery's defense attorneys agreed that the note was dark—they accused Sarah of writing it to frame him for her suicide. Historians agree that the note seems damning against Avery, or it appears to be evidence that, perhaps, Sarah Cornell **did** frame the Methodist minister. But surprisingly Catharine Williams disagreed about the intention of Sarah's note. The women in her boardinghouse, as well as her coworkers, agreed that she was in a fine mood on December 20.

"She (S. M. C.) told them several times that she was only waiting for some money she was expecting to receive, when she should leave Fall River," wrote Catharine. "The flutter of spirits, which made her on the last day of her life more cheerful than usual may be easily accounted for."

Sarah seemed happy to make the visit, to finally demand something for herself and her child.

"She came out of the mill early and changed her clothes, and then probably wrote that little strip of paper, 'If I am missing enquire of Rev. E. K. Avery,'" wrote Catharine. "Turning to the oldest sister, she said as she went out, 'I think I shall be back as soon now, as Lucy returns from the factory.'"

Sarah appeared more animated that night than she had for weeks, perhaps because a weight would soon be lifted. The grim note didn't seem to match her upbeat mood.

This note, assessed Catharine, was likely not a surreptitious, haunting note about her possible murder. Catharine believed that Sarah was simply being polite, letting her roommates know where she was heading. A woman **that** optimistic, that cheerful, contended Catharine, was not in fear of her life. But something concerned both of us: if Sarah penned the benign message on the small slip of paper that night out of consideration for her landlady, why tuck it inside her locked trunk when she had the only key?

Sarah was bright but also shrewd, like when she copied Ephraim Avery's letter after he ordered her to burn it. During her angst-ridden conversations with Dr. Wilbur, she refused to express resentment toward the Methodist minister, even vowing to protect him and his family. Her deference to him after the sexual assault was perplexing to Catharine Williams, but not to modern-day victims' advocates, particularly since capitulation to men in the nineteenth century for women was the norm.

Sarah Cornell expressed no ill feelings toward Avery during the first two initial examinations by Dr. Wilbur, only panic over her pregnancy. If that were the case, Catharine asked the reader, why did she write that cryptic note on the night of her death?

"To that we answer, that . . . something within us, that never fails to warn us of approaching danger," wrote Catharine, "some call it 'a presentiment of evil.'"

Sarah Cornell was naive but also wary of devious men. When she revealed to Dr. Wilbur that Avery had suggested that she take tansy oil, Dr. Wilbur immediately forbade her from taking the stuff. Avery's urging was suspicious, Sarah knew, and she sought to distance herself from him for her own safety. She promised Dr. Wilbur that she would protect herself. Catharine sensed that Sarah's contradictory reactions to Avery were confusing to the public, so she sought to clarify the note's purpose. Yes, Sarah had seemed reticent at first to publicly expose Avery, despite the sexual assault. But Dr. Wilbur's worry over the oil of tansy deepened her mistrust. The secreted note, Catharine believed, was a result of fear. **What if he did try to hurt me tonight, like Dr. Wilbur warned?**

"If her tale was true," wrote Catharine, "if she had once had poison recommended her, and been warned by him who told her not to take it, neither to go to Bristol, nor to put herself in his power, but to have him come to her fairly and honourably, and settle it—if she had received this warning, she could not but have some fear."

Sarah **must** have been afraid. Catharine contended that no moral man would have asked a young woman to a clandestine meeting on a dark evening on a farm.

"She knew, probably, it was a fearful thing under such circumstances, or indeed under any, to go there to an assignation," Catharine wrote.

Sarah felt she was putting herself at risk that night, Catharine concluded, but she was trusting that her fears were unfounded. If Avery agreed to support her and the child, then perhaps her own life had hope. As she swiftly wrote at her wooden desk in Providence, Rhode Island, during the trial, Catharine grew concerned.

During cross-examination, Ephraim Avery's defense team focused heavily on several lines of questioning. Richard Randolph sought to discredit the parade of witnesses who testified to seeing the minister in Tiverton or Fall River on December 20, 1832. He attacked the veracity of those who claimed that Avery was the author of the anonymous letters to Sarah—surely, belonging to the man who murdered her. Randolph began to frame Sarah as promiscuous and unstable. He hinted to the jury during the State's section of the trial that Sarah was suicidal, that she had a vendetta against Avery for expelling her from the church in Lowell. There was no evidence of a rape, such as witnesses, or that Avery was the father of her baby. In fact, Randolph had witnesses who claimed to see Sarah at the campground that August in various stages of undress and that she was apparently pregnant then. This was despite the testimony of her sister, who proclaimed that she had ended her menstrual cycle two weeks before. His experts believed that the baby was not conceived at the end of August, despite the claims of Albert Greene.

On Wednesday, May 15, the attorney general rested, and Avery's defense attorneys began to present their case the next day. Richard Randolph's witness list was longer than that of the attorney general, more than double. As Catharine Williams sat in court that morning, she felt sickened. She listened to Richard Randolph present his opening statements; as she scribbled notes, she became saddened. Ephraim Avery's well-heeled, aggressive attorneys were plotting to free their client by viciously dismantling a murder victim's character.

Catharine Williams eyed Richard Randolph as he moved around the courtroom, gesturing to the jury. The tall fifty-two-year-old with the long, pointy nose came from the distinguished and wealthy Randolph family in Virginia, a clan that boasted a list of wealthy politicians, landowners, and war heroes. Attorney General Albert Greene had been ill for much of the trial, his stamina waning as he slowly chipped away at his own witness list. But despite being a decade older than his rival, Richard Randolph was certainly the more able attorney in the courthouse in Newport. Catharine described the attorney general as "a gentleman of good law knowledge, of amiable manners, and feeling heart, but whose plain good sense was no match for the subtlety of his antagonist." The State needed to be prepared for a character assassination never seen in America in a case where the victim was a woman, and Catharine was concerned that Greene and his team were not ready for a lawyer as combative as Randolph.

"His argument was, that this girl, the deceased, was utterly bad, capable of any sort of wickedness,"

Catharine wrote, "that she owed the prisoner a grudge for his share in turning her out of meeting, and that she had, wreaked her vengeance upon him in this manner."

Randolph indicated that he would present witnesses claiming to hear from Sarah herself that she would make Avery pay for expelling her. The defense said that she did this by writing those anonymous letters herself or by asking someone to do it for her.

"Then by pretending he was her betrayer," Catharine told her readers, "and finally hanging herself after writing a billet, 'if she was missing to inquire of the Rev. E. K. Avery.'"

Randolph claimed that Sarah Cornell had declared that "she would be revenged upon him if it cost her, her life." Sarah settled on taking her own life and executed her revenge that night, alone, on John Durfee's farm. Ephraim Avery was never there. The bruises discovered by the matrons were naturally occurring in a rapidly decomposing body. Besides, what would the matrons know about the decomposition process? As Catharine listened to Randolph's opening remarks, the author watched him with disgust; her deep emotions spilled onto the pages of her book. Randolph insinuated that the good people of Fall River had propelled this preposterous murder trial forward when it was a simple, sad suicide.

"All the rest was the effect of the heightened imagination of 'the Fall River folks,' and the excitement he politely styled the 'Fall River fever,'" she wrote of

Randolph's remarks. "He attempted to establish it as a fact that the deceased was insane too."

That claim made Catharine livid. Randolph hoped to frame Sarah as mentally unstable for the jury, yet could an insane woman really develop such a nefarious, clever plot against a Methodist minister?

"That she was capable of a plot of revenge deeper and of a more diabolical character than any ever related before of woman," wrote Catharine, "a plot which, in conception and execution, surpassed all human credibility."

Catharine refused to delve more deeply into the defense's argument, dismissing much of it as misogynistic and immaterial to the case of Sarah Cornell's murder. She's correct—much of it reads like a haughty speech determined to disparage a young woman. But Catharine's book aimed to be persuasive, while mine is journalistic. Richard Randolph made some excellent points, some assertions that we should consider. The defense attorney questioned if the knot had been a clove hitch.

"It was not discovered until partly picked out," Randolph contended, "and what was the difference between a clove hitch and a slipping noose, that would be distinguished, when partly untied?"

Even if it **had been** a clove hitch, Sarah could have tightened it using her own body weight, as other people taking their own lives have done, according to Paul Holes. There appeared to be signs of a struggle on her body, but the defense contended that those assessments from the matrons were inaccurate, and that decomposition could have caused some of the discoloration. Holes refuted that, but he also said that people who take their own lives can accidentally hurt their bodies in the process. There appeared to be no signs of a struggle in the stack-yard, which seemed odd if she had been strangled by someone.

All the State's so-called evidence, said Richard Randolph, was also evidence of a suicide. The puzzling note on the slip of paper naming Ephraim Avery proved nothing, except that Sarah had been bent on framing him for her murder. Randolph blamed that paper, discovered by the matrons of Fall River, for all of Avery's troubles. Randolph asked the jury something interesting about the bonnet that Sarah was wearing that night, which was still neatly on her head, the strings tied beneath the twine used in her death.

"How could a man have strangled her against her will, without throwing off the calash?" Randolph retorted to Albert Greene, sitting at the opposite table. Randolph didn't mention that a calculating criminal might have strangled Sarah with the twine, then untied the knot, straightened the calash, and then retied it before hanging her. Or perhaps she had tied her calash so tightly to brace against the cold night that it moved little.

And we still haven't answered the most crucial

question of whether Sarah Cornell was murdered, and if so, by whom. In his opening statement, Richard Randolph issued a sobering demand to the jury—a statement that is at the crux of this case.

"The government must prove it is not suicide," Randolph said. "So long as a doubt exists as to the act, there can be nothing to charge any one as the perpetrator. If, therefore, the jury doubted whether this was murder or suicide, they need go no further. They must acquit the prisoner."

Do we, right now, have definitive proof that this was murder? Richard Randolph's rebuttal of the physical evidence might have been enough to create reasonable doubt, except most of the defense's argument did not address the circumstantial evidence, the lost forensic clues, or the unreliable witnesses. Richard Randolph had focused his vitriol on Sarah Maria Cornell—**she was so devious, she did this to herself. Look at her history of deceptive and vulgar tendencies.**

"I will now state what we expect to prove of this unfortunate girl. That she was once a member of E. K. Avery's church, in Lowell," said Richard Randolph to the jury. "There tried for fornication and expelled from the church. That she confessed her guilt, and that she declared she would be revenged of Avery, if it cost her life. That she was afflicted with an odious disease, to a great degree, and passed from the church to the doctor's shop. That this miserable woman made repeated threats of suicide, and attempted to effect it," he told the jury. "That her conduct was so strange, she was believed to be deranged." Randolph promised to provide the jury with witnesses who heard Sarah's threats, and he certainly did. The attorney referenced multiple times the sexually transmitted infection that Sarah supposedly carried.

Randolph assured the men on the panel that he could trace Sarah's path of lewdness and odd character over a fourteen-year period across New England. She had considered suicide, Randolph insisted to the jury. She hated Avery for thwarting her efforts to be welcomed back to the Methodist church, despite her confessions to him about her unseemly relationships with men.

"When you learn these facts," said Randolph, "I am greatly mistaken if you will not then think that of all women, she was the most likely to commit suicide."

Sarah Cornell, insisted the defense attorney, was a malicious, manipulative, promiscuous woman, determined to ruin a man she had once claimed to idolize. Before calling his first witness, Richard Randolph walked over to the panel and narrowed his eyes. Seemingly in all earnestness, the defense attorney called the prosecution of Ephraim Avery . . . a witch hunt.

"In my honest and serious opinion, if you, gentlemen of the jury, should convict Avery, and he should suffer, future generations will regard the act with as much abhorrence as we now do the hanging of the witches at Salem," said Randolph. "The infatuation with which Avery is pursued, is the same kind of infatuation."

With that, Ephraim Avery's defense team began an assault on Sarah Maria Cornell that had been unprecedented in American courts. Randolph called a string of physicians to the stand, all questioning whether the matrons could correctly identify the signs of violence found on Sarah's body. Cocounsel Jeremiah Mason asked one doctor, "Are the women competent to judge whether the marks they saw were appearances of violence, or arising from death by suicide?"

"I should suppose that females examining a body would give a good account of the appearance, but would not be good judges of the cause of it," replied Dr. Nathaniel Miller. "The change in the parts after death is very great."

Mason and Randolph tried to dismantle the State's contention that the marks on Sarah were caused by physical violence, asserting that instead they could have been the result of decomposition, though Paul Holes argued that most people would not mistake bruises for decomposition, particularly matrons used to dressing dead women who might have suffered domestic violence. The defense contended that measuring the length and the weight of a fetus was not an accurate way to determine its age, but we know that isn't true.

Much of the medical testimony devolved into a battle of the experts, a legal technique leveraged to sway the jury your way, but which oftentimes simply confuses jurors. The physicians debated where the knot on Sarah's neck was placed, how quickly her skin blackened, where the blood pooled within her body, and whether there were definitive signs of an attempted abortion. After eight days of testimony including a litany of medical terms, the jury appeared fatigued. The defense had exhausted its medical experts, except for several who could testify to Sarah's wicked character.

The first one up was Dr. William Graves, the doctor and sometime-abortionist who later killed a patient during a botched pregnancy termination. Sarah had accused him of trying to sexually assault her during a late-night visit, but Dr. Graves took the stand and issued his official version of that office visit in 1831, one year before her death.

"Her disease was lues venerea, a very severe case, so bad as I have seen," said Graves on the stand, referring to syphilis. "This young woman came in and inquired in reference to a young man, who she said had treated her improperly and deserted her. She wished to know if he was under my treatment. He was not so. I furnished her with a prescription."

Dr. Graves told the court that Sarah acted strangely, insinuating that she was insane, yet he couldn't be specific.

"Her language was so different from what I ever

heard from a female," said Dr. Graves; "I should not be willing to give it as my opinion she was deranged."

The physician's statements were just vague enough to cause rumblings in the jury box. Graves said he also saw Sarah at a tavern in Lowell when she was talking loudly about Avery.

"She seemed to be blaming him for turning her out of the church," said Graves, "called him a rascal, villain, and I believe she said he ought to be hung."

Dr. Graves claimed that on another visit, Sarah had asked about the status of two other young men who might have purportedly given her the disease. He warned Avery about his unstable parishioner. And when she didn't pay her bill, Graves came to the minister looking for her. If the jury believed Dr. Graves, then Sarah had not only slept with several men and contracted a disease; she had also skipped out on the bill. But according to Sarah Cornell herself, only the last digression was true. None of the men that Sarah had supposedly inquired about were called to the stand—why? Either Dr. Graves fabricated them, or the men weren't credible as witnesses. Sarah had accused Dr. Graves of trying to sexually assault her after she came to him one night with a strong cold that had developed during a camp meeting on Cape Cod—not a venereal disease. Graves tried to trap her, and she escaped, but then she refused to pay the bill. And though she later admitted to having an STI in her confession letters to Avery, Sarah had made it clear to her family that none of it was true—she was desperate to be received back in the church. She had to confess to **something** for that to happen. Catharine Williams wasn't sure; Sarah might have had a horrid disease, but if she did, would the Methodists **really** allow her to attend meetings? Catharine cried indignantly: **What kind of religious society held such low standards?** Sarah might have made moral mistakes, but how could the Methodists tolerate those mistakes in their church?

"We do not know but a part of the charges against her may be true, because we have no means of positively knowing," she concluded. "To receive again a woman upon probation who had once been expelled upon such a charge as Doctor Graves made against her. Gracious heaven!"

Either the Methodists were lying about Sarah's disease, or they were willing to take in a fornicator—both were awful options to Catharine. And yet, as self-righteous as she was, Catharine believed that Sarah was a good person. She was disgusted with the procession of people on the defense's witness list—they were virtually all Methodists, each loyal to the popular preacher, according to the author. And none could be trusted, especially Dr. Graves, who made an important disclosure on the stand.

"I was the family physician of Mr. Avery, I should

think, at the time this girl applied to me," he said. "I am not positive that I have prescribed for Mr. Avery. Think I have."

Could Dr. Graves's testimony be trusted? No, particularly given the physician's relationship with Ephraim Avery—he should have never been allowed to testify. Another physician took the stand after Graves and parroted the first doctor's claims that Sarah was being treated for a disease, this time gonorrhea. He also served two purposes for the defense, labeling her as both unchaste and seemingly demented.

"The transition was sudden," said Dr. Noah Martin. "She would perhaps be talking of her ailment, and be in a flood of tears, and in five minutes change the subject, and be in a state of laughter. I thought at the time, she appeared like a person whose mental operations appeared to be considerably deranged."

Catharine found Dr. Graves repulsive and Dr. Martin unreliable—both men were hired by the defense to lie. Dr. Graves's relationship with the Avery family and Sarah's story about his attempted rape should have convinced the jury to dismiss his testimony. But what about Dr. Martin? Was he lying? After the trial, a newspaper report—widely believed—suggested that Martin had confused Sarah Cornell with a woman named Maria Snow Cornell, who was known to be promiscuous. **Fall River Outrage** author David Kasserman wrote,

"Although not believed by all, the story did much to reduce the image of Sarah Cornell's depravity—and to call into question the bulk of the testimony on which the defense's assertion of suicide was based."

But neither physician gave credence to the idea that Sarah Cornell took her own life. If she did have venereal diseases, did that matter? To a modern-day jury, probably not. But in 1833, twelve men likely felt some modicum of disgust for a woman who defiled herself, then contracted diseases and reacted irrationally. In mid-May 1833, Catharine rued the following weeks as the defense painted a grotesque portrait of Sarah Cornell. None of the slander could be believed, she contended.

"Had two or three respectable persons of good standing in society stated that the character of S. M. Cornell was not good, and that she was plotting, revengeful, &c. it would have gone farther toward convincing the minds of the public than all this array of questionable evidence," Catharine wrote. "A great deal of it was entirely irrelevant to the case; a vast deal appeared to have no object but to blacken the character."

After the pair of physicians accused Sarah of carrying on various affairs and requiring treatment for two different venereal diseases, a parade of women strode past Ephraim Avery and swore an oath to tell the truth. They all represented different eras in Sarah Cornell's life—and each one was in court to diminish Sarah's credibility. The jury watched closely as woman after woman, all Methodists, explained their relationship with Sarah and what they had learned during their time with her—little of it was positive. **How could so many people have drastically different opinions of her?** Catharine Williams asked herself. The answer, the author believed, was simple: the Methodists were colluding against Sarah Cornell. Asaneth Bowen worked in a weaving room in Waltham, Massachusetts, with Sarah three years earlier when the twenty-seven-year-old began acting erratically; she retrieved a piece of twine and disappeared into a room before Bowen discovered her.

"She immediately went out of the room," Bowen testified. "I then went out of the room and remarked to someone that I did believe Maria would make way with herself. There were nails and spikes in the room, where she might have hung a line up to."

Mary Ann Lary worked with Sarah Cornell in 1830 in Dover after Avery had Sarah expelled from the church in Lowell. Lary reported finding Sarah anguished one night, cursing the Methodist minister and threatening to take her own life.

"She said she had gone out to make away with herself, but when she came to the place her courage failed," Lary testified. "She said it was because Mr. Avery had not used her well in expelling her from the Methodist church."

Lary admitted that a Methodist minister in Dover had suggested that she testify when the defense was rounding up witnesses. Didn't that make her biased? Ezra Park claimed that he knew Sarah almost a decade earlier in Thompson, Connecticut, where she appeared eight or nine months pregnant at his tavern and bellowed to a man that he was the father—but Mr. Park was dead by the time of the trial. The attorney general quickly discredited Park's story for the jury; no one else in Sarah's life, on either side, would swear that she had been pregnant before 1832. Besides, said Greene, Park had disclosed that he was Baptist, a congregation that often joined with the Methodists during camp meetings—another potentially biased witness.

Next up for the defense was Sarah's overseer in a mill in Lowell, where her troubles with Avery began in 1830; she had been initially fired there for breaking a loom, and he rehired her but then dismissed her again after she admitted to fornication.

"She acknowledged to me that she had had intercourse with one or two individuals in the place," said Brooks Shattuck on the stand. "As many as two."

Sarah had confessed to Avery that she had slept with several men, but later recanted to her family. What was the truth? It didn't matter—what mattered was what could be proved by the attorneys: murder or suicide? The jury was at risk of being distracted by the dubious gossip that horrified nineteenth-century society, the label that made Hawthorne's **Scarlet Letter** so terrifyingly real.

"'I can teach my little Pearl what I have learned

from this!' answered Hester Prynne, laying her finger on the red token," wrote Hawthorne. "'Woman, it is thy badge of shame!' replied the stern magistrate. 'It is because of the stain which that letter indicates, that we would transfer thy child to other hands.'"

The list of witnesses continued over the following days, each person disparaging Sarah. She had been unstable for years, they said. Nathan Howard said she appeared irrational. "How?" asked the defense attorney.

"Her eyes appeared fiery, and looked red."

"Was there any appearance of wildness?" asked Jeremiah Mason, in a leading question.

"Yes, sir," replied Howard.

More people took the stand. "She told me she had been tempted to make way with herself," reported Lucy Davol. Lydia Pervere testified that Sarah Cornell was so upset with Avery for ejecting her from the church in Lowell that she refused to attend a camp meeting.

"She said she did not wish to go where Avery was, because someone had told him about her." Pervere, one of Avery's church members, said she once saw Avery burn a letter, supporting his contention that he had no intentions of blackmailing Sarah.

Ellen Griggs claimed that Sarah was so furious with Avery that she openly plotted against him: "She said, 'I will have revenge of him if it costs me my life.'" On cross-examination, Griggs admitted that she didn't ask Sarah any details about her threats, or report them to anyone else, which seemed strange to the attorney general.

One of the most disturbing parts of the trial, aside from the barrage of victim blaming and shaming, came when Sarah Worthing, a coworker, took the stand and claimed that Sarah had designs on her own brother-in-law, Grindall Rawson. Worthing said that Grindall had initially wanted to be with Sarah, not Lucretia, whom he would eventually marry. This disclosure stunned the courtroom, it seemed so disturbing. Sarah, Worthing claimed, had stopped visiting the family by 1828.

"She said she did not like to go because her sister felt disagreeable," Worthing testified, "was jealous of her husband and her; that her sister had often told her she would come to the gallows, there were so many men after her."

Worthing said that Sarah loved her family, but Lucretia made it difficult because of the mutual attraction between Grindall and Sarah.

"She said that Mr. Rawson had said she was more attractive than her sister (his wife)," said Worthing. "That there was something very attractive in her eyes."

In 1830, when her troubles really began, Sarah wrote to her mother and did indicate that Grindall and Lucretia had stopped writing to her recently.

"I have been in Lowell so long that I should feel lonesome anywhere else. My love to my sister, tell

---

her I long to see her and the children," she wrote. "I shall write to Mr. Rawson as soon as I return from the Cape, though I never received a line from him or Lucretia since they were married, but I expect my sister's time is pretty much taken up with her children."

There were similar letters, all lamenting her lack of contact with the couple but promising a visit, including one a year earlier.

"The bell rings for meeting and I must draw my letter to a close," she wrote to Lucretia. "I do not know why you or Mr. Rawson have not written to me. I want one of you to answer this previous to the first of June and let me know what your wishes are, and I shall act accordingly."

But, as you will recall, Lucretia invited Sarah to live with them in Connecticut for several months just weeks before she became pregnant in 1832, and then for two months after. If Sarah had tried to steal away Grindall, would he really request that she work in his tailor shop? Would her sister allow it? Lucretia and her husband denied the rumors, but it was too late to unring the bell for the jurors.

Sarah supposedly told Worthing that she had once been accused of stealing fabric and decided to hang herself; that testimony effectively addressed multiple themes for the defense. Lucy Howe testified that Sarah confessed this: "O! I have been a very bad girl, but it is nothing to what I have been guilty of." Elizabeth Shummway knew Sarah in Slatersville in

1825. She testified that Sarah lamented the loss of Grindall Rawson as a suitor to her sister. She had thought of drowning herself over lost love.

"She said because she had been disappointed in marriage—that Grindall Rawson had courted her, and her sister got him away from her by art and stratagem, and he married her," Shumway testified. "But he had one thing to comfort her. He liked her best now, for he had owed it to her, and her sister was jealous."

Shumway leaned forward on the stand and disclosed something scandalous from Sarah's own words, Shumway claimed.

"We have been intimate as husband and wife," Sarah allegedly told Shumway. "She said he composed some verses for her, and wrote them in the blank leaf of a testament, and presented it to her."

Another woman testified that Sarah admitted she could imitate most anyone's handwriting, including Avery's, thus the anonymous notes might have been written in her own hand. Others said that Ephraim Avery was virtually never alone at the Thompson camp meeting when the sexual assault supposedly took place. Each woman who took the stand turned on Sarah Cornell, depicting her as a criminal, a fornicator, and an unstable harlot who often threatened to take her own life while framing the minister who had expelled her from her beloved Methodist church. They detailed why Ephraim Avery could never be a killer or a rapist—his character was beyond reproach. Even though the defense couldn't provide any witnesses to Avery's solo trip on December 20, there were enough people who spotted him that day to piece together an alibi, they believed.

The attorney general, desperate to counter some of the damage, leaned on the physical clues. He called veteran weavers to the stand who testified that weavers used a square knot, not a clove hitch—**where would Sarah have learned how to tie that knot if not at work?** But the defense presented weavers who contradicted them—yes, they had all used a clove hitch. As an aside, I spoke with two forensic knot experts who said that, in a struggle, the knot could have inadvertently become a clove hitch during either scenario.

Sarah's friends took the stand again to testify to her good character, but they had been outnumbered by those women who aimed to convince the jury that she was someone of ill repute and had been for more than a decade. Virtually every witness who had taken the stand for the State was countered by a witness for the defense. The sheer number of people in court, all swearing an oath, was incredible. The jury was exhausted by the end, and Sarah Cornell had been betrayed by so many people. In life, Sarah certainly would have never suspected that so many women thought so little of her—she truly lacked advocates. But would all these witnesses for the defense **really** lie for Ephraim Avery? Richard Randolph and his team called more than 150 people to the stand over two weeks.

With that, it's best to end the narrative of the defense's version of events, because to both Catharine and me, it lacked credibility. The questions at hand for the jury remained: Was this murder or suicide? And if murder, was Ephraim Avery her killer? Both sides closed just before seven o'clock at night on Saturday, June 1, summarizing their arguments one final time. Catharine watched as Richard Randolph returned to his table. While Ephraim Avery watched from his chair, Chief Justice Samuel Eddy turned toward the jury box and issued a long edict for the panel; he concluded with these suggestions:

"It is your duty to go into the consideration of this case, with candor, firmness, and impartiality. If satisfied of the guilt of the prisoner, upon your oaths, you will say so, without regard to consequences. If not fully satisfied, you will acquit. With these remarks, I leave the case with you."

Seventeen hours later, at noon the next day, the jury foreman knocked on the door. Avery was retrieved from his cell, and people filed into the crowded courtroom, including Catharine Williams. The clerk asked the foreman, "Have you agreed on a verdict?"

"We have" was the reply.

"Prisoner, look on the foreman. Foreman, look

at the prisoner. What say you, Mr. Foreman, is the prisoner guilty or not guilty?"

"Not guilty," the man replied.

The courtroom gasped, and Catharine Williams sighed.

CHAPTER TWELVE

⁓ ⁓

WICKED CREATURES

IN THE END, THE JURY could not find enough evidence to convict Ephraim Avery of murdering Sarah Cornell, and the panel found him not guilty. Avery's defense team reminded jurors that they must consider if he were guilty beyond a **reasonable doubt**; there was an abject lack of evidence in the case, according to legal experts that I spoke with.

No one could conclusively report that Avery was seen at Durfee's farm that night, if ever. In 1833, there was no way to prove that the minister penned the mystery note to Sarah, requesting a visit on the night of December 20. Multiple people provided him with alibis (though those were unreliable). The notes found in Sarah's trunk were circumstantial. There were no witnesses to the rape. Medical experts couldn't agree on the age of the fetus and whether the timing of the tent revival would match up. Investigators had not explored other suspects, like a stranger who might have wandered in and out of town. Their contention that the clove hitch knot, which tied the cord around her neck, proved murder was incorrect—the defense said that it could have been suicide. And we know that forensic investigator Paul Holes agreed. She **could have** physically done it. And Sarah's coworkers reported that she had been depressed.

According to the legal experts I spoke with, the jury in the criminal trial was correct in their verdict. One thing that my father once told his law school classes is this: the cold lesson of the law means that no matter what we think, we must pursue what we can prove. There are elements of proof that you must present in court; sometimes you have the evidence and sometimes you don't. There's a substantial difference between "not guilty" and "innocent," and for the legal system to remain credible, guilty people must sometimes go free.

Author Catharine Williams found the jury's verdict outrageous.

Ephraim Avery left court for Bristol ahead of the public announcement of the verdict. He did not remain there long; by June 5, 1833, Avery was in Boston awaiting a Methodist Church trial, likely set to "officially" clear his name. He was acquitted by the church of the charges of murder and "improper connexion." Catharine and other leaders in Providence cried that the Methodist Church's "investigation" was a whitewash, a farce. She rushed to finish her book, what would be titled **Fall River: An Authentic Narrative**.

Avery returned to Bristol and tried to preach, but his congregation was now divided, with many opposed to his continuing there. After Catharine's book was published in 1833, it was widely read, and it created a fervor. Avery was burned in effigy twice in Bristol and at least four times in Fall River. After 1834 Avery was never again stationed in the New England Conference of the Methodist Episcopal Church. His role gradually diminished, and by 1837 he was dropped and then shunned. He and his wife and six children moved to Ohio, where he became a farmer, a Methodist preacher . . . and a coroner, whose sprawling farmhouse still stands across the road from the cemetery where he is buried. By all accounts, Avery never had any legal issues after his dual acquittals. He lived a quiet life in northern Ohio, raising his large family. When he died in 1869 at almost seventy, several local obituaries were printed, and each had praise for him, but they did detail the case. The headline of **The Weekly Marysville Tribune**, "Death of a Notorious Preacher," was a good example. It described how, after the trial, hundreds of people traveled great distances to hear him preach, "but it was evident that curiosity, more than anything else, tended to swell his audiences, and he could not outgrow or outlive the suspicion that existed against him."

When Avery had left Massachusetts, the obituary read, he had hoped to travel to Ohio to escape the attention.

"For the last twenty or thirty years, Mr. Avery has led the life of an industrious and quiet farmer, at Pittsfield, Ohio, where he died," it read, "going to the grave with the respect and regret of his neighbors and acquaintances."

By the time of his death, accusations were all but forgotten—but not by the minister's own family, whom I interviewed at length. Ephraim Avery was Ray Avery's third great-uncle, and the reason why his family was reared in Ohio. Ray's mother was fascinated with the case and even printed an extensive booklet about the family's history before she died, as I mentioned before. Ray Avery had done plenty of digging himself on the story, but I updated him on my own research. I asked him, did he think he had a murderer in the family or was Ephraim Avery unjustly painted a pariah?

"I actually once got a piece of rope, and it was very difficult to tie around my neck on my own," Ray said. "Yeah, she probably could have done that. But the likelihood is probably very, very slim that she did."

Ray believed it was murder and, if so, concluded that his relative was the killer. He reminded me that coworkers testified that Sarah had seemed upbeat on the days leading to her death, casting doubt on the possibility of suicide. But we both wondered if

Sarah and Ephraim Avery had a contentious argument that night that might have led her to take her own life.

My parallel investigation with Catharine uncovered weaknesses in the case against the minister, but despite that, she and I shared the same conclusion: Ephraim Avery killed Sarah Cornell. Was she capable of tying the clove hitch herself to die by suicide? Perhaps, but not easily, and suicidal people aren't apt to make things more difficult. There are simpler knots to tie. The markings on her body indicated a struggle, according to Paul Holes and the matrons who dressed her in 1832. Avery had allegedly already attempted to force Sarah into taking poison. No one else had a motive. Holes said that we had conducted what he calls a "psychological autopsy" on Sarah. And the conclusion was clear.

"No, it doesn't seem like she was in a position in life where she seemed likely she would have killed herself," he said. "And then you take a look at the other side, and he has everything to lose. I imagine this would be disgraceful to him, his congregation, his reputation in the community."

But evidence against Avery did not meet the burden of the legal system—which is why the law can be so maddening. After I presented all the evidence to Holes, he agreed with me. And the witnesses who had convinced him were the matrons.

"You can't accuse somebody of homicide unless you actually have evidence of homicide. And with everything you've told me, probably the most significant thing I've heard is [the testimony of] the matrons dressing on the same day her body was found," he said. "They are saying she had bruises all over her body. There's nothing within the decomposition process that I or a pathologist would confuse as bruising. You're dealing with matrons who are familiar with dead bodies. So they know what they're seeing."

The matrons had sealed it for a modern forensic investigator. Paul Holes told me that the results of a modern document examination of those anonymous letters might help further convince him of Avery's guilt, and I agreed. This was the singular clue that I was most interested in. I believed that veteran document examiner Eileen Page could help me understand more about these anonymous letters. If she could tell us whether Avery authored them, then that would mean something.

A little about Eileen Page: She's been at work as a handwriting expert for more than forty years, with much of her work involving hundreds of wills and trusts. Page is on the board of the International Association of Document Examiners. She's examined anonymous letters, fraudulent signatures, and every kind of fraud involving handwriting that you can think of. But this is her first murder case.

A little about her method: "I just look at everything, so that I can see what jumps off the page at me and what might be worth making a note of," said Page. "I use highlighters, sometimes I use different color codes I like on the copies that I print off, so that I can zoom right in on things."

I asked Page to examine letters that we proved to be written by Ephraim Avery and notes from Sarah Cornell, and then compare the variations in the writing to the variations in the anonymous letters—the loops of certain letters, the abnormalities of others, and even the misspellings. Here's what she determined:

"Evaluating the abundance of **similarities** between the anonymous note and Rev. E. K. Avery's writing and the abundance of **differences** between the anonymous note and Sarah M. Cornell's writing, I have determined with a high degree of professional certainty that the writer of the anonymous note was Rev. E. K. Avery."

Page felt certain that Avery was the author of the anonymous notes. She sensed his desperation in his writing—she thought that he didn't disguise his writing because he never thought he would get caught. He incorrectly spelled her name "Connell" in both the anonymous note and in the letter that he acknowledged was written in his hand.

"He was just hurried or just didn't care enough to make a difference," said Page. "It just becomes his way of doing things. . . . So everything, you know, just seems to fall in line."

And it turns out that Sarah Cornell was very helpful to Page. I sent her a high-quality copy of the letter that Sarah last wrote to her family in which she quotes the anonymous letter, word for word. Page could compare the writings.

"It's rare that you get a writing sample that covers almost the word-for-word," said Page. "I know she paraphrased something, so it's not exact, but it was close enough that, you know, it was significant to do that match."

She could see how Sarah's letters curve and compared that to the curves written in the letters. Page is certain: Ephraim Avery was the person luring Sarah from her home that night in December. Yes, document examination is subjective. And it shouldn't be used exclusively in court to convict or acquit. But this is pretty convincing to me—Ephraim Avery was certainly a liar, and almost definitely a killer.

———

As we both stood at the murder site, separated by 190 years, Catharine and I reflected on the life of a young woman who seemed to be careening through her world before meeting a tragic death and a public humiliation. Sadly, there would be no justice for Sarah Maria Cornell. Ephraim Avery carried on with his life, had two more children, and then died without making another public statement about Sarah. Sarah had been excised from his history, like a dream that had faded into the night. Catharine concluded her book in a solemn tone, directly addressing those readers who attempted to vilify Sarah.

"The trial has been published, and the evidence is before the public," wrote Catharine. "Those who wished to make her appear a monster of wickedness, have continually said all that is possible to say against any individual."

Perhaps Catharine could relate to the public condemnation. In her final pages, she attacked factory owners for employing women in low-wage jobs with backbreaking working conditions. Catharine applauded women for pursuing independence, but factory work was grueling, even demeaning. She chided women for sleeping with married men, a reminder that despite her incredible empathy for Sarah, she would always defer to the Bible. Catharine believed that all religious houses could survive this type of scandal and that Avery didn't represent all ministers. But she did believe that the Methodist Church was unseemly and suspect.

"The publication of this matter has had one good tendency which is obvious," she concluded. "It has generated a suspicion of those noisy, ranting professors, who go about interrogating everyone they meet, to know 'if they love the Lord? If they are not ashamed of Jesus?' . . . We hope and trust it has not lessened the respect felt for those modest, practical and retiring Christians, who mind their own concerns and pursue the even tenor of their way, without seeking to obtrude themselves or their religion."

At home in her house on Olney Street in Providence, Rhode Island, about thirty miles from Newport, Catharine Williams skimmed her notes in late summer of 1833. She glanced at her daughter, Amey, who would turn eight in August. She had been baptized at an Episcopal church five years earlier as Amey Reed, named after Catharine's beloved mother. The author thought about her mission in publishing her **Fall River** book; she had felt obligated to persuade her readers of Sarah Cornell's violation, that this case was centered on the victim of murder. In her heart, Catharine felt outrage over Sarah's misuse, first at the hands of Ephraim Avery and then from many of the society that she had supported and revered for much of her life. But Catharine Williams was a practical woman, as I soon learned—and it was problematic to her credibility.

She had done well as an author, but she was compelled to continue writing almost incessantly to support her young daughter. I wondered what specifically had compelled her to undertake such an ambitious narrative: months of interviews, twenty-seven days of testimony, and frantic organizing of an incredible amount of material to produce a book almost two hundred pages long. Surely there must have been some type of financial support. **Who had hired her?** The trial concluded in early June

1833; she interviewed John Durfee on his farm just weeks later, as well as many of the other witnesses. She needed time to analyze the court documents. Catharine had been given the edict, apparently, to publish as soon as possible. At the end of August, she had alerted the press that she was preparing a book about the Avery case.

"We understand the subject of the late unhappy affair in that village will be treated in quite a new way," read **The Rhode-Island Republican**. "Mrs. Williams has been urged against her inclination to undertake this subject."

No word on who had urged her to turn down the assignment, but perhaps they were referring to the Methodists. She had taken time to gather Sarah Cornell's letters from her family, stated the article.

"Several very interesting anecdotes are related of her," said the article, "and some facts tending to throw light on this mysterious affair."

The reporter said he had reviewed the partial manuscript, and he was impressed.

"The style we observe is to be that of the 'Revolutionary Tales,'" he wrote, referring to her widely read narrative.

The writer assumed that his readership was familiar with Catharine's most reviewed book to date. The new volume would go on sale in the fall for 50 cents a copy, which is almost $20 today. In October, its scheduled publishing month, it was delayed, "for the purpose of publishing a much larger edition than was at first contemplated, owing to the increasing demand for the work."

Fall River was published by the end of the year and then it was popular enough that a second run was published in 1834. This all seemed to happen swiftly, especially because Catharine had traditionally taken at least one year to write each of her previous books. It wasn't until I closely read the preface that I realized that Catharine had been hired by someone—and I wasn't pleased.

"It was not until after long and reiterated persuasion, that the author was induced to attempt it," she wrote. "Who first proposed it, is of no consequence."

It's very likely, though, that Catharine had been hired by someone on the Fall River Committee, based on her incredible access to witnesses and factory tours. She had been hired by the people who represented the interests of the mill workers—the factory owners, the Congregationalists. Catharine might have felt impassioned by Sarah's cause, but she was not an independent journalist.

"The problem that arises from a sentimental conception of justice . . . has to do with the unreliability of the observations, whether first-hand or mediated, on which sympathetic identification depends," wrote Jon W. Blandford in "Known Criminals: Nineteenth-Century U.S. Crime Literature and the Epistemology of Notoriety." "The spectatorial, performative dimension of sympathy makes it difficult, if not impossible, to discern authentic feeling from fraudulent displays designed to manipulate observers."

Catharine had been paid to be persuasive, to sway the public against Ephraim Avery. And her writing, deemed by many as sentimental, even emotional, now felt calculating—even if she was justified. This was more than just a writing assignment to Catharine Williams. Sarah Cornell's story was every woman's future without guidance and protection. Catharine might have traveled down the same road after her divorce, had writing not saved her. She memorialized her whole experience as Sarah's advocate in a poem:

> **Where shall the murderer appear?**
> **My God thy judgements are most deep:**
> **No verdict can the monster clear**
> **Who dies a hypocrite must wake to weep.**

The tale of Sarah Cornell's murder isn't itself unusual, but its contribution to the annals of crime, despite being forgotten for almost two centuries, is crucial. The evisceration of Sarah's character was a precursor to other high-profile, modern cases where the victim's character became central to an accused killer's defense. The battle between two major denominations (and more broadly, between charismatic religion versus more staid, sober traditions) detracted from the issue that men exploited women in a society that already restricted them to lives of propriety. Both the killer and the victim were used.

It was in the interest of the Congregationalist factory owners to prevent Sarah Cornell from being smeared in the press, and to push for the arrest and conviction of her murderer. Conversely, the Methodists wanted to earn respectability and win more converts; to that end, it was essential that they avoid at all costs a criminal and sexual scandal involving one of their own ministers. Consequently, both groups contributed a great deal of effort, money, and publicity to the trial.

After two years of research, I've concluded my investigation into the murder of Sarah Cornell, a victim whose case has been largely forgotten by both society and her own family—something that happens often with murder victims. I've reviewed numerous Leffingwell wills, deeds, and journals: none mention Sarah in her family's papers.

Two years after the publication of **Fall River**, Catharine Williams sat for that painter, who immortalized her in a portrait. Aside from publishing her major books, Catharine became an activist: she was a close ally of Thomas Wilson Dorr, an American politician and former governor of Rhode Island, in his crusade for political reform; Catharine organized a women's group dedicated to his liberation from prison. He had been arrested for treason after attempting to overthrow the state government over universal suffrage (voting rights). In 1844, Dorr was sentenced to life imprisonment, but he was released a year later. Catharine had the distinction of being elected an honorary member of several Rhode Island learned societies—an honor not conferred, she once remarked, upon women in Rhode Island.

When Catharine's daughter, Amey, grew older, she married and had a child named Lewis; when the boy was ten, Catharine became his guardian and raised him as her own son, later formally adopting him. We don't know why. Lewis was Alexandra Washburn's great-grandfather, a guiding light in her family generations earlier—thanks to the foundation provided by Catharine. Catharine Williams died in 1872, not in obscurity, but with the respect of most everyone she knew, despite her retirement from writing about twenty-five years earlier.

In her time, Catharine's books placed her alongside some of New England's major literary figures. She was an inspiration for Nathaniel Hawthorne, Henry Wadsworth Longfellow, and other esteemed writers. Her ardent advocacy of Sarah Cornell, a female crime victim, as well as her condemnation of abuse in New England's industrial age, was far ahead of its time; her passionate defense of Sarah was unprecedented in American journalism. But it is also a cautionary tale for me: not all advocates are altruistic. There are lessons to be learned about bias in journalism and the need to offer a balanced, nuanced evaluation of a crime story, one that doesn't exploit the victims. **Be careful whose true crime content you consume.**

True crime should educate, explain, and illuminate, not simply entertain. From the time "penny dreadfuls" drew in readers with cheap serial literature in nineteenth-century London until now, readers have consumed true crime voraciously. In the twenty-first century, there is chatter about "this new resurgence of true crime," but true crime has always been popular—media other than books, like TV shows and podcasts, are finally catching up. Yet to some, it's inexplicable that a family's horror, like Sharon Tate's murder by the Manson family, continues to be voraciously consumed by millions of "fans." Now many contemporary readers and critics are making some long-needed demands of true crime creators: cease glorifying the criminal and his crimes; respect the victim and their family; complete due diligence so there is accurate reporting. True crime can be insightful, even engrossing, but it must be truthful, and much of it is not.

Catharine's advocacy of female crime victims, in her first and only true crime book, was admirable and inspirational to me, though it was likely not fully appreciated in her time. **Fall River** was published in 1833 and, like many books of its day, may have disappeared, but it's had a revival as a historical and cultural artifact, as well as a literary production. In 1994, **Fall River** was selected as the first

American book in the prestigious Brown University Women Writers Project and the Oxford University Press "Women Writers in English, 1350–1850" texts, introducing early women writers to modern writers—a huge honor for Catharine Williams. In 2002, she was posthumously inducted into the Rhode Island Heritage Hall of Fame as one of the state's most well-known writers. Williams has been the focus of more than a dozen academic articles about religion, women's rights, female writers, women's sexuality, and how female crime victims are depicted in the media. Her influence has been far-reaching, even two hundred years later.

There were then, and continue to be, people who blame the victim, particularly the female victim.

"We have some federal laws on the book, but I think that those are being eaten away by some of the judicial decisions, certainly decisions at the Supreme Court," said attorney Sharon Vinick. "Even if you're not going to have the introduction of evidence about how many people she slept with, they still have that in their minds. They're still going to be making the same sort of arguments. It's all about the fact that we don't believe victims."

But books like Catharine's **Fall River** and my book **The Sinners All Bow** will continue to push forward a new agenda: to return a voice to victims who have been silenced for centuries. Catharine Williams refused to sensationalize the story and glorify the killer. Sarah Cornell's plight is all too familiar to us today. My examination of this case has reminded me of the value of shining my own light on themes in society that are darkened.

Catharine reserved her most damning words for Ephraim Avery, the monster who she believed had hidden behind the facade of a pious man of the cloth, a predator who had escaped the noose and thwarted justice for Sarah Maria Cornell.

"We have always believed that the existence of counterfeits, was itself a proof there was real coin somewhere, and have been accustomed to consider the Christian Church as a net cast into the sea which gathered fish of every kind both bad and good," she wrote. "Our Bibles tell us 'there will be deceivers in the last days.'"

We offer one final parallel between Sarah Cornell and the fictional Hester Prynne. Nathaniel Hawthorne seemed to paint the portrait of his heroine with Sarah in mind, perhaps wistfully. If Sarah had been offered grace, perhaps good would have triumphed over evil.

"By having the magistrates commute Hester's sentence, Hawthorne imagines what might have been possible for the real-life transgressor, Sarah Cornell, had she survived her fall from chastity and faced her community," wrote Kristin Boudreau.

I think that's true. The narrator of **The Scarlet Letter** says, "With a burning blush, and yet a haughty smile, and a glance that would not be abashed, [Hester] looked around at her townspeople and neighbors."

Sarah Cornell was never offered that chance at pride and redemption, at least in life; instead, her legacy as the fallen woman, subjected to abuse before and after death, is hopefully expunged in our book, as well as that of Hawthorne's.

I'll reserve my own final words about the story for Sarah Maria Cornell: She was a strong worker turned hopeful expectant mother; she was a sexual assault survivor and then a murder victim. But most important, she was a self-advocate, even until the final moments of her death. Witnesses reported hearing screams from the Durfee stackyard. Her body was bruised, as if she were defending herself. She left behind a note, indicating whom she intended to visit, perhaps out of fear. She copied letters from Ephraim Avery as evidence, even revealing his name to her sister and brother-in-law. She kept them secured in a locked trunk. Sarah demanded child support from Avery. She demanded his respect and he answered with deadly violence. Sarah Cornell, as an advocate for her child, was indeed the real Hester Prynne—the object of contempt for so many in life, whose legacy in literature endures today. They both provided for writers the framework to paint a portrait of a victim turned survivor. Like so many other victims and survivors before and after her, Sarah Cornell had been abandoned that wintry night in December 1832—voiceless. Not anymore.

"I have enough of the good things of this life," Sarah Cornell wrote to her family, two years before her murder. "I brought nothing into this world, and I expect to carry nothing out, a stranger and a pilgrim here."

ACKNOWLEDGMENTS

~~~

THE LIST IS LONG OF people and places to thank for this book. "The 'Scarlet Letter' and the 1833 Murder Trial of the Reverend Ephraim Avery" by Kristin Boudreau was invaluable to me as a source for all things Hawthorne and how he viewed the Cornell case. I plumbed the archives of several wonderful institutions including the Rhode Island Historical Society, the Fall River Historical Society, and the Brown University Library. The wonderful folks at the Leffingwell House Museum in Norwich, Connecticut, were helpful tour guides as I gathered information on Sarah Cornell's family.

Many thanks to Catharine Williams's relative Alexandra Washburn, and to Ephraim Avery's relative Ray Avery. Sarah Cornell's relative Carrie Nolte helped me with invaluable genealogy research.

I leaned on several experts for this book, including

attorney Sharon Vinick, handwriting consultant Eileen M. Page, defense attorney David Sheppard, Episcopal priest David Peters, forensic pathologist Judy Melinek, poison expert Dr. Neil Bradbury, and forensic investigator Paul Holes.

I would be remiss not to thank some folks at the University of Texas, particularly the dean of the Moody College of Communication, Rachel Davis Mersey, and School of Journalism director David Ryfe.

To my wonderful team at G. P. Putnam's Sons: this is our third book together and I'm always stunned by the amount of work that you put into my projects. I'm grateful for Ivan Held, president; Lindsay Sagnette, vice president and editor-in-chief; Alexis Welby, director of publicity; Katie Grinch, associate director of publicity; Ashley McClay, vice president, associate publisher, and director of marketing; Brennin Cummings, assistant director of marketing; and Ashley Di Dio, assistant editor. I also appreciate all the production and managing editorial team members who brought this book to market: Emily Mileham, Maija Baldauf, Tal Goretsky, and Claire Sullivan.

I will forever be indebted to executive editor and good friend Michelle Howry—her skill as an editor offers me security that I'm not sure I could find anywhere else.

As always, I'm grateful for my literary agent, Jessica Papin, with Dystel, Goderich & Bourret.

She's the best in the business and I'm thankful for her guidance.

To my Texas girls, Lorena, Tina, Robbynn, Monica, Angie, Valerie, and Leticia: thanks for the Tex-Mex, the wine, and the laughs.

And finally, to Jenny, Ella, and Quinn; as well as my parents, Lynn and Jack Lefevre; my in-laws, Sandra and Charlie Winkler; and my brothers-in-law, Chuck Winkler and Shelton Green—thanks for tolerating me during my "writing phase."

BIBLIOGRAPHY

~⌇~

Aristides. **Strictures on the Case of Ephraim K. Avery.** Providence, Rhode Island, 1833.

Avery, Ephraim. Series 5: Avery Trial, Box 11 (122 folders). Rhode Island Historical Society, Providence, Rhode Island.

Baldwin, Eric. "'The Devil Begins to Roar': Opposition to Early Methodists in New England." **Church History** 75, no. 1 (March 2006): 94–119.

Barbour, Judith. "Letters of the Law: The Trial of E. K. Avery for the Murder of Sarah M. Cornell." **Law Text Culture** 2 (1995): 118–33.

Baron, Kassie Jo. "'A Jury Ye Young Fools Is Nothing. What's to Be Done with Public Opinion!': True Crime, Individual Responsibility, and Two Averys on Trial." **Journal of the Midwest Modern Language Association** 55, no. 2 (Fall 2022): 35–64.

Barton, George. **Celebrated Crimes and Their Solution: Famous Detective Mysteries.** London: St. Paul, 1926.

Blandford, Jon W. "Known Criminals: Nineteenth-Century U.S. Crime Literature and the Epistemology of Notoriety." Dissertation, Department of English, Indiana University, 2011.

Boudreau, Kristin. "The 'Scarlet Letter' and the 1833 Murder Trial of the Reverend Ephraim Avery." **ESQ: A Journal of the American Renaissance** 47, no. 2 (2001): 89–112.

"Broadside: The Death of Sarah M. Cornell" (poem). Boston: Burnham's, [1833].

Brownson, O. A. The Laboring Classes: An Article from the "Boston Quarterly Review." 3rd ed. Boston: Benjamin H. Greene, 1840.

Caldwell, Patricia. "In 'Happy America': Discovering Catharine Williams's Fall River for the Women Writers Project." South Central Review 11, no. 2 (Summer 1994): 79–98.

DeWaard, Jeanne Elders. "'Indelicate Exposure': Sentiment and Law in Fall River: An Authentic Narrative." American Literature 74, no. 2 (June 2002): 373–401.

Drury, Luke. A Report of the Examination of Rev. Ephraim K. Avery. 1833.

Durfee Family Papers. Tiverton, Rhode Island, 1771–1902. Rhode Island Historical Society, Providence, Rhode Island.

Durfee, Job. Papers. Box 2, folder 12, Avery Trial, ca. 1833. Rhode Island Historical Society, Providence, Rhode Island.

Ela, David H. Report of a Committee of the New England Annual Conference of Methodists. 1833.

———. A Vindication of the Result of the Trial of Rev. Ephraim K. Avery. Boston: Russell, Odiorne and Co., 1834.

Fall River Historical Society. Box containing the Ephraim K. Avery murder trial collection (call number: Avery Papers in Stacks).

Frost, Rebecca. "Identity and Ritual: The American Consumption of True Crime." Ph.D. dissertation, Michigan Technological University, 2015.

Gedge, Karin E. Without Benefit of Clergy: Women and the Pastoral Relationship in Nineteenth-Century American Culture. New York: Oxford University Press, 2003.

Graham, Susan. "'A Warm Polititian and Devotedly Attached to the Democratic Party': Catharine Read Williams, Politics, and Literature in Antebellum America." Journal of the Early Republic 30, no. 2 (Summer 2010): 253–78.

Greene, Albert C. Papers. Lawyer and Statesman of East Greenwich and Providence, R.I. Papers, 1804–1863. Catalog number: MSS 452. Rhode Island Historical Society, Providence, Rhode Island.

Hallett, Benjamin F. A Full Report of the Trial of Ephraim K. Avery: The Arguments of Counsel in the Close of the Trial, and Avery's Trial, supplementary edition. Boston, 1833.

Harnden, Harvey. Narrative of the Apprehension in Rindge, N.H. of the Rev. E.K. Avery, Charged with the Murder of Sarah M.

Cornell, Together with the Proceedings of the Inhabitants of Fall River. Providence, Rhode Island, 1833.

Hawthorne, Nathaniel. The Scarlet Letter. Boston: J. R. Osgood, 1878.

Hessinger, Rodney. "Mixing 'the Poison of Lust with the Ardor of Devotion': Conjuring Fears of the Reverend Rake and the Rise of Anti-Enthusiasm Literature." Chap. 4 in Smitten: Sex, Gender, and the Contest for Souls in the Second Great Awakening. Ithaca, New York: Cornell University Press, 2022.

Hildreth, Richard. A Report of the Trial of the Rev. Ephraim K. Avery. 1833.

Holliday, Charles, and J. F. Wright. "Letter from Charles Holliday & J. F. Wright to James B. Finley," 1833. Finley Letters. 136.

Ingram, Eleonore Maria. "Dissolution of Community in the New Republic: Changing Social Order for Single Working Women in Catharine Williams Fall River." B.A. dissertation, University of Missouri, 1978.

Kasserman, David Richard. Fall River Outrage: Life, Murder, and Justice in Early Industrial New England. Philadelphia: University of Pennsylvania Press, 1986.

Kerstetter, Earl E. "The Glorious Camp Meetings of the Nineteenth Century." Publication details unknown.

Leffingwell, Albert. The Leffingwell Record, 1637–1897: A Genealogy of the Descendants of Lieut. Thomas Leffingwell, One of the Founders of Norwich, Conn. 1897.

Livengood, Nicole C. "'Thus Did Restell Seal This Unfortunate Lady's Lips with a Lie': George Washington Dixon's Polyanthos and the Seductive Abortion Narrative." American Journalism 33, no. 3 (2016): 289–316.

Mahan, Russell. Thomas Leffingwell: The Connecticut Pioneer Who Rescued Chief Uncas and the Mohegans. Historical Enterprises Press, 2018.

McLoughlin, William G. "Untangling the Tiverton Tragedy: The Social Meaning of the Terrible Haystack Murder of 1833." Journal of American Culture 7, no. 4 (Winter 1984): 75–84.

Melvill, David. "A Fac-simile of the Letters Produced at the Trial of the Rev. Ephraim K. Avery." Newport, Rhode Island, 1833.

Member of the Massachusetts Bar. "The Trial of Rev. Ephraim K.

Avery." In **Mysteries of Crime, as Shown in Remarkable Capital Trials.** 1870.

Peterson, Orville C. T. "Early Methodist Education: The Conversion of American Methodism to Higher Education in the Period from 1816 to 1868." M.A. thesis, Fresno State College, January 1969.

Pilarczyk, Ian C. "The Terrible Haystack Murder: The Moral Paradox of Hypocrisy, Prudery and Piety in Antebellum America." **American Journal of Legal History** 41, no. 1 (January 1997): 25–60.

Pollitt, Katha. "Abortion in American History." The Atlantic, May 1997.

Rider, Sidney S. **Bibliographical Memoirs of Three Rhode Island Authors, Joseph K. Angell, Frances H. (Whipple) McDougall, Catharine R. Williams.** Providence, RI: S. S. Rider, 1880.

Rhode Island Supreme Court. **The Trial at Large of Ephraim Avery.** 1833.

———. **The Correct, Full and Impartial Report of the Trial of Rev. Ephraim K. Avery Before the Supreme Judicial Court of the State of Rhode Island at Newport.** 1833.

Rowen, Leslie. "True Crime as a Literature of Advocacy." Undergraduate thesis, Bellarmine University, 2017, 14.

Samuels, Shirley. "Black Rivers, Red Letters, and White Whales: Mobility and Desire in Catharine Williams, Nathaniel Hawthorne, and Herman Melville." Chap. 4 in **Reading the American Novel, 1780–1865.** New York: John Wiley and Sons, 2012.

Saunders, Robert M. "Crime and Punishment in Early National America: Richmond, Virginia, 1784–1820." **Virginia Magazine of History and Biography** 86, no. 1 (January 1978): 33–44.

Schechter, Harold. **True Crime: An American Anthology.** New York: Library of America, 2008, 69–71.

Staples, W. M. R. **A Correct Report of the Examination of Rev. Ephraim K. Avery.** 1833.

State of Rhode Island Department of Education. **Points of Historical Interest in the State of Rhode Island.** Department of Education, Rhode Island Education Circulars Historical Series 5, 1911.

Stodart, William. **Report of the Trial of the Rev. Ephraim K. Avery, Methodist Minister, for the Murder of Sarah Maria Cornell.** 1833.

Temin, Peter. "The Industrialization of New England: 1830–1880." NBER Historical Paper No. 114, February 1999, Development of the American Economy.

Turner, Frederick Jackson. "New England, 1830–1850." **Huntington Library Bulletin**, University of Pennsylvania Press, no. 1 (May 1931): 153–98.

Updike, Wilkins. **Memoirs of the Rhode Island Bar**. Boston: Thomas H. Webb, 1842.

Williams, Catharine Read Arnold. Catharine Read Williams Collection. Brown University Library, Special Collections Department, Manuscripts Division, Ms. 2-E, W668 Rider, Ms. 2-FD-D73c Rider, Ms. Dorr.

———. **Aristocracy, or the Holbey Family: A National Tale**. Providence, Rhode Island, 1832.

———. **Fall River: An Authentic Narrative**. Boston: Lilly, Wait & Co.; Providence, RI: Marshall, Brown & Co., 1833.

———. **Original Poems, on Various Subjects**. Providence, RI: H. H. Brown, 1828.

———. **Tales: National and Revolutionary**. Providence, Rhode Island, 1830.

Zlomke, Briony D. "Death Became Them: The Defeminization of the American Death Culture, 1609–1899." M.A. thesis, University of Nebraska–Lincoln, 2013.

INDEX

ABOUT THE AUTHOR

❧

KATE WINKLER DAWSON is a seasoned documentary producer and podcaster whose hit podcasts **Wicked Words** and **Buried Bones** appear on the Exactly Right network. She is the author of **Death in the Air, American Sherlock,** and **All That Is Wicked,** and is a professor of journalism at the University of Texas at Austin.

Facebook KateWinklerDawson
X KWinklerDawson
Instagram KateWinklerDawson